MCP Python

A Hands-On Beginner's Guide to Building Your First Context-Aware MCP Server

Written By

James Wiglow

MCP Python: A Hands-On Beginner's Guide to Building Your First Context-Aware MCP Server
First Edition, April 2025

Table of Content

Chapter 1: Introduction to MCP & Context-Aware Architectures

Overview & Objectives
By the end of this chapter you will:

1. Understand what the Model Context Protocol (MCP) is and why it exists.
2. See a real-world scenario that shows the value of context-aware AI servers.
3. Learn core MCP terms (JSON-RPC, tool manifest, capabilities).
4. Visualize the basic MCP request flow.

Motivation & Context

Imagine you chat with a personal assistant that can:

- Read your calendar to suggest meeting times.
- Pull data from your CRM to draft customer emails.
  A vanilla AI model can't do that on its own. It needs a
  context-aware server to connect to external tools and data sources.
  That's exactly what MCP provides—a standard way for AI clients to
  call and coordinate these tools securely and reliably.

1.1 What Is the Model Context Protocol (MCP)?

Definition:
MCP (Model Context Protocol) is an open, JSON-RPC–based standard that
lets AI clients and servers exchange structured requests and responses for
external "tools." It defines:

- **Message formats** (how to ask for a tool, and how to return results)
- **Tool manifests** (what each tool can do, its parameters)
- **Capability registration** (how servers advertise available tools)

Key Terms

Term	Definition
JSON-RPC 2.0	A lightweight, transport-agnostic remote procedure call protocol using JSON for messages.
MCP Manifest	A JSON schema listing each tool's name, description, input/output parameters, and version.
Capability	A single function or service that an MCP server offers (e.g., "read_calendar", "send_email").

MCP vs. Plain JSON-RPC

Aspect	JSON-RPC Only	MCP Extension
Message payload	arbitrary method & params	method, params **plus** manifest-driven validation
Tool discovery	ad-hoc	standardized manifest in server startup
Versioning	none	semver in manifest, explicit compatibility checks

Request/Response Flow (ASCII Diagram)

```
scss
```

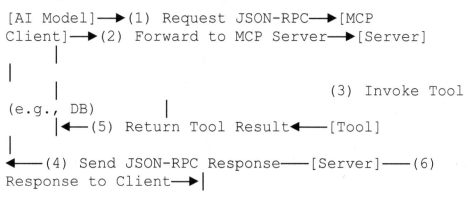

1. **AI Model** issues a JSON-RPC call to the client.
2. **MCP Client** forwards it to the server.
3. **Server** invokes the requested tool.
4. Tool returns data to the server.
5. **Server** packages it as a JSON-RPC response.

6. **Client** delivers it back to the AI model.

1.2 Evolution of JSON-RPC and MCP's Role

Motivation & Context

Imagine you've built a microservice that exposes weather data via HTTP, then another that offers currency exchange rates. You find yourself inventing new conventions—URL paths, query parameters, response formats—for each service. As systems multiply, integration becomes a tangle of bespoke adapters. That's why **JSON-RPC** was born: a simple, transport-agnostic way to call procedures over JSON. MCP builds on this foundation to bring consistency and discoverability to AI tool integrations.

Fundamentals

- **JSON-RPC 2.0**
  - A lightweight RPC protocol using JSON objects for requests and responses.
  - **Request** must include:

    jsonc

    ```jsonc
    {
      "jsonrpc": "2.0",
      "method": "subtract",
      "params": [42, 23],
      "id": 1
    }
    ```

  - **Response** example:

    jsonc

    ```jsonc
    {
      "jsonrpc": "2.0",
      "result": 19,
      "id": 1
    }
    ```

- **Limitations of Plain JSON-RPC**
  - No standardized discovery of available methods.
  - No built-in versioning or manifest.
  - Adapters still required for describing input/output schemas.
- **MCP's Extension Points**

  0. **Tool Manifest:** A JSON schema listing every method, its params, and output types.
  1. **Capability Registration:** Servers advertise available tools automatically.
  2. **Semantic Versioning:** Ensures client–server compatibility checks at startup.

Historical Timeline (ASCII)

```csharp
[2010] JSON-RPC 1.0 ──▶ Lightweight RPC over
HTTP/WS
   │
[2013] JSON-RPC 2.0 ──▶ Standardized error codes,
batch calls
   │
[2023] MCP v1.0  ──▶ Tool manifests, capability
discovery, semver
```

Feature Comparison

Feature	JSON-RPC 2.0 Only	JSON-RPC + MCP Extensions
Method Discovery	none	manifest-driven
Parameter Validation	ad-hoc	enforced by manifest schema
Version Compatibility	manual checks	semantic versioning in manifest
Batch Support		
Tool Metadata		description, input/output types

MCP's Role in the Landscape

- **From Unstructured to Structured:** Clients no longer guess method names or param shapes.
- **Built-In Safety:** Manifest validation prevents runtime errors from malformed calls.
- **Future-Proofing:** Semver lets you evolve tools without breaking existing clients.

1.3 Why Python for Context-Aware Servers?

1. Understand why Python is an ideal choice for building context-aware MCP servers.
2. Compare Python's strengths against other popular languages for JSON-RPC services.
3. See a minimal Python JSON-RPC handler example.
4. Learn best practices for writing scalable, maintainable Python MCP servers.

Motivation & Context

When you need to connect AI models to external data and tools, you want a language that lets you:

- Rapidly prototype new handlers and message flows.
- Leverage a rich ecosystem of JSON, HTTP, and AI-integration libraries.
- Scale from a single script to a production deployment with minimal friction.

Python ticks all these boxes, which is why most MCP server examples and community tools are written in Python.

Fundamentals

Why Python?

Criterion	Python	Node.js	Go
Ease of Learning	Simple syntax, readable	JavaScript familiarity	Steeper learning curve
Async Support	`asyncio` + `await`	Native `async/await`	Goroutines
JSON Handling	Built-in `json` module	Built-in `JSON`	`encoding/json`
Ecosystem for AI/HTTP	`requests`, `aiohttp`, `openai`, `fastapi`	`axios`, `express`	`net/http`, third-party
Packaging & Deployment	venv/poetry, Docker support	npm, Docker	`go modules`, static bin

Step-by-Step Tutorial

Here's a minimal Python MCP-style JSON-RPC handler using `asyncio` and the built-in `json` module:

```python
python

import asyncio
import json

HOST = '127.0.0.1'
PORT = 4000

async def handle_client(reader, writer):
    data = await reader.read(4096)          #
Read raw JSON-RPC payload
    request = json.loads(data.decode())          #
Parse to Python dict
```

12

```python
    # Minimal JSON-RPC response: echoes method name
    response = {
        "jsonrpc": "2.0",
        "result": f"Called {request['method']}",
        "id": request.get("id")
    }

    writer.write(json.dumps(response).encode())  #
Send JSON back
    await writer.drain()
    writer.close()

async def main():
    server = await
asyncio.start_server(handle_client, HOST, PORT)
    addr = server.sockets[0].getsockname()
    print(f"Serving on {addr}")
    async with server:
        await server.serve_forever()

if __name__ == "__main__":
    asyncio.run(main())
python

#  Watch out: forgetting `await
server.serve_forever()` means your server stops
immediately.
```

Deep Dive & Best Practices

- **Use asyncio for Concurrency:**

Pattern	When to Use
asyncio coroutines	High-concurrency I/O (network, disk)
Thread pool (concurrent.futures)	CPU-bound tasks or blocking libraries

- **Dependency Management:**

13

- o Pin versions in a `poetry.lock` or `requirements.txt`.
- o Separate dev dependencies (tests, linters) from runtime.
- **Logging & Error Handling:**
  - o Use Python's built-in `logging` with JSON output for observability.
  - o Catch `json.JSONDecodeError` and return standard JSON-RPC error codes.
- **Project Layout:**

```
arduino

mcp_server/
├── mcp_server/
│   ├── __init__.py
│   ├── handlers.py
│   └── server.py
├── tests/
│   └── test_handlers.py
├── pyproject.toml  # or requirements.txt +
setup.py
└── README.md
```

Hands-On Exercise

Challenge: Extend the sample server above to support a `multiply` method that accepts two numbers and returns their product.

- **Test input:**

```json
json

{"jsonrpc":"2.0","method":"multiply","params":
[6,7],"id":2}
```

- **Expected output:**

```json
json

{"jsonrpc":"2.0","result":42,"id":2}
```

Section 1.3 Summary & Cheat Sheet

- **Why Python?** Rapid prototyping, vast ecosystem, clear syntax.
- **Key module:** `asyncio` + `json` for lightweight JSON-RPC servers.
- **Best practices:** Use coroutines for I/O, structured logging, version-pin dependencies.
- **Code snippet:** Minimal async server that echoes method names.

Further Reading / Next Steps

- Python `asyncio` documentation: https://docs.python.org/3/library/asyncio.html
- JSON-RPC 2.0 spec: https://www.jsonrpc.org/specification
- FastAPI for building HTTP-based MCP proxies: https://fastapi.tiangolo.com/

1.4 Real-World Use Cases & Case Study Preview

Overview & Objectives

By the end of this section you will:

1. Identify three core real-world applications for MCP servers.
2. Understand how each case study illustrates MCP's value.
3. Preview the hands-on projects you'll build later.

Motivation & Context

In production AI systems, context makes the difference between generic replies and truly helpful automation. Consider:

- A financial analyst who needs daily PDF reports generated and emailed without manual intervention.
- A support chatbot that pulls a user's order history before answering questions.

- A research portal that searches internal documents, summarizes findings, and returns concise answers.

MCP makes these workflows seamless by standardizing how AI models call external tools.

Fundamentals

Use Case	Description	Key Tools
Business Report Agent	Periodically query a database, generate analysis in Python/Pandas, export to PDF, and email it.	Database connector, PDF exporter, Email sender
Contextual Chatbot	Retrieve user profile or session data, enrich LLM prompt, and deliver personalized responses.	Key-value store, LLM client, Session tracker
Enterprise Search Agent	Index documents in a vector database, perform similarity search, and synthesize answers via LLM.	Vector DB tool, LLM client, RAG pipeline

Case Study Preview

```java

Case Studies You'll Build:
1. Business Report Agent (Chapter 13)
2. Context-Aware Chatbot Server (Chapter 6)
3. Enterprise Search Agent with RAG (Chapter 13)
4. Contextual Calendar Assistant (Chapter 13)
```

Deep Dive & Best Practices

- **Choose the right data store:** For fast lookups, use Redis or a key-value tool.
- **Keep context minimal:** Store only necessary session fields to reduce memory use.
- **Secure sensitive data:** Encrypt credentials and sanitize all inputs.

Hands-On Exercise

Challenge: Think of one process in your work or hobby that could be automated with MCP.

- List the external tools it would need (e.g., database, email API).
- Sketch a minimal manifest entry (tool name + one param).

Section 1.4 Summary & Cheat Sheet

- MCP shines when AI models need external data or actions.
- Three flagship use cases: reporting, chat, and RAG search.
- Case studies guide you from concept to production.

Term	Quick Definition
Use Case	A real-world automation scenario for MCP and AI models.
Case Study	Step-by-step project illustrating a use case.

Further Reading / Next Steps

- Explore MCP community examples: https://github.com/open-rpc/mcp
- Read about RAG architectures: https://www.rag.research/overview
- In **Section 1.5**, we'll walk through core MCP artifacts—tool manifests, capabilities, and message flows—so you can start writing your first manifest.

1.5 How to Use This Book

Overview & Objectives

By the end of this section you will:

1. Know how each chapter is structured for maximum learning.
2. Learn to navigate code samples, exercises, and reference tables.
3. Understand how to run the companion GitHub examples.
4. See tips for getting the most out of hands-on exercises and cheat sheets.

Motivation & Context

This book is designed as a guided, hands-on tutorial. Rather than reading straight through, you'll work side-by-side with the code, exercises, and reference tables. Knowing the layout up front helps you jump directly to examples, revisit key concepts, or tackle exercises at your own pace.

Fundamentals

Section	Purpose
Overview & Objectives	Sets clear, outcome-focused goals ("By the end of this chapter...").
Motivation & Context	Real-world scenario that shows why the topic matters.
Fundamentals	Plain-English definitions and short tables/flowcharts.
Tutorial	Code-first walkthroughs with inline comments and pitfalls.
Deep Dive & Best Practices	Security tips, performance notes, and extension points.
Hands-On Exercise	Small challenge with test inputs and expected outputs.
Summary & Cheat Sheet	Bullet-list takeaways and mini reference tables.
Next Steps	Links to advanced chapters, StackOverflow threads, or GitHub.

Book Structure Flow (ASCII Diagram)

css

```
[ Chapter N ]
 ├─ Objectives
 ├─ Motivation
 ├─ Fundamentals
 ├─ Tutorial
 ├─ Best Practices
 ├─ Exercise
 ├─ Summary
 └─ Next Steps
```

Step-by-Step Tutorial for Getting Started

1. **Clone the Companion Repo**

   bash

   ```
   git clone
   https://github.com/your-org/mcp-python-example
   s.git
   cd mcp-python-examples
   ```

2. **Install Dependencies**

   bash

   ```
   python3 -m venv venv
   source venv/bin/activate
   pip install -r requirements.txt
   ```

3. **Run the First Example**

   bash

   ```
   python examples/basic_server.py
   ```

   You should see:

   nginx

   ```
   Serving on ('127.0.0.1', 4000)
   ```

Hands-On Exercise

Challenge: Run the first example in chapter 4 (basic MCP server).

- Confirm you see the "Serving on …" message.
- Send a test JSON-RPC request using `curl` or a simple Python client.
- Verify the response matches the expected echo format.

Section 1.5 Summary & Cheat Sheet

- Every chapter follows the same eight-step structure for consistency.
- Use the table of contents and ASCII diagram to jump to what you need.
- Clone and run the companion repo before diving into code.
- Exercises reinforce learning; cheat sheets speed up reference.

Further Reading / Next Steps

- **Companion GitHub:** https://github.com/your-org/mcp-python-examples
- **Community Forum:** Join the MCP Slack channel for support.
- In **Chapter 2**, we'll dive into **JSON-RPC 2.0**, the protocol underpinning MCP.

1.6 Glossary of Terms

Overview & Objectives

By the end of this section you will:

1. Have a quick reference for all key terms introduced so far.
2. Be able to look up definitions as you work through tutorials and exercises.

Glossary of Terms

Term	Definition
MCP	**Model Context Protocol**, an open JSON-RPC–based standard for AI clients to discover and invoke external "tools" (services) in a structured, versioned way.
JSON-RPC 2.0	A lightweight, transport-agnostic RPC protocol using JSON objects for requests, responses, and notifications.

Term	Definition
Request	A JSON-RPC object sent by the client to invoke a method on the server. Includes `jsonrpc`, `method`, `params`, and `id`.
Response	A JSON-RPC object returned by the server containing either a `result` (on success) or an `error` object, matched to the original `id`.
Notification	A JSON-RPC message without an `id`, used for one-way signals (no response expected).
Tool Manifest	A JSON schema that lists each tool's name, description, input parameters, output types, and semantic version.
Capability	A single function or service that an MCP server offers (e.g., `read_calendar`, `send_email`).
Context-Aware	The ability of an AI system to use external data or services (tools) to produce more informed, personalized, or automated responses.
Batch Request	A JSON-RPC feature allowing multiple requests or notifications to be sent in a single array payload.
Semantic Versioning	A versioning scheme (MAJOR.MINOR.PATCH) ensuring backward compatibility: increases in MAJOR version may introduce breaking changes.
Asyncio	Python's standard library for writing concurrent code using the `async`/`await` syntax, ideal for high-concurrency I/O tasks like JSON-RPC servers.
Handler	A function in the MCP server that processes a specific method call and returns a result or error.
Client	The component that sends JSON-RPC requests/notifications and receives responses from the MCP server.
Server	The component that registers capabilities, listens for incoming JSON-RPC messages, invokes tools, and returns responses.

Keep this glossary handy as you move into Chapter 2, where we'll dive deeper into **JSON-RPC 2.0** fundamentals.

Chapter 2: Core Concepts: JSON-RPC 2.0 Deep Dive

2.1 JSON-RPC Message Structure

Overview & Objectives

By the end of this section you will:

1. Identify the three core JSON-RPC message types: **Request**, **Response**, and **Notification**.
2. Understand required vs. optional fields in each message.
3. Construct and parse each message type in Python.
4. Spot common pitfalls, like missing `id` or malformed error objects.

Motivation & Context

When your MCP client and server exchange JSON-RPC messages, even a tiny typo can break the entire flow. Clear knowledge of the message structure helps you debug issues fast and build reliable integrations.

Fundamentals

Field	Description	Required in...
`jsonrpc`	Protocol version string. Must be `"2.0"`.	All message types
`method`	The name of the method to invoke on the server.	Request, Notification
`params`	Positional (array) or named (object) parameters for the method.	Request, Notification
`id`	Unique identifier matching requests to responses. Can be string, number, or `null`.	Request
`result`	The value returned on success.	Response (success)
`error`	An object with `code`, `message`, and optional `data` on failure.	Response (error)

Comparison: Request vs. Response vs. Notification

Aspect	Request	Response	Notification
method	must include	must omit	must include
params	optional or required per method	must omit	optional or required per method
id	required	must match request's id	must omit
result	must omit	if success	must omit
error	must omit	if failure	must omit

Message Flow (ASCII Diagram)

pgsql

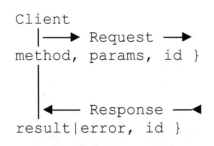
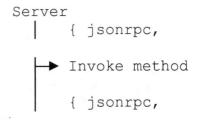

```
Client                          Server
    |——→ Request ——→               |    { jsonrpc,
method, params, id }
                                   ├→ Invoke method
    |←—— Response ——◄               |    { jsonrpc,
result|error, id }
```

Step-by-Step Tutorial

python

```python
import json

# 1. Build a Request
request = {
    "jsonrpc": "2.0",
    "method": "add",
    "params": [4, 5],
    "id": 1
}
raw = json.dumps(request)
print("Request JSON:", raw)

# 2. Simulate Server Reply
response = {
```

23

```python
    "jsonrpc": "2.0",
    "result": 9,
    "id": 1
}
print("Response JSON:", json.dumps(response))

# 3. Build a Notification (no id, no response
expected)
notification = {
    "jsonrpc": "2.0",
    "method": "logEvent",
    "params": {"event": "user_login", "user_id":
42}
}
print("Notification JSON:",
json.dumps(notification))
python

#  Pro Tip: Always use simple integers or UUID
strings for `id` to avoid collisions.
```

Deep Dive & Best Practices

- **id Types & Uniqueness**
  - Use incremental integers for simple flows.
  - Use UUID strings for high-concurrency systems.
- **Batching**
  - You can send an array of requests/notifications in one payload.
  - Responses array may arrive out of order—match by id.
- **Error Object Structure**

```jsonc
"error": {
  "code": -32602,
  "message": "Invalid params",
  "data": {"param": "age", "reason": "must be
integer"}
}
```

  - Follow standard error codes:

Code	Meaning
-32700	Parse error
-32600	Invalid Request
-32601	Method not found
-32602	Invalid params
-32603	Internal error

Hands-On Exercise

Challenge:

1. Write a Python snippet that:
    o   Sends a batch of two requests: `subtract(10,3)` with `id=1`, and `multiply(3,7)` with `id=2`.
    o   Prints each parsed response from a simulated server reply array.
2. Create a notification `notifyUser` with a `message` param—no response is expected.

Section 2.1 Summary & Cheat Sheet

*   **Three message types:** Request (needs `id`), Response (`result` or `error`), Notification (no `id`).
*   **Core fields:** `jsonrpc`, `method`, `params`, `id`, `result`, `error`.
*   **Pitfall:** Missing or duplicated `id` breaks matching.
*   **Best practice:** Use UUIDs for `id` in concurrent systems; follow standard error codes.

2.2 Batch Requests & Notifications

Overview & Objectives

By the end of this section you will:

1. Send and receive **batch** JSON-RPC calls in one payload.
2. Mix **requests** and **notifications** in a batch.
3. Parse batch responses and handle out-of-order replies.
4. Spot pitfalls like missing responses or mismatched `id`s.

Motivation & Context

Imagine your AI client needs to:

- Fetch user profile
- Retrieve recent transactions
- Log an analytics event

Instead of three separate HTTP calls, you wrap them in one **batch** payload. This reduces network overhead and keeps related operations together.

Fundamentals

Concept	Description
Batch Request	An **array** of Request and/or Notification objects sent in a single payload.
Batch Response	An array of Response objects for the Requests in the batch (no entries for Notifications).
Mixed Payload	You can include Requests (with `id`) and Notifications (without `id`) together.
Empty Batch	Sending `[]` is invalid—servers must return an error.

JSON-RPC Batch Example

jsonc

```
[
  { "jsonrpc":"2.0", "method":"getProfile",
"params": [42],  "id": 1 },
  { "jsonrpc":"2.0", "method":"getHistory",
"params": [42,10], "id": 2 },
  { "jsonrpc":"2.0", "method":"logEvent",
"params": {"evt":"login"} }
]
```

Step-by-Step Tutorial

python

```
import json
import uuid
```

```python
# 1. Build batch payload
batch = [

{"jsonrpc":"2.0","method":"getProfile","params":[42
],"id":1},

{"jsonrpc":"2.0","method":"getHistory","params":[42
,10],"id":2},

{"jsonrpc":"2.0","method":"logEvent","params":{"evt
":"login"}}
]
raw_batch = json.dumps(batch)

# 2. Simulate server reply (only for Requests)
server_reply = json.dumps([
    {"jsonrpc":"2.0","result":
{"name":"Alice"},"id":1},
    {"jsonrpc":"2.0","result":
[{"amt":100},{"amt":50}],"id":2}
])

# 3. Parse and match responses
responses = json.loads(server_reply)
for resp in responses:
    print(f"Response for id={resp['id']}:
{resp['result']}")
python

#  Watch out: Notifications produce no response—
don't loop over missing ids!
```

Deep Dive & Best Practices

- **Out-of-Order Replies:**

Scenario	Handling Strategy
Server reorders results	Match each resp["id"] to your original request

Scenario	Handling Strategy
Missing response entries	Check that each request's `id` appears once

- **Error in Batch:**
  - If any request fails, server may return only error objects for those ids.
  - You must still handle successful and failed entries separately.
- **Payload Size Limits:**
  - Monitor total byte size to avoid HTTP limits.
  - Split large batches into smaller chunks if needed.

Hands-On Exercise

Challenge:

1. Send a batch of three requests:
   - `add(1,2)` → id="a"
   - `subtract(5,3)` → id="b"
   - `multiply(2,4)` → id="c"
2. Simulate a server reply where `subtract` fails with code `-32602`.
3. Print each result or error with a clear label.

Section 2.2 Summary & Cheat Sheet

- **Batch** = array of Requests + Notifications.
- **Notifications** produce no response entries.
- **Match by `id`**—order is not guaranteed.
- **Handle partial failures** in the same batch.

Item	Note
Batch format	`[ {...}, {...}, {...} ]`
Missing Responses	Normal for Notifications
Error Handling	Look for `error` field in each response

Further Reading / Next Steps

- JSON-RPC spec on batch calls: https://www.jsonrpc.org/specification

28

- In **Section 2.3**, we'll cover **Error Handling & Standard Error Codes** in depth.

2.3 Error Handling & Standard Error Codes

Overview & Objectives

By the end of this section you will:

1. Understand the structure of a JSON-RPC error object.
2. Know the five standard error codes and when to use each.
3. Write Python code to generate and handle errors gracefully.
4. Distinguish between server-side and application-level errors.

Motivation & Context

When a client sends a malformed request or a method invocation fails, you need a consistent way to inform the caller what went wrong. JSON-RPC's error model—and MCP's use of it—ensures clients can programmatically react to failures, retry operations, or surface user-friendly messages.

Fundamentals

A JSON-RPC **error** response looks like this:

jsonc

```
{
  "jsonrpc": "2.0",
  "error": {
    "code": -32602,
    "message": "Invalid params",
    "data": { "param": "age", "reason": "must be
integer" }
  },
  "id": 3
}
```

Field	Description
`code`	A numeric error code. Standard codes are negative integers.
`message`	A short, human-readable description of the error.
`data`	(Optional) Additional information about the error, such as which parameter failed validation.

Standard JSON-RPC Error Codes

Code	Name	Meaning
-32700	Parse error	Invalid JSON was received by the server.
-32600	Invalid Request	The JSON sent is not a valid Request object.
-32601	Method not found	The method does not exist or is not available.
-32602	Invalid params	Invalid method parameter(s).
-32603	Internal error	Internal JSON-RPC error.

Step-by-Step Tutorial

```python
python

import json

def make_error_response(request_id, code, message,
data=None):
    """Build a JSON-RPC error response."""
    error_obj = {"code": code, "message": message}
    if data is not None:
        error_obj["data"] = data

    response = {
        "jsonrpc": "2.0",
        "error": error_obj,
        "id": request_id
    }
    return json.dumps(response)

# 1. Simulate invalid JSON parse error (id is null
for parse errors)
parse_error = make_error_response(None, -32700,
"Parse error")
```

```python
print("Parse Error Response:", parse_error)

# 2. Simulate invalid params for a known method
(id=5)
invalid_params = make_error_response(
    5, -32602, "Invalid params", {"param": "age",
"reason": "must be integer"}
)
print("Invalid Params Response:", invalid_params)

# 3. Simulate method not found (id=7)
method_not_found = make_error_response(7, -32601,
"Method not found")
print("Method Not Found Response:",
method_not_found)
python

#  Pro Tip: Use `None` as `id` for parse errors so
clients know the server couldn't extract an id.
```

Deep Dive & Best Practices

- **Distinguish Protocol vs. Application Errors**
  - Use **standard codes** (-32700...-32603) for protocol violations.
  - For domain-specific errors (e.g., "user not authorized"), pick codes $\geq$ -32000 and document them in your manifest.
- **Logging & Monitoring**
  - Log every error with full stack trace on the server side.
  - Expose metrics for counts of each error code to detect regressions.
- **Graceful Degradation**
  - For non-critical tools, consider returning a fallback result instead of an error.
  - Notify clients of partial failures via the data field.
- **Validation Layer**
  - Validate params against your manifest schema before invoking handlers.
  - Return -32602 immediately on schema mismatch to avoid executing invalid logic.

Hands-On Exercise

Challenge:

1. Extend your MCP server to validate incoming requests against a simple manifest schema:

```jsonc
{
  "methods": {
    "add": { "params": ["number", "number"] }
  }
}
```

2. If validation fails, return a -32602 error with `data` indicating which param failed.
3. Write a pytest unit test that sends a bad request (`add("x", 3)`) and asserts the correct error response.

Section 2.3 Summary & Cheat Sheet

- **Error object fields:** `code`, `message`, optional `data`.
- **Standard codes:**
    - -32700 Parse error
    - -32600 Invalid Request
    - -32601 Method not found
    - -32602 Invalid params
    - -32603 Internal error
- **Best practices:**
    - Log errors, monitor metrics, validate early.
    - Use domain codes (-32000 to -32099) for application-level faults.

Code	Use Case
-32700	Malformed JSON

Code	Use Case
-32600	Bad Request object
-32601	Unknown method
-32602	Schema/parameter mismatch
-32603	Unexpected server exception

2.4 MCP Specific Extensions to JSON RPC

Overview & Objectives

By the end of this section you will:

1. Recognize the three key MCP extensions to JSON-RPC: **tool manifests, capability registration**, and **semantic versioning**.
2. See how manifests drive request validation and discovery.
3. Implement basic manifest loading and request validation in Python (high-level).
4. Know where to find the full manifest schema in Chapter 4.

Motivation & Context

Plain JSON-RPC leaves clients guessing method names and parameter shapes. MCP adds structure so clients can:

- **Discover** what methods a server offers before calling them.
- **Validate** inputs/outputs against a shared schema.
- **Manage** evolving APIs safely via versioning.

This prevents runtime surprises and streamlines tool orchestration in AI workflows.

Fundamentals

Extension	Purpose
Tool Manifest	JSON schema listing every method, its parameters, return types, and metadata.
Capability Registration	Server advertises its manifest on startup so clients can fetch it.
Semantic Versioning	Clients and servers check manifest versions to avoid incompatibilities.

ASCII Flow: Manifest-Driven Call

```scss
[AI Client]──▶ fetchManifest() ──▶[MCP Server]──▶
manifest.json

   │
   │── Validate method & params ──▶
   │
   │── sendValidatedRequest() ──▶
```

Step-by-Step Tutorial

```python
import json

def load_manifest(path):
    """Load tool manifest metadata (simplified)."""
    with open(path) as f:
        return json.load(f)

def validate_request(request, manifest):
    """Check method and params against manifest
(outline only)."""
    method = request.get("method")
    entry = manifest["methods"].get(method)
    if not entry:
        raise ValueError(f"Unknown method:
{method}")
    # Further param checks would go here (see
Chapter 4)
```

```python
    return True

# Example usage
manifest = load_manifest("manifest.json")
request =
{"jsonrpc":"2.0","method":"add","params":[1,2],"id"
:1}

try:
    validate_request(request, manifest)
    # proceed to handler invocation
    print("Validation passed")
except ValueError as e:
    print("Validation error:", e)
python

#  Pro Tip: Always fetch the latest manifest at
server startup and cache it for validation.
```

Deep Dive & Best Practices

- **Manifest Location:**
  - Serve your manifest at a well-known HTTP endpoint (e.g., /mcp/manifest.json).
  - Clients fetch once and refresh only on version change.
- **Version Checks:**
  - Include manifest["version"] in your validation.
  - Reject or warn when client's expected version ≠ server's.
- **Incremental Updates:**
  - Use semver rules: MAJOR bumps for breaking changes, MINOR for feature additions.
- **Lightweight Validation:**
  - For performance, validate only method existence and param count in hot paths, defer deep schema checks to test suites.

Hands-On Exercise

Challenge:

1. Extend the sample server to:
    o Serve `manifest.json` at
      `http://localhost:4000/manifest`.
    o On each request, compare `request["method"]` against
      `manifest["methods"]`.
2. Write a quick client script that:
    o Fetches the manifest,
    o Attempts to call a non-existent method,
    o Prints a user-friendly error when validation fails.

Section 2.4 Summary & Cheat Sheet

- **MCP adds:** Tool manifests, capability registration, semantic versioning.
- **Manifest** drives discovery and input validation.
- **Version guard** protects clients from incompatible changes.

Concept	Quick Note
Tool Manifest	JSON schema of available methods (see Chapter 4).
Capability Registration	Server advertises manifest to clients.
Semantic Versioning	MAJOR.MINOR.PATCH; clients check before calling tools.

Chapter 3: Designing an MCP Server Architecture

3.1 Server vs. Client Responsibilities

Overview & Objectives

By the end of this section you will:

1. Distinguish the roles of an MCP **server** and an MCP **client**.
2. See a real-world scenario illustrating server vs. client duties.
3. Examine the minimal code for registering a capability (server) and invoking it (client).
4. Learn best practices for clear separation of concerns.

Motivation & Context

In a context-aware AI system:

- The **MCP Server** hosts tools (e.g., database queries, file readers) and advertises them.
- The **MCP Client** lives alongside your AI model, fetching the manifest and forwarding calls.

Imagine you build a chatbot that needs weather data:

- The server implements a `getWeather` tool by calling an external API.
- The client takes the model's JSON-RPC call, looks up `getWeather` in the manifest, and sends it to the server.

Properly dividing responsibilities keeps your code modular, testable, and secure.

Fundamentals

Role	Responsibilities
Server	• Load and serve the manifest • Register and invoke tool handlers • Validate inputs against schema • Return JSON-RPC responses/errors
Client	• Fetch and cache the manifest • Validate outgoing calls against manifest • Send JSON-RPC requests/notifications to server • Receive responses

ASCII Flow: Server vs. Client

```scss
scss

[AI Model]━━▶(1) Build Request━━▶[MCP Client]━━▶(2)
Validate & Forward━━▶[MCP Server]

|

┠━▶(3) Invoke Tool Handler

|

◀━(4) Tool Result━━◀
        ◀━━━━━━(5) Send Response━━[MCP Client]━━(6)
Return to AI Model━━━━━▶
```

1. Model calls client.
2. Client fetches manifest, validates, forwards.
3. Server invokes handler.
4. Handler returns result.
5. Server wraps result in JSON-RPC response.
6. Client returns response to model.

Step-by-Step Tutorial

```python
python
```

```python
# server.py
from mcp_framework import MCPServer

def add_handler(params):
    a, b = params
    return a + b

server = MCPServer(host="127.0.0.1", port=5000)
server.register_tool("add", add_handler)     #
Server advertises "add"
server.serve()                               #
Starts listening

# client.py
from mcp_framework import MCPClient

client =
MCPClient(manifest_url="http://127.0.0.1:5000/manif
est")
result = client.call("add", [3, 4])          #
Client validates & sends
print("3 + 4 =", result)                      # => 7
python

#  Watch out: Registering after server.serve() may
mean the tool isn't advertised.
```

Deep Dive & Best Practices

- **Manifest Caching**
  - o Cache on startup; refresh only on version bump.
  - o Avoid fetching per request to reduce latency.
- **Validation Layers**
  - o Client-side: quick check for method existence & param count.
  - o Server-side: deep schema validation before handler invocation.
- **Error Boundaries**
  - o Clients should catch transport errors (connection timeouts).
  - o Servers should catch handler exceptions and return -32603 internal errors.

Concern	Server Approach	Client Approach
Latency	Optimize handler code, use async I/O	Batch calls where possible
Fault Tolerance	Return fallback results for non-critical tools	Retry with backoff on transient failures
Security	Sandbox untrusted code, validate inputs	Never expose credentials to model code

Hands-On Exercise

Challenge:

1. Build an MCP server that offers two tools:
   - o echo (returns its input)
   - o reverse (reverses a string)
2. Write a client script that:
   - o Fetches the manifest
   - o Calls both tools in a single batch
   - o Prints each result

Test Input (batch):

jsonc

```
[

{"jsonrpc":"2.0","method":"echo","params":["hello"]
,"id":1},

{"jsonrpc":"2.0","method":"reverse","params":["worl
d"],"id":2}
]
```

Section 3.1 Summary & Cheat Sheet

- **Server**: hosts tools, validates, invokes, responds.
- **Client**: fetches manifest, validates, forwards, returns to model.
- **Flow**: Model → Client → Server → Tool → Server → Client → Model.

Component	Key Method	Main Duty
Server	`register_tool(name)`	Advertise & handle tool calls
Client	`call(name, params)`	Validate & forward requests

Further Reading / Next Steps

- MCP Spec: Server vs. Client patterns – https://github.com/open-rpc/mcp
- In **Section 3.2**, we'll compare **Synchronous vs. Asynchronous Designs** using `asyncio`.

3.2 Synchronous vs. Asynchronous Designs

Overview & Objectives

By the end of this section you will:

1. Distinguish **synchronous** (blocking) from **asynchronous** (non-blocking) server designs.
2. Know when to choose each model based on workload characteristics.
3. Implement a simple **synchronous** MCP server in Python.
4. Rewrite it as an **asynchronous** server using `asyncio`.
5. Recognize common pitfalls and performance considerations.

Motivation & Context

A synchronous server handles one request at a time—simple but limited under concurrent load. An asynchronous server can interleave many connections without dedicating a thread per client, improving throughput and resource use. For MCP servers that often wait on I/O (databases, APIs, file systems), `asyncio` can dramatically boost responsiveness.

Fundamentals

Aspect	Synchronous	Asynchronous (`asyncio`)
Concurrency model	One thread/process per request (or sequential)	Single thread, event loop interleaves tasks
Resource usage	Higher (threads/processes consume memory/CPU)	Lower (coroutines are lightweight)
Complexity	Simpler control flow	Requires async/await, callbacks
I/O-bound performance	Poor under many concurrent waits	Excellent for I/O-heavy workloads
CPU-bound performance	Similar; consider thread/process pools	Requires offloading to executors or processes

Step-by-Step Tutorial

python

```
# sync_server.py
import json
import socket

HOST, PORT = '127.0.0.1', 5001

def handle_request(conn):
    raw = conn.recv(4096)
# Blocking read
    request = json.loads(raw.decode())
    result = {"jsonrpc":"2.0", "result": "pong",
"id": request.get("id")}
    conn.sendall(json.dumps(result).encode())
# Blocking write
    conn.close()

def main():
    sock = socket.socket(socket.AF_INET,
socket.SOCK_STREAM)
    sock.bind((HOST, PORT))
    sock.listen()
    print(f"Synchronous server listening on
{HOST}:{PORT}")
```

```python
    while True:
        conn, _ = sock.accept()
# Blocks until client connects
        handle_request(conn)

if __name__ == '__main__':
    main()
python

#  Watch out: In the synchronous server, a slow
handler blocks all other clients!
python

# async_server.py
import asyncio
import json

HOST, PORT = '127.0.0.1', 5002

async def handle_client(reader, writer):
    data = await reader.read(4096)
# Non-blocking read
    request = json.loads(data.decode())
    response = json.dumps({
        "jsonrpc":"2.0", "result": "pong", "id":
request.get("id")
    }).encode()
    writer.write(response)
# Buffer write
    await writer.drain()
# Wait until sent
    writer.close()

async def main():
    server = await
asyncio.start_server(handle_client, HOST, PORT)
    addr = server.sockets[0].getsockname()
    print(f"Asynchronous server listening on
{addr}")
    async with server:
        await server.serve_forever()
```

```
if __name__ == '__main__':
    asyncio.run(main())
python
```

```
#  Pro Tip: Use `await reader.read()` instead of a
fixed loop to handle variable payload sizes.
```

Deep Dive & Best Practices

Concern	Synchronous Approach	Asyncio Approach
Simplicity	Easier to reason about; no event loop needed	Requires understanding of coroutines and event loop
Scalability	Limited by thread/process count	Can handle thousands of concurrent clients
Blocking pitfalls	One slow call stalls entire server	Non-blocking I/O keeps server responsive
Error handling	Use try/except around handler per connection	Wrap handler code in try/except within coroutine
CPU-bound tasks	Offload to thread/process pool	Offload to loop.run_in_executor()
Debugging	Standard stack traces and debuggers	Use asyncio debug mode (PYTHONASYNCIODEBUG=1)

- **When to use synchronous**: simple scripts, low concurrency, CPU-bound tasks.
- **When to use asyncio**: many I/O-bound connections, real-time streaming, long-lived sessions.

Hands-On Exercise

Challenge:

1. Run both sync_server.py and async_server.py locally.

2. Write a Python script that spawns **10 concurrent** clients to call each server with a simple ping JSON-RPC request (`{"jsonrpc":"2.0","method":"ping","id":1}`).
3. Measure and compare total time taken for each server (use `time.perf_counter()`).
4. Report which model handled concurrency more efficiently.

Section 3.2 Summary & Cheat Sheet

- **Synchronous servers** are straightforward but block on each connection.
- **Asyncio servers** use a single event loop to interleave many connections.
- **Key code changes**: replace `socket.accept()`/`recv()` with `asyncio.start_server()`, `await reader.read()`.
- **Best practice**: offload CPU-heavy work to executors when using `asyncio`.

Pattern	Sync Code	Asyncio Code
Listen & accept	`socket.accept()`	`await asyncio.start_server()`
Read data	`conn.recv()`	`await reader.read()`
Send response	`conn.sendall()`	`writer.write()` + `await writer.drain()`
Close connection	`conn.close()`	`writer.close()`

Further Reading / Next Steps

- Official `asyncio` docs: https://docs.python.org/3/library/asyncio.html
- Deep dive into `run_in_executor()`: https://docs.python.org/3/library/asyncio-eventloop.html#asyncio.loop.run_in_executor
- In **Section 3.3**, we'll cover **Directory Layout & Module Organization** for clean, maintainable MCP projects.

3.4 Dependency Management

Overview & Objectives

By the end of this section you will:

1. Understand the role of virtual environments and why dependency isolation matters.
2. Create and manage dependencies using **venv** + **pip** and with **poetry**.
3. Compare workflows and features of **pip** vs. **poetry**.
4. Apply best practices for pinning versions and sharing lock files.

Motivation & Context

When multiple projects live on the same machine, or when you onboard a new collaborator, unpinned or global dependencies lead to "it works on my machine" problems. Virtual environments isolate project packages, while lock files ensure everyone installs identical versions. **venv** + **pip** is built into Python and lightweight; **poetry** adds richer project metadata and lock-file management.

Fundamentals

Toolchain	Environment Creation	Dependency Install	Metadata & Lock File	Dev vs. Prod Deps
venv + pip	`python3 -m venv venv`	`pip install pkg==1.2.3`	`pip freeze > requirements.txt`	Manual requirements-dev.txt
poetry	`poetry init`	`poetry add pkg@^1.2`	`poetry lock` creates poetry.lock	`poetry add --dev pkg`

ASCII Flow: pip vs. poetry

```
pgsql

venv + pip                          poetry
───────────                         ────────

python3 -m venv venv                poetry init
activate venv                       poetry add <pkg>
```

```
pip install all                    poetry install
pip freeze > requirements.txt   / | \
                                       |
                                  poetry.lock +
pyproject.toml
```

Step-by-Step Tutorial

A. Using venv + pip

bash

```
# 1. Create & activate virtual environment
python3 -m venv venv
source venv/bin/activate       # Windows:
venv\Scripts\activate

# 2. Install dependencies
pip install fastapi aiohttp

# 3. Pin versions
pip freeze > requirements.txt

# 4. Install from lock file (fresh setup)
pip install -r requirements.txt
python

#  Watch out: Forgetting to activate 'venv' means
you install globally!
```

B. Using poetry

bash

```
# 1. Initialize project
poetry init --name mcp-python-project \
   --dependency fastapi --dependency aiohttp \
   --dev-dependency pytest

# 2. Install dependencies & lock
poetry install
```

```
# 3. Add a new package later
poetry add pydantic

# 4. Install dev dependencies
poetry add --dev black flake8

# 5. Run commands within poetry shell
poetry shell
python main.py
bash

#  Pro Tip: Commit both pyproject.toml and
poetry.lock to version control.
```

Deep Dive & Best Practices

- Pin **exact versions** (==1.2.3) in requirements.txt for production releases.
- Use **semantic version constraints** (^1.2) in poetry to allow safe minor updates.
- Separate **dev** and **runtime** dependencies to keep production images lean.
- Recreate environments often (e.g., CI pipelines) to catch drift early.
- Use tools like **dependabot** or **renovate** to automate lock-file updates.

Hands-On Exercise

1. In your project directory, create a **venv** and install at least two packages; generate `requirements.txt`.
2. Tear down the venv, recreate it from `requirements.txt`, and confirm imports succeed.
3. Initialize a **poetry** project; add the same two packages and a dev package.
4. Verify that `poetry.lock` lists exact versions and run `poetry install --no-dev` to see only runtime deps.

Section 3.4 Summary & Cheat Sheet

- **venv + pip**: Built-in, minimal. Use `requirements.txt` for locks.
- **poetry**: All-in-one project + lock management (`pyproject.toml` + `poetry.lock`).

- Pin exact versions for reproducibility; use semantic constraints for maintenance.
- Always commit lock files and clear env recreation in CI.

Command	Description
`python3 -m venv venv`	Create virtual environment
`pip install -r requirements.txt`	Install pinned deps
`poetry init`	Scaffold project & dependencies
`poetry add <pkg>`	Add runtime dependency
`poetry add --dev <pkg>`	Add development dependency
`poetry lock`	Generate/update lock file

Further Reading / Next Steps

- Python Packaging User Guide: https://packaging.python.org/
- pip documentation: https://pip.pypa.io/
- Poetry documentation: https://python-poetry.org/docs/

3.4 Dependency Management

Overview & Objectives

By the end of this section you will:

1. Grasp why dependency isolation matters for reliable MCP projects.
2. Create and activate virtual environments using **venv**.
3. Install and pin dependencies with **pip** and `requirements.txt`.
4. Initialize, manage, and lock dependencies with **poetry**.
5. Compare workflows and choose the right tool for your project.

Motivation & Context

When multiple Python projects coexist, installing packages globally leads to conflicts and "works on my machine" bugs. Virtual environments isolate each project's packages. Lock files (`requirements.txt` or `poetry.lock`) guarantee reproducible installs—vital when collaborating or deploying MCP servers in production.

Fundamentals

Toolchain	Create Env	Install Packages	Lock File	Dev vs. Prod Dependencies
venv + pip	`python3 -m venv venv`	`pip install` `fastapi`	`pip freeze > requirements.txt`	Manually maintain separate `requirements-dev.txt`
poetry	`poetry init`	`poetry add` `fastapi`	`poetry lock →` `poetry.lock`	`poetry add --dev pytest`

Workflow Comparison (ASCII)

```pgsql
venv + pip                              poetry
_____                             _____
python3 -m venv venv                    poetry init
source venv/bin/activate                poetry add <pkg>
pip install <pkg>                       poetry install
pip freeze > requirements.txt           poetry lock +
pyproject.toml
```

Step-by-Step Tutorial

A. venv + pip

```bash
# 1. Create & activate environment
python3 -m venv venv
```

```
source venv/bin/activate        # Windows:
venv\Scripts\activate

# 2. Install runtime packages
pip install aiohttp pydantic

# 3. Pin versions to lock file
pip freeze > requirements.txt

# 4. Recreate environment elsewhere
python3 -m venv venv
source venv/bin/activate
pip install -r requirements.txt
python

#  Watch out: Forgetting `source venv/bin/activate`
installs globally!
```

B. poetry

```
bash

# 1. Initialize project metadata
poetry init --name mcp-server --dependency aiohttp
--dependency pydantic

# 2. Install & generate lock
poetry install

# 3. Add new dependencies
poetry add fastapi

# 4. Add development tools
poetry add --dev pytest black

# 5. Run within poetry shell
poetry shell
python -m mcp_server.server
bash

#  Pro Tip: Always commit both pyproject.toml and
poetry.lock to VCS.
```

Deep Dive & Best Practices

- **Pin Exact vs. Range**
  - Use exact versions (==1.2.3) in production requirements.txt.
  - Use semantic ranges (^1.2) in pyproject.toml to allow safe updates.
- **Separate Dev Dependencies**
  - Keep linters, test frameworks out of your production image.
- **CI Integration**
  - In CI pipelines, recreate env from lock files to catch drift.
- **Automated Updates**
  - Use Dependabot or Renovate to auto-bump your lock files.

Hands-On Exercise

1. In a new folder, create a **venv** and install two packages; generate requirements.txt.
2. Tear down and recreate the venv from requirements.txt, ensuring imports succeed.
3. Initialize a **poetry** project in the same folder, add the same two packages plus a dev tool.
4. Verify that poetry.lock contains exact versions and run poetry install --no-dev to see only runtime deps.

Section 3.4 Summary & Cheat Sheet

- **venv + pip**: Built-in, simple isolation; use pip freeze for locks.
- **poetry**: Comprehensive project management with lock file (poetry.lock).
- Pin exact versions for reproducibility; use semantic ranges for maintenance.
- Always commit lock files and test env recreation in CI.

Command	Description
`python3 -m venv venv`	Create isolated environment
`pip install -r requirements.txt`	Install pinned dependencies
`poetry init`	Scaffold project & initial dependencies
`poetry add <pkg>`	Add runtime dependency
`poetry add --dev <pkg>`	Add development dependency
`poetry lock`	Generate or update `poetry.lock`

Further Reading / Next Steps

- Python Packaging Guide: https://packaging.python.org/
- pip Documentation: https://pip.pypa.io/
- poetry Documentation: https://python-poetry.org/docs/
- In **Section 3.5**, we'll cover **Configuration & Environment Variables** for flexible deployments.

3.5 Configuration & Environment Variables

Overview & Objectives

By the end of this section you will:

1. Understand why separating configuration from code is critical.
2. Use environment variables to store host, port, and secrets.
3. Load settings in Python via the built-in `os` module and via `python-dotenv`.
4. Validate required variables and provide sensible defaults.

Motivation & Context

Imagine deploying your MCP server in development versus production:

- In development you bind to `localhost:4000` and use a local SQLite file.

- In production you need $0.0.0.0:80$, connect to a managed database, and hide API keys.

Hard-coding these values forces code changes and risks leaking secrets. Instead, environment variables decouple configuration and let you manage settings per environment securely.

Fundamentals

Concept	Description
Environment Variable	A key/value pair provided by the OS to configure applications (e.g., `MCP_HOST`, `DB_URL`).
Default Value	A fallback used when the environment variable is not set (e.g., `4000` for `MCP_PORT`).
`.env` File	A local file (ignored by VCS) containing key/value pairs; loaded at runtime by `python-dotenv`.
Validation	Checking that required variables are present and correctly typed (e.g., converting ports to `int`).

ASCII Flow: Config Loading

```csharp
[OS Env] ──▶ Python (os.getenv or dotenv) ──▶
Settings object ──▶ Server uses settings.HOST,
settings.PORT
```

Step-by-Step Tutorial

A. Using `os.getenv`

```python
# config.py
import os

class Settings:
```

```python
    def __init__(self):
        # Bind address and port with defaults
        self.HOST = os.getenv("MCP_HOST",
"127.0.0.1")
        self.PORT = int(os.getenv("MCP_PORT",
4000))

        # Database URL is required
        self.DB_URL = os.getenv("DB_URL")
        if not self.DB_URL:
            raise ValueError("Missing required
environment variable: DB_URL")

        # Log level with a default
        self.LOG_LEVEL = os.getenv("LOG_LEVEL",
"INFO")

settings = Settings()
python
```

\# Watch out: Converting PORT to int avoids passing a string to your server bootstrap.

B. Using `python-dotenv`

1. **Install**

   bash

   ```bash
   pip install python-dotenv
   ```

2. **Create** a `.env` file at project root (add `.env` to `.gitignore`):

   ini

   ```ini
   MCP_HOST=0.0.0.0
   MCP_PORT=8080
   DB_URL=postgresql://user:pass@db:5432/mcp
   LOG_LEVEL=DEBUG
   ```

3. **Load & use**

```python
# config.py
from dotenv import load_dotenv
import os

load_dotenv()  # Reads .env before accessing os.environ

class Settings:
    HOST = os.getenv("MCP_HOST", "127.0.0.1")
    PORT = int(os.getenv("MCP_PORT", 4000))
    DB_URL = os.getenv("DB_URL") or \
        (_ for _ in
()).throw(ValueError("DB_URL is required"))
    LOG_LEVEL = os.getenv("LOG_LEVEL", "INFO")

settings = Settings()
```
```bash
#  Pro Tip: Commit a `.env.example` with
placeholders but never commit your actual `.env`.
```

Deep Dive & Best Practices

Concern	Recommendation
Secret Management	Use environment variables or a secrets manager (e.g., AWS Secrets Manager) rather than checking secrets into code.
Type Conversion	Always cast strings to the needed type (int, float, bool) and raise clear errors on failure.
Validation & Fail-Fast	Validate required variables at startup to catch misconfigurations early.
Configuration Reload	For long-running servers, consider watching .env or using a file watcher to reload config on change (advanced).
Documentation & Examples	Provide a .env.example and clear README instructions so new contributors know which variables are needed and their formats.

Hands-On Exercise

Challenge:

1. Create a `.env` file with:

   ```ini
   MCP_HOST=0.0.0.0
   MCP_PORT=9000
   DB_URL=sqlite:///mcp.db
   ```

2. Write a `config.py` using `python-dotenv` that loads these values into a `Settings` class.
3. In `server.py`, import `settings` and print `HOST`, `PORT`, and `DB_URL` when the server starts.
4. Run `python server.py` and confirm the output matches your `.env` values.

Section 3.5 Summary & Cheat Sheet

- **Keep config separate**: no hard-coded secrets or host/port.
- **Environment variables**: primary method for production settings.
- **Use `python-dotenv`**: for local development convenience.
- **Validate early**: fail at startup if required vars are missing.

Setting	Env Var	Default	Required?
Host	MCP_HOST	127.0.0.1	No
Port	MCP_PORT	4000	No
Database URL	DB_URL	—	Yes
Log Level	LOG_LEVEL	INFO	No

Further Reading / Next Steps

- **Python `os` module**: https://docs.python.org/3/library/os.html

- **python-dotenv docs**: https://github.com/theskumar/python-dotenv
- In **Chapter 4**, we'll start building your first MCP server—defining manifests and handlers.

Chapter 4: First MCP Server

4.1 Project Initialization & Packaging

Overview & Objectives

By the end of this section you will:

1. Initialize a new Python project directory for your MCP server.
2. Choose and configure a packaging tool (setuptools vs. poetry).
3. Create a minimal `pyproject.toml` (or `setup.py`) to make your code installable.
4. Understand how to install your package in "editable" mode for development.

Motivation & Context

Without packaging, running your MCP server relies on ad-hoc `PYTHONPATH` hacks or manual copies. Packaging lets you:

- **Install** your server and its dependencies consistently.
- **Import** your modules cleanly (`import mcp_server`).
- **Distribute** or containerize with confidence that all metadata (version, dependencies) is declared.

Fundamentals

Term	Definition
Package	A directory with an `__init__.py`, installable via pip or other tools.
Distribution	A built artifact (wheel or sdist) that can be uploaded to PyPI or installed locally.
pyproject.toml	Standard metadata file defining build requirements and package info (PEP 518).

Term	Definition
setup.py	Legacy script that calls setuptools to define package metadata and dependencies.
Editable Mode	Installs your package as a link so changes in source reflect immediately (`pip install -e .`).

Project Skeleton (ASCII)

```
arduino

mcp-python-project/
├── mcp_server/              # Your package source
│   ├── __init__.py
│   └── server.py
├── pyproject.toml           # OR setup.py + setup.cfg
├── README.md
└── .gitignore
```

Step-by-Step Tutorial

A. Using poetry

```bash
bash

# 1. Initialize Poetry project interactively
poetry init --name mcp-server --author "Your Name"
--dependency aiohttp

# 2. Confirm prompts and create pyproject.toml
#     - Defines name, version, description,
dependencies automatically

# 3. Install current package in editable mode
poetry install          # installs dependencies +
your package

# 4. Run your MCP server entry point
poetry run python -m mcp_server.server
bash
```

```
#  Pro Tip: Use `poetry version patch` to bump your
package version before releases.
```

B. Using setuptools (legacy)

1. **Create `setup.py` at project root:**

   ```python
   python

   # setup.py
   from setuptools import setup, find_packages

   setup(
       name="mcp_server",
       version="0.1.0",
       description="Context-Aware MCP Server in
   Python",
       packages=find_packages(),
       install_requires=[
           "aiohttp>=3.8.0",
       ],
       entry_points={
           "console_scripts": [
               "mcp-server =
   mcp_server.server:main"
           ]
       },
   )
   ```

2. **Generate `requirements.txt` (optional):**

   ```bash
   bash

   pip install -r requirements.txt
   ```

3. **Install in editable mode:**

   ```bash
   bash

   pip install -e .
   mcp-server          # runs your server via
   console_scripts
   ```

```
python

#  Watch out: Forgetting `find_packages()` may skip
submodules—verify your package is discovered.
```

Deep Dive & Best Practices

- **Single Source of Truth:**
  - With poetry, `pyproject.toml` holds metadata,
    dependencies, and build settings in one file.
  - With setuptools, consider adding `setup.cfg` for declarative
    metadata and minimization of `setup.py` code.
- **Version Management:**
  - Automate version bumps (e.g., poetry's `version` command
    or bump2version for setuptools).
- **Entry Points:**
  - Define console scripts so users can launch your server without
    `python -m`.
- **Lock Files:**
  - Commit `poetry.lock` or `requirements.txt` to
    version control to ensure reproducible builds.

Toolchain	Metadata File	Install Command	Entry Point Config
poetry	pyproject.toml	`poetry install`	`[tool.poetry.scripts]`
setuptools	setup.py / setup.cfg	`pip install -e .`	`entry_points` in setup

Hands-On Exercise

1. Create a new folder `mcp-python-project` and add the
   `mcp_server/` package directory.
2. Choose **one** toolchain:
   - **poetry**: run `poetry init` and follow promts.
   - **setuptools**: write a `setup.py` as above.

3. Install your package in editable mode (`poetry install` or `pip install -e .`).
4. Confirm you can launch the server via `poetry run python -m mcp_server.server` or `mcp-server`.

Section 4.1 Summary & Cheat Sheet

- **Packaging** ensures your MCP server is installable and importable.
- **poetry** centralizes metadata in `pyproject.toml`; **setuptools** uses `setup.py`.
- **Editable installs** (`-e .` or `poetry install`) let you iterate on code without reinstalling.
- **Entry points** simplify launching your server.

Action	poetry	setuptools
Initialize project	`poetry init`	create `setup.py`
Install dependencies + package	`poetry install`	`pip install -e .`
Define CLI entry point	`[tool.poetry.scripts]` in TOML	`entry_points` in setup.py
Lockfile	`poetry.lock`	`requirements.txt`

Further Reading / Next Steps

- **poetry docs**: https://python-poetry.org/docs/
- **setuptools guide**: https://setuptools.pypa.io/
- In **Section 4.2**, we'll define and validate your **Tool Manifest** schema so your server knows what capabilities to advertise.

4.2 Defining the Tool Manifest

Overview & Objectives

By the end of this section you will:

1. Understand the JSON Schema that defines an MCP tool manifest.

2. See a minimal `manifest.json` example with core fields.
3. Load and validate a manifest in Python using `jsonschema`.
4. Learn best practices for extending and versioning your manifest.

Motivation & Context

A manifest tells clients exactly what tools your server offers, what parameters each tool accepts, and what type of data it returns. Without a shared schema, clients guess method names and param shapes—leading to runtime errors. Defining your manifest with JSON Schema brings consistency, discoverability, and validation.

Fundamentals

Field	Type	Description
`version`	string	Semantic version of the manifest (e.g., `"1.0.0"`).
`name`	string	Human-readable name of this set of tools (e.g., `"My MCP Server"`).
`description`	string	Brief summary of what your tools do.
`methods`	object	Map of method names to their parameter and return schemas.
`methods.<m>.params`	array	List of parameter schemas (type, description) for method <m>.
`methods.<m>.result`	object	JSON Schema describing the return value of <m>.

Minimal `manifest.json` Example

jsonc

```
{
  "version": "1.0.0",
  "name": "mcp-python-demo",
  "description": "Basic tools for demo purposes",
  "methods": {
```

```json
    "add": {
      "params": [
        { "name": "a", "type": "number" },
        { "name": "b", "type": "number" }
      ],
      "result": { "type": "number" }
    },
    "echo": {
      "params": [
        { "name": "message", "type": "string" }
      ],
      "result": { "type": "string" }
    }
  }
}
```

ASCII Flow: Manifest Validation

pgsql

```
[manifest.json] ──▶ jsonschema.validate() ──▶
Valid? ──▶ True ──▶ Server starts
                                        └──▶ False ──▶

Error + exit
```

Step-by-Step Tutorial

python

```python
# manifest_validator.py
import json
from jsonschema import validate, ValidationError

# 1. Load JSON Schema (simplified)
manifest_schema = {
    "type": "object",
    "required": ["version", "methods"],
    "properties": {
        "version": {"type": "string"},
```

```
            "name": {"type": "string"},
            "description": {"type": "string"},
            "methods": {
                "type": "object",
                "minProperties": 1,
                "additionalProperties": {
                    "type": "object",
                    "required": ["params", "result"],
                    "properties": {
                        "params": {
                            "type": "array",
                            "items": {
                                "type": "object",
                                "required": ["name",
"type"],
                                "properties": {
                                    "name": {"type":
"string"},
                                    "type": {"type":
"string"}
                                }
                            }
                        },
                        "result": {"type": "object"}
                    }
                }
            }
        }
    }
}

# 2. Load and validate your manifest
with open("manifest.json") as f:
    manifest = json.load(f)

try:
    validate(instance=manifest,
schema=manifest_schema)
    print("Manifest is valid ")
except ValidationError as e:
    print("Manifest validation error:", e.message)
python
```

```
#  Watch out: a missing "methods" key will raise a
ValidationError and prevent your server from
starting.
```

Deep Dive & Best Practices

- **Semantic Versioning:**
  - o Bump MAJOR for breaking changes (e.g., param renames).
  - o Bump MINOR when adding new methods.
- **Rich Metadata:**
  - o Add `"deprecated": true` or an `"examples"` array under each method for client guidance.
- **Strict vs. Lenient Validation:**
  - o In production, disable `additionalProperties` to catch typos early.
  - o During development, allow extras to experiment with extensions.
- **Hosting the Schema:**
  - o Expose your JSON Schema at `/mcp/manifest/schema` so clients can validate locally.

Hands-On Exercise

1. Extend the example manifest to add a `multiply` method with two numeric params and a number result.
2. Update `manifest_schema` to require each param include a `"description"` field.
3. Run the validator and fix any validation errors.

Section 4.2 Summary & Cheat Sheet

- **Key fields:** `version`, `methods`, each method's `params` and `result`.
- **Validation:** Use `jsonschema.validate()` before server startup.

- **Best practice:** Host your manifest and schema via HTTP for dynamic clients.

Concept	Quick Note
`manifest.json`	Describes tools and data shapes
JSON Schema	Enforces manifest structure and prevents runtime bugs
`jsonschema` lib	Python package for JSON Schema validation

Further Reading / Next Steps

- Full JSON Schema spec: https://json-schema.org/
- OpenRPC manifest extension: https://spec.open-rpc.org/
- In **Section 4.3**, we'll implement **basic request handlers** and wire them into your MCP server.

4.3 Implementing Basic Request Handlers

Overview & Objectives

By the end of this section you will:

1. Define what a **request handler** is in an MCP server.
2. Write and register simple handlers (e.g., `add`, `echo`).
3. Return results or errors in correct JSON-RPC format.
4. Understand how handlers fit into your server's workflow.

Motivation & Context

Handlers are the core "tools" your MCP server offers. Each handler is a Python function that:

- Receives `params` from a client's JSON-RPC request.
- Performs some work (computation, I/O, API call).
- Returns a Python value (or raises an error) that the server wraps in a JSON-RPC response.

Without clear, well-written handlers, even a perfectly configured server can't do anything useful.

Fundamentals

Concept	Description
Handler	A Python function tied to a method name (e.g., `"add"`) that processes `params` and returns a result.
Signature	`def handler_name(params: Any) → Any:`
Return Value	Any JSON-serializable Python object (`dict`, `list`, `str`, `int`, etc.).
Error	Raise an exception or return a JSON-RPC error object to signal failure.
Registration	Linking a handler to its method name so the server knows which function to invoke.

Handler Registration Flow (ASCII)

pgsql

```
[ server.start() ]
       ├── server.register_tool("add", add_handler)
       ├── server.register_tool("echo", echo_handler)
       |
[ client request ]
       └── server looks up handler by method name →
invokes function(params)
```

Step-by-Step Tutorial

1. **Define simple handlers** in `mcp_server/handlers/basic.py`:

   python

```
# mcp_server/handlers/basic.py

def add(params):
    """Return the sum of two numbers."""
    a, b = params
    return a + b

def echo(params):
    """Return the same value back."""
    (value,) = params
    return value
```

2. **Register handlers** in your server bootstrap
   (`mcp_server/server.py`):

   python

```
from mcp_framework import MCPServer
from mcp_server.handlers.basic import add,
echo

server = MCPServer(host="0.0.0.0", port=4000)
server.register_tool("add", add)        #
Advertise "add"
server.register_tool("echo", echo)    #
Advertise "echo"
server.serve()
python

#  Watch out: If you register *after* calling
serve(), tools won't be advertised.
```

3. **Invoke via a simple client** (`client.py`):

   python

```
from mcp_framework import MCPClient

client =
MCPClient(manifest_url="http://127.0.0.1:4000/
manifest")
```

```
result_add = client.call("add", [5, 7])
print("5 + 7 =", result_add)          # => 12

result_echo = client.call("echo", ["hello"])
print("echo:", result_echo)           # => hello
```

Deep Dive & Best Practices

Concern	Recommendation
Input Validation	Validate `params` length and types early; raise -32602 for invalid inputs.
Error Handling	Catch exceptions in handlers and return JSON-RPC error codes instead of tracebacks.
Idempotence	Ensure handlers produce consistent results for same inputs to simplify retries.
Separation of Concerns	Keep business logic in separate modules; handlers should be thin wrappers.

- **Returning Errors:**

python

```python
from mcp_framework import RPCError

def divide(params):
    a, b = params
    if b == 0:
        raise RPCError(code=-32001,
message="Division by zero")
    return a / b
```

- **Logging Inside Handlers:**

python

```python
import logging
logger = logging.getLogger(__name__)

def add(params):
    logger.debug(f"Adding {params}")
```

```
return sum(params)
```

Hands-On Exercise

Challenge:

1. Add a new handler `multiply` that multiplies two numbers.
2. Write a pytest in `tests/handlers/test_basic.py` to verify `add`, `echo`, and `multiply`.
3. Enhance `add` to reject non-numeric inputs with a `-32602` error.

Section 4.3 Summary & Cheat Sheet

- **Handlers** are Python functions tied to method names.
- **Signature**: `handler(params: Any) → Any`.
- **Registration**: `server.register_tool("name", handler)`.
- **Error**: Raise `RPCError` or return a JSON-RPC error object.

Step	Code Snippet
Define handler	`def add(params): return params[0] + params[1]`
Register handler	`server.register_tool("add", add)`
Call handler	`client.call("add", [1,2])`

Further Reading / Next Steps

- In **Section 4.4**, we'll cover **Registering Handlers & Capabilities** in detail, including grouping tools and dynamic registration.
- Review the MCP spec's handler guidelines: https://github.com/open-rpc/mcp#tool-manifest
- Explore advanced handler patterns: dependency injection, middleware hooks, and batching.

4.4 Registering Handlers & Capabilities

Overview & Objectives

By the end of this section you will:

1. Know how to register individual handlers and group multiple tools as capabilities.
2. Use decorator-based and programmatic approaches to registration.
3. Dynamically discover and register all handlers in a module.
4. Understand how capability metadata (names, descriptions, versions) flows into your manifest.

Motivation & Context

A robust MCP server may offer dozens of tools—database queries, file I/O, analytics routines—each exposed via a handler. Manually calling `register_tool` for each one gets tedious and error-prone. Instead, you can automate registration, keep handler definitions close to business logic, and ensure your manifest always reflects the server's capabilities.

Fundamentals

Concept	Description
register_tool	Method on `MCPServer` that ties a handler function to a `method` name and records metadata.
Capability	A named tool (method + handler) that appears in the manifest and can be invoked by clients.
Decorator syntax	`@server.tool(name, description, version)` above a function to register it automatically.
Bulk registration	Programmatically iterate a module's functions and register each as a capability.
Metadata propagation	Name, description, and version passed at registration time show up in the tool manifest.

ASCII Flow: Dynamic Registration

```
python

[ handlers/basic.py ]                    [ server.py
]
  ┌─────────────────────────────────┐
  ┌─┴───────────────────────────────┴─┐
  │  @server.tool("add",...)  │──import──▶│ for fn in
handlers_module:           │
  │  def add(params): …       │           │
server.register_tool(fn)   │
  └─────────────────────────────────┘
  └──────────────────────────────────────┘
            │                              │
            ▼                              ▼
    manifest.json ←— auto-generate from registrations
```

Step-by-Step Tutorial

1. **Manual registration** (we saw this in 4.3):

   ```python
   server = MCPServer(...)
   server.register_tool("add", add_handler,
                         description="Add two
   numbers",
                         version="1.0.0")
   server.register_tool("echo", echo_handler,
                         description="Echo input
   value",
                         version="1.0.0")
   ```

2. **Decorator-based registration**:

   ```python
   # mcp_server/server.py
   from mcp_framework import MCPServer
   server = MCPServer(...)
   ```

```python
# handlers/decorated.py
@server.tool(name="multiply",
description="Multiply two numbers",
version="1.0.0")
def multiply(params):
    a, b = params
    return a * b

@server.tool(name="reverse",
description="Reverse a string",
version="1.0.0")
def reverse(params):
    return params[0][::-1]
python
```

Pro Tip: Decorators must be applied before server.serve() to ensure capabilities appear in the manifest.

3. **Bulk registration from a module**:

python

```python
# utils/auto_register.py
import inspect
from importlib import import_module

def register_all(server, module_name):
    mod = import_module(module_name)
    for name, fn in inspect.getmembers(mod,
inspect.isfunction):
        meta = getattr(fn, "_mcp_meta", None)
        if meta:
            server.register_tool(meta["name"],
fn,

description=meta["description"],

version=meta["version"])

# server.py
```

```
from utils.auto_register import register_all

# After importing handlers module to trigger
decorator attachments:
import mcp_server.handlers.decorated
register_all(server,
"mcp_server.handlers.decorated")
server.serve()
```

- o Here, each decorated function carries _mcp_meta that
  register_all reads.

Deep Dive & Best Practices

- **Consistent Metadata**
  - o Always include description and version when
    registering; these fields populate the manifest.
- **Avoid Name Collisions**
  - o Enforce unique name per handler; log or raise on duplicates.
- **Lazy Loading**
  - o For large handler modules, consider lazy imports so startup
    cost remains low.
- **Grouping by Namespace**
  - o Use module prefixes (e.g., "db.query", "fs.read") to
    categorize capabilities.
- **Hot-Reload Support**
  - o In development, watch handler files and re-register changed
    functions without restarting the server.

Pattern	Benefit
Decorator registration	Keeps handler and metadata together
Programmatic bulk register	Scales to many handlers automatically
Namespaced method names	Organizes manifest for discoverability

---

Hands-On Exercise

1. In `mcp_server/handlers/decorated.py`, decorate two new functions:
   - `uppercase` (uppercases a string)
   - `square` (squares a number)
2. Implement `register_all` in a `utils/` module, then call it in your server bootstrap.
3. Start the server, fetch `/manifest`, and verify that `uppercase` and `square` appear with correct metadata.

Section 4.4 Summary & Cheat Sheet

- **register_tool(name, fn, description, version)** ties a handler to a manifest entry.
- **Decorator** approach attaches metadata to functions for auto-registration.
- **register_all(server, module_name)** inspects and registers decorated functions in bulk.
- **Metadata** flows into manifest, enabling client discovery and validation.

Method	Usage
`server.register_tool(...)`	Manual, explicit registration
`@server.tool(...)`	Declarative, decorator-based registration
`register_all(server, module)`	Bulk, programmatic registration via introspection

Further Reading / Next Steps

- In **Section 4.5**, we'll explore **Handling Notifications & Subscriptions** so your server can receive one-way signals and push updates.
- Review MCP spec on capability metadata: https://github.com/open-rpc/mcp#tool-manifest

- Check out decorator utilities in popular frameworks (e.g., FastAPI's `@app.get`) for inspiration.

4.5 Handling Notifications & Subscriptions

Overview & Objectives

By the end of this section you will:

1. Distinguish **notifications** (one-way messages) from **requests**.
2. Implement server-side handlers for incoming notifications.
3. Build a simple **subscription** mechanism so clients can receive server-initiated notifications.
4. Integrate subscription logic into your async MCP server.

Motivation & Context

Beyond on-demand calls, AI systems often need **push** updates—e.g., new log entries, file changes, or timed events.

- **Notification**: client → server, no response expected (e.g., `logEvent`).
- **Subscription**: client tells server "notify me of X," then server → client via notifications when X occurs.

Handling these improves real-time workflows: your chatbot can push alerts, your report agent can notify completion, and more.

Fundamentals

Concept	Description
Notification	JSON-RPC message without id (`{jsonrpc, method, params}`), no response sent.
Subscription	Pattern where client requests to listen for events; server maintains subscriber list.

Concept	Description
Unsubscribe	Client sends notification or request to stop receiving updates.
Push Notification	Server sends JSON-RPC notification to each subscribed client when event occurs.

Notification vs. Subscription Flow

```scss
Client                          Server
Client (subscriber)
  |———▶  logEvent()              |

  |   (notify only)             |

  |                             |

  |———▶  subscribeAlerts()———▶|

  |         (notification)     | register subscriber

  |                             |

  |                             |———▶(event
occurs)————————————▶| receive notification
  |                       |          send
alertNotification       |
  |                       |
  |
  |———▶  unsubscribeAlerts()▶| remove subscriber
  |
```

Step-by-Step Tutorial

```python
# server.py (excerpt)
import asyncio
import json
```

```python
from collections import defaultdict
from mcp_framework import MCPServer

server = MCPServer(host="0.0.0.0", port=4000)
subscribers = defaultdict(set)  # topic → set of
writer transports

@server.notification("logEvent")
def handle_log(params):
    """Process a one-way logEvent from client (no
response)."""
    user, evt = params
    print(f"[LOG] {user}: {evt}")

@server.notification("subscribeAlerts")
async def subscribe(params, client_writer):
    """Client asks to subscribe to 'alerts'. Keep
writer to push."""
    topic = params[0]
    subscribers[topic].add(client_writer)

@server.notification("unsubscribeAlerts")
async def unsubscribe(params, client_writer):
    topic = params[0]
    subscribers[topic].discard(client_writer)

async def alert_generator():
    """Periodically send alerts to subscribers."""
    while True:
        await asyncio.sleep(10)  # every 10s
        msg =
{"jsonrpc":"2.0","method":"alertNotification","para
ms":["An event occurred"]}
        raw = json.dumps(msg).encode()
        # push to all writers for 'alerts'
        for writer in set(subscribers["alerts"]):
            writer.write(raw + b"\n")
            await writer.drain()

# bootstrap
server.serve(background_tasks=[alert_generator()])
python
```

```
#  Pro Tip: Always include a newline or delimiter
so async clients know where a notification ends.
python

# client.py (excerpt)
import asyncio, json

async def listen():
    reader, writer = await
asyncio.open_connection('127.0.0.1', 4000)
    # send a subscription notification
    sub =
{"jsonrpc":"2.0","method":"subscribeAlerts","params
":["alerts"]}
    writer.write(json.dumps(sub).encode()+b"\n")
    await writer.drain()

    while True:
        line = await reader.readline()
        note = json.loads(line.decode())
        print("Received notification:", note)

asyncio.run(listen())
```

Deep Dive & Best Practices

- **Delimiter Strategy**

Choice	Pros	Cons
Newline (\n)	Simple, low overhead	Avoid JSON strings with \n
Length prefix	Precise framing	More complex to implement

- **Subscriber Cleanup**
  - Detect broken connections (catch `writer.write` errors) and remove writer from set.
- **Backpressure Handling**
  - If a client is slow, consider queuing or dropping messages.
- **Security**
  - Authenticate subscribers before adding.

o   Rate-limit event generation to prevent DoS.

Hands-On Exercise

1. Modify your server to support two topics: `"alerts"` and
    `"statusUpdates"`.
2. Write a client that subscribes to `"statusUpdates"` and prints
    incoming messages.
3. Trigger manual pushes via a one-off script: send a notification to
    server's special `publish` endpoint to broadcast a message.

Section 4.5 Summary & Cheat Sheet

-   **Notification:** client → server, no `id`, no response.
-   **Subscription:** client notifies server to register; server pushes
    JSON-RPC notifications back.
-   **Push notification:** server sends {`jsonrpc`, `method`,
    `params`} to each subscriber.
-   **Maintain subscriber list** (e.g., dict of sets).

Action	JSON-RPC Example
Send notification	`{"jsonrpc":"2.0","method":"logEvent","params" :["user1","🚀"]}`
Subscribe	`{"jsonrpc":"2.0","method":"subscribeAlerts"," params":["alerts"]}`
Push to subscribers	`{"jsonrpc":"2.0","method":"alertNotification" ,"params":["Alert!"]}`

Further Reading / Next Steps

-   Explore WebSocket-based JSON-RPC for bidirectional
    streams: https://www.jsonrpc.org/specification#notification

- In **Chapter 5**, we'll build a **robust MCP client** that handles batches, streams, and subscriptions.
- Review advanced subscription patterns in JSON-RPC libraries (e.g., `rpc-websockets`).

4.6 Batch Requests in Practice

Overview & Objectives

By the end of this section you will:

1. Send mixed **batch** JSON-RPC calls (requests + notifications) to your MCP server.
2. Ensure your server correctly processes each entry and responds with an array of results.
3. Handle partial failures within a batch without aborting the entire payload.
4. Measure and tune batch performance for high-throughput scenarios.

Motivation & Context

Imagine your AI client needs to:

- Add two numbers
- Echo a message
- Log an event

Rather than three separate calls, bundling these into a single batch reduces latency and groups related operations. In high-throughput systems, efficient batch handling can drastically cut network overhead and improve responsiveness.

Fundamentals

Concept	Description
Batch Request	JSON-RPC array containing `Request` and/or `Notification` objects.

Concept	Description
Batch Response	Array of Response objects for each Request in the same order (notifications omitted).
Partial Failure	Some requests succeed, others error; server must return individual success/error entries.
Size Limits	Constrain batch size to avoid overwhelming server or hitting transport limits.

ASCII Flow: Batch Handling

nginx

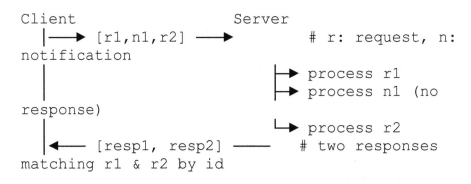

```
Client                    Server
   |──▶ [r1,n1,r2] ──▶            # r: request, n:
notification
   |                      ┠▶ process r1
   |                      ┠▶ process n1 (no
response)
   |                      ┗▶ process r2
   |◀── [resp1, resp2] ──    # two responses
matching r1 & r2 by id
```

Step-by-Step Tutorial

python

```python
# server.py (excerpt)
from mcp_framework import MCPServer, RPCError

server = MCPServer(...)

# Handlers
def add(params):
    a, b = params
    return a + b

def echo(params):
    return params[0]

def divide(params):
```

```python
    a, b = params
    if b == 0:
        # Raise an RPCError to include code/message
in batch response
        raise RPCError(code=-32001,
message="Division by zero")
    return a / b

# Register tools
server.register_tool("add", add)
server.register_tool("echo", echo)
server.register_tool("divide", divide)

# Start server—batch support is built-in
server.serve()
python

#  Watch out: Notifications in a batch produce no
response entries—ensure client ignores gaps.
python

# client.py (excerpt)
from mcp_framework import MCPClient

client =
MCPClient(manifest_url="http://127.0.0.1:4000/manif
est")

# Build mixed batch: add, divide by zero, echo, and
a notification
batch = [

{"jsonrpc":"2.0","method":"add","params":[2,3],"id"
:1},

{"jsonrpc":"2.0","method":"divide","params":[5,0],"
id":2},

{"jsonrpc":"2.0","method":"echo","params":["hi"],"i
d":3},
```

```json
{"jsonrpc":"2.0","method":"logEvent","params":["bat
chTest"]}  # notification
]
```

```python
# Send batch and parse responses
responses = client.send_batch(batch)
for resp in responses:
    if "result" in resp:
        print(f"id={resp['id']} →
result={resp['result']}")
    else:
        print(f"id={resp['id']} →
error={resp['error']['message']}")
```

Deep Dive & Best Practices

Concern	Recommendation
Order of Responses	Match by id rather than array index; servers may reorder internally.
Error Isolation	Catch and return errors per request; don't let one failure abort others.
Batch Size	Limit to 50–100 entries or based on payload byte size.
Concurrency	Process entries concurrently (async) if handlers are I/O-bound.

- **Concurrent Handling Example** (asyncio):

  python

  ```python
  async def handle_batch(requests):
      # Dispatch all requests concurrently
      tasks =
  [asyncio.create_task(process_single(r)) for r
  in requests]
      return await asyncio.gather(*tasks,
  return_exceptions=True)
  ```

- **Logging**: Tag each log entry with the batch id for traceability.

86

Hands-On Exercise

Challenge:

1. Extend your server with a new handler `multiply`.
2. Send a batch of four entries:
   - `add(1,2)` id="a"
   - `multiply(3,4)` id="b"
   - `divide(10,2)` id="c"
   - Notification `logEvent("batchTest")`
3. Simulate a failure by calling `divide(1,0)` as id="d".
4. Print each response or error, and verify no response for the notification.

Section 4.6 Summary & Cheat Sheet

- **Batch Request**: array of mixed requests/notifications.
- **Batch Response**: array of per-request results or errors.
- **Notifications**: omitted from responses.
- **Best practices**: match by `id`, limit size, isolate errors.

Step	Action
Build batch	`[ {...}, {...}, {...} ]`
Send batch	`client.send_batch(batch)`
Handle responses	Loop over `resp["id"]`, check for `result` vs. `error`
Pitfall	Notifications → no response entries

Further Reading / Next Steps

- JSON-RPC spec on batch processing: https://www.jsonrpc.org/specification
- In **Section 4.7**, we'll perform **Local Testing with a Minimal Python Client** to validate your server before deployment.

4.7 Local Testing with a Minimal Python Client

Overview & Objectives

By the end of this section you will:

1. Write a minimal Python client to test your MCP server locally.
2. Send single and batch JSON-RPC calls and parse responses.
3. Automate basic smoke tests to verify server behavior.
4. Integrate your client into a simple test script for rapid feedback.

Motivation & Context

Before deploying your MCP server, you need a quick way to validate that each handler, manifest entry, and error case works as expected. A minimal Python client gives you tight feedback loops and confidence that your server meets the contract defined in your manifest.

Fundamentals

Concept	Description
Test Client	A lightweight script that opens a connection, sends JSON-RPC payloads, and prints/parses responses.
Smoke Test	Basic checks that verify core functionality (e.g., "add" returns correct sum).
Batch Verification	Ensuring mixed requests + notifications produce expected multi-response arrays.
Automated Script	A runnable Python file (or pytest) that sequences tests and asserts outcomes.

ASCII Flow: Local Test Cycle

pgsql

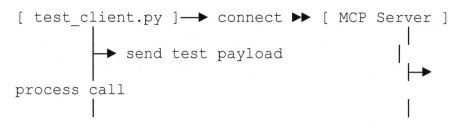

└◄ read and validate response ──┘

Step-by-Step Tutorial

python

```python
# test_client.py
import json
import socket
import sys

HOST, PORT = "127.0.0.1", 4000

def send_payload(payload):
    """Send JSON-RPC payload and return parsed
responses."""
    with socket.create_connection((HOST, PORT)) as
sock:
        raw = json.dumps(payload).encode() + b"\n"
        sock.sendall(raw)                          #
send request or batch
        data = sock.recv(8192)                     #
read response(s)
    return json.loads(data.decode())               #
parse JSON

def test_add():
    req =
{"jsonrpc":"2.0","method":"add","params":[10,5],"id
":1}
    resp = send_payload(req)
    assert resp.get("result") == 15, f"add test
failed: {resp}"

def test_echo():
    req =
{"jsonrpc":"2.0","method":"echo","params":["hello"]
,"id":2}
    resp = send_payload(req)
    assert resp.get("result") == "hello", f"echo
test failed: {resp}"
```

```python
def test_batch():
    batch = [

{"jsonrpc":"2.0","method":"add","params":[1,2],"id"
:3},

{"jsonrpc":"2.0","method":"echo","params":["x"],"id
":4},

{"jsonrpc":"2.0","method":"logEvent","params":["tes
t"]}  # notification
    ]
    responses = send_payload(batch)
    # responses should be list
    assert isinstance(responses, list), "Batch did
not return list"
    results = {r["id"]: r.get("result") for r in
responses}
    assert results[3] == 3 and results[4] == "x",
f"batch failed: {responses}"

if __name__ == "__main__":
    for fn in (test_add, test_echo, test_batch):
        try:
            fn()
            print(f"{fn.__name__} passed")
        except AssertionError as e:
            print(str(e))
            sys.exit(1)
    print("All local tests passed ")
python
```

```python
#  Pro Tip: Add newline delimiters so recv()
returns complete JSON; adjust recv buffer size as
needed.
```

Deep Dive & Best Practices

- **Timeouts & Retries**: wrap `socket.create_connection` with a timeout to avoid hanging tests.
- **Isolated Environments**: run your server in a separate terminal or background process before testing.

90

- **Test Frameworks**: migrate to `pytest` by replacing `assert` + print loops with test functions and fixtures.
- **Mocking Error Cases**: send invalid params to confirm error codes (e.g., `{"jsonrpc":"2.0","method":"add","params":["x"],"id":5}`).

Improvement	Benefit
Use `unittest` or `pytest`	Better reporting, fixtures, and parameterization
Wrap client logic in a class	Reuse connection setup and teardown code
Parameterize tests	Auto-generate combinations of methods and params

Hands-On Exercise

1. Enhance `test_client.py` to include:
   - A test for your `multiply` handler.
   - A test that invalid parameters return error code `-32602`.
2. Convert `test_client.py` into a `pytest` module with fixtures for `HOST` and `PORT`.
3. Add a CI step (e.g., GitHub Actions) that runs your tests on every push.

Section 4.7 Summary & Cheat Sheet

- **send_payload:** open socket, send JSON, read, parse.
- **Single test:** assert `result` matches expected.
- **Batch test:** ensure list of responses and correct mapping by `id`.
- **Automation:** exit non-zero on failure to integrate with CI.

Function	Purpose
`send_payload`	Encapsulates connection, send/receive, JSON parse
`test_add`	Validates `add` handler
`test_batch`	Verifies mixed batch behavior

Further Reading / Next Steps

- Move to **Chapter 5**: building a full-featured Python MCP client library.
- Explore pytest fixtures: https://docs.pytest.org/en/stable/fixture.html
- Integrate tests into CI:
  https://docs.github.com/actions/languages/python

Chapter 5: Building Robust MCP Clients in Python

5.1 Client Initialization & Connection Patterns

Overview & Objectives

By the end of this section you will:

1. Initialize both **synchronous** and **asynchronous** MCP clients in Python.
2. Compare **connection patterns**: ad-hoc vs. persistent connections.
3. Implement reconnect and timeout strategies.
4. Choose the right transport (`socket`, `asyncio`, or HTTP) for your workflow.

Motivation & Context

Your MCP client sits between the AI model and the MCP server. A reliable connection layer ensures:

- Low latency for interactive scenarios (e.g., chatbots).
- High throughput for batch operations (e.g., report generation).
- Resilience in face of network blips or server restarts.

Picking the right initialization and connection pattern lays the foundation for all subsequent calls.

Fundamentals

Pattern	Description	Use Case
Ad-Hoc Sync	Open socket, send single request, close socket	One-off scripts, simple tests

Pattern	Description	Use Case
Persistent Sync	Keep a socket open across multiple calls	Low-latency pipelines, minimal overhead
Ad-Hoc Async	`asyncio.open_connection` per call, then close	Lightweight, I/O-bound batch clients
Persistent Async	Reuse `StreamReader/Writer` across calls	Real-time streams, subscriptions
HTTP Transport	Use `aiohttp` or `requests` to wrap JSON-RPC over HTTP	HTTP-only environments, proxies, firewalls

Connection Flow (ASCII)

```scss
scss

[Client Init]
       ┣━▶ open_connection()              # sync or
async
       ┃
       ┣━▶ send JSON-RPC payload(s)
       ┃
       ┣━▶ receive & parse response(s)
       ┗━▶ close or reuse connection
```

Step-by-Step Tutorial

A. Synchronous Ad-Hoc Client

```python
python

import json
import socket

HOST, PORT = "127.0.0.1", 4000

def call_sync(method, params, req_id=1, timeout=5):
```

```python
    """Open, send, receive, and close a TCP socket
per call."""
    payload = json.dumps({
        "jsonrpc":"2.0", "method": method,
"params": params, "id": req_id
    }).encode() + b"\n"
    with socket.create_connection((HOST, PORT),
timeout=timeout) as sock:
        sock.sendall(payload)                    #
send request
        data = sock.recv(8192)                   #
receive response
    return json.loads(data.decode())             #
parse JSON

# Usage
resp = call_sync("add", [2, 3], req_id=42)
print("Sync call result:", resp.get("result"))
python
```

```
#  Watch out: Ad-hoc sockets incur connection
overhead per call—use sparingly.
```

B. Asynchronous Persistent Client

python

```python
import asyncio
import json

HOST, PORT = "127.0.0.1", 4000

class AsyncMCPClient:
    def __init__(self):
        self.reader = None
        self.writer = None

    async def connect(self):
        """Establish and reuse a single
connection."""
        self.reader, self.writer = await
asyncio.open_connection(HOST, PORT)
```

```python
    async def call(self, method, params, req_id):
        """Send a request and await the
response."""
        payload = json.dumps({
            "jsonrpc":"2.0", "method": method,
"params": params, "id": req_id
        }).encode() + b"\n"
        self.writer.write(payload)
        await self.writer.drain()
        raw = await self.reader.readline()
        return json.loads(raw.decode())

    async def close(self):
        self.writer.close()
        await self.writer.wait_closed()

# Usage
async def main():
    client = AsyncMCPClient()
    await client.connect()
    res = await client.call("echo", ["hello"],
req_id=7)
    print("Async echo:", res.get("result"))
    await client.close()

asyncio.run(main())
python

#  Pro Tip: Use `asyncio.wait_for(client.call(...),
timeout=5)` to avoid stalled reads.
```

C. HTTP Transport with aiohttp

```python
python

import json
import aiohttp
import asyncio

API_URL = "http://127.0.0.1:5000/jsonrpc"
```

```python
async def http_call(method, params, req_id,
session):
    payload = {
        "jsonrpc":"2.0", "method": method,
"params": params, "id": req_id
    }
    async with session.post(API_URL, json=payload)
as resp:
        resp.raise_for_status()
        data = await resp.json()
        return data

async def main_http():
    async with
aiohttp.ClientSession(timeout=aiohttp.ClientTimeout
(total=10)) as session:
        out = await http_call("add", [10,20],
req_id=100, session=session)
        print("HTTP call result:",
out.get("result"))

asyncio.run(main_http())
python

#  Watch out: HTTP may add latency; use persistent
sessions to reuse TCP connections.
```

Deep Dive & Best Practices

Concern	Recommendation
Timeouts	Always specify timeouts (`socket`, `asyncio.wait_for`, `ClientTimeout`) to avoid hangs.
Retries	Implement exponential backoff (e.g., retry up to 3× with delays 0.5s,1s,2s).
Connection Pooling	For HTTP, use a single `ClientSession`; for TCP, reuse a single socket or connection per client instance.
Error Handling	Catch `ConnectionRefusedError`, `asyncio.TimeoutError`, or `aiohttp.ClientError` and surface as retries or abort.

Concern	Recommendation
Thread Safety	Sync clients must not share a socket across threads without locks.

Hands-On Exercise

1. **Implement a persistent sync client** that opens one socket in `__init__`, reuses it for five calls to `add`, then closes it.
2. **Add retry logic**: for transient errors, retry up to 2× with 1 s delay.
3. **Benchmark**: compare average latency of ad-hoc vs. persistent calls (run 10 calls each, measure with `time.perf_counter()`).

Section 5.1 Summary & Cheat Sheet

- **Ad-Hoc Sync:** `socket.create_connection` per call—simple but higher overhead.
- **Persistent Async:** `asyncio.open_connection` once, reuse reader/writer.
- **HTTP Transport:** `aiohttp` session for JSON-RPC over HTTP.
- **Best practices:** timeouts, retries, connection pooling.

Pattern	Open	Send/Recv	Close	Note
Ad-Hoc Sync	per-call	`sock.sendall`	auto on exit	simple, high overhead
Persistent Async	once	writer.write/read	`writer.close`	low latency, requires event loop
HTTP w/ aiohttp	session	`session.post`	session close	firewall/proxy friendly, slightly slower

Further Reading / Next Steps

- In **Section 5.2**, we'll dive into **Sending Requests & Parsing Responses**, including batch calls and error handling from the client side.

- Explore `tenacity` for robust retry decorators:
  https://github.com/jd/tenacity
- See `aiohttp` advanced patterns: https://docs.aiohttp.org/

5.2 Sending Requests & Parsing Responses

Overview & Objectives

By the end of this section you will:

1. Build functions to **send** JSON-RPC requests (single & batch) using your client.
2. **Parse** responses, distinguishing **results** from **errors**.
3. Map responses back to original `id`s for correct handling.
4. Handle partial failures gracefully in mixed batches.

Motivation & Context

Your MCP client must not only open connections—it must also interpret what the server sends back. Mis-parsing an error as a success (or vice versa) can lead to silent failures or crashes. By standardizing your parsing logic, you ensure that each call yields the expected outcome or a clear exception.

Fundamentals

Field	Meaning
`jsonrpc`	Always `"2.0"`—verifies protocol version.
`id`	Matches the original request's `id`; lets you correlate responses in batches.
`result`	Present on success; any JSON-serializable value the handler returned.
`error`	Present on failure; object with `code`, `message`, and optional `data`.

99

Response vs. Error Example

```jsonc
jsonc

// Success
{ "jsonrpc":"2.0", "id":1, "result": 42 }

// Error
{
  "jsonrpc":"2.0",
  "id":2,
  "error": { "code": -32602, "message": "Invalid
params", "data": { "param":"b" } }
}
```

Step-by-Step Tutorial

1. **Single-call parsing**

```python
python

def parse_response(resp: dict):
    """
    Given a JSON-RPC response dict, return
result or raise error.
    """
    if "error" in resp:
        err = resp["error"]
        # Raise a Python exception
encapsulating the RPC error
        raise Exception(f"RPC Error
{err['code']}: {err['message']}")
    return resp.get("result")

# Usage with sync client
raw = call_sync("add", [3,4], req_id=5)   #
from Section 5.1
result = parse_response(raw)
print("3+4 =", result)  # => 7
python
```

Watch out: Always check "error" before "result"—some servers may include both fields erroneously.

2. **Batch parsing**

python

```python
def parse_batch(responses: list):
    """
    Given a list of JSON-RPC response dicts,
return a mapping id→result or raise on errors.
    """
    results = {}
    for resp in responses:
        rid = resp.get("id")
        if "error" in resp:
            err = resp["error"]
            # Attach the error to the id for
client-side handling
            results[rid] = Exception(f"RPC
Error {err['code']}: {err['message']}")
        else:
            results[rid] = resp.get("result")
    return results

# Usage with sync batch
batch = [

{"jsonrpc":"2.0","method":"add","params":[1,2]
,"id":1},

{"jsonrpc":"2.0","method":"divide","params":[5
,0],"id":2},
]
raw_batch = client.send_batch(batch)   #
returns list of dict
outcomes = parse_batch(raw_batch)
for rid, val in outcomes.items():
    if isinstance(val, Exception):
        print(f"id={rid} failed:", val)
    else:
```

101

```
        print(f"id={rid} → {val}")
python

#  Pro Tip: Use a custom exception class
(e.g., RPCError) to carry code/data for richer
handling.
```

Deep Dive & Best Practices

Concern	Recommendation
Out-of-Order Responses	Always map by id, never rely on list position.
Missing Response	If a request's id is absent, retry or raise a timeout error after a wait period.
Error Propagation	Surface errors immediately or collect them for aggregate reporting—avoid silent swallowing.
Custom Error Data	Inspect error["data"] for domain-specific info (e.g., validation failures) and handle accordingly.

Hands-On Exercise

1. **Implement** a helper send_and_parse(method, params, req_id) that:
    o Sends a single call, receives the response, parses it, and returns the result or raises an exception.
2. **Extend** it to send_batch_and_parse(batch_list) that returns two dicts:
    o successes: id→result
    o failures: id→error
3. **Write tests** using your test_client.py script to verify correct parsing for both success and error cases.

Section 5.2 Summary & Cheat Sheet

- **Check "error" first**—raise on any RPC error.
- **Map batch responses by id** into results or exceptions.

- **Handle missing IDs** or timeouts explicitly to avoid silent bugs.

Function	Purpose
`parse_response(resp)`	Return `result` or raise on `error`
`parse_batch(resps)`	Return mapping `id→(result`

Further Reading / Next Steps

- In **Section 5.3**, we'll explore **Streaming, Subscriptions & Callbacks** on the client side for real-time notifications.
- Learn about structured exception classes in Python: https://docs.python.org/3/library/exceptions.html
- Review advanced batch patterns: https://www.jsonrpc.org/specification#batch_processing

5.3 Streaming, Subscriptions & Callbacks

Overview & Objectives

By the end of this section you will:

1. Implement **streaming** of incoming notifications alongside request/response calls.
2. Register **subscription callbacks** to handle specific notification methods.
3. Manage a **listener loop** that demultiplexes responses vs. notifications.
4. Integrate callback invocation into both synchronous and asynchronous clients.

Motivation & Context

In many AI workflows, your client not only sends requests but must also react in real time to server-initiated events—status updates, alerts, or progress notifications. Without a streaming listener and callback mechanism, your client would miss these vital signals or block on requests, degrading the end-user experience.

Fundamentals

Concept	Description
Streaming	Continuously reading from the open connection to capture both responses and notifications.
Notification	A JSON-RPC message without `id` that carries event data from server → client.
Callback	A user-provided function that the client invokes when a matching notification arrives.
Demultiplexing	Separating incoming JSON messages into **responses** (with `id`) and **notifications** (without).
Listener Loop	An event loop or background thread/task dedicated to reading and dispatching incoming messages.

ASCII Flow: Client Listener Loop with Callbacks

```scss
scss

[Client.connect()]
        |
        |──▶ send request → [Server]
        |                ◀── response (id=1)
        |                ◀── notification
(method="alert")
        |
[ listener ]
while True:
  msg = read_next_json()
  if "id" in msg: dispatch to
pending_futures[msg["id"]]
  else: dispatch to callback_map[msg["method"]]
```

Step-by-Step Tutorial

A. Asynchronous Streaming Client with Callbacks

```python
python
```

```python
import asyncio
import json
from typing import Callable, Dict

class StreamingMCPClient:
    def __init__(self, host: str, port: int):
        self.host = host
        self.port = port
        self.reader = None
        self.writer = None
        self.pending: Dict[int, asyncio.Future] =
{}
        self.callbacks: Dict[str, Callable] = {}

    async def connect(self):
        self.reader, self.writer = await
asyncio.open_connection(self.host, self.port)
        # Start background listener
        asyncio.create_task(self._listener())

    async def call(self, method: str, params,
req_id: int):
        """Send a request and return a future for
the response."""
        payload = json.dumps({
            "jsonrpc":"2.0", "method": method,
"params": params, "id": req_id
        }).encode() + b"\n"
        fut =
asyncio.get_event_loop().create_future()
        self.pending[req_id] = fut
        self.writer.write(payload)
        await self.writer.drain()
        return await fut

    def on_notification(self, method: str,
callback: Callable):
        """Register a callback for a notification
method."""
        self.callbacks[method] = callback
```

```python
    async def _listener(self):
        """Continuously read lines and dispatch to
response futures or callbacks."""
        while True:
            raw = await self.reader.readline()
            if not raw:
                break  # connection closed
            msg = json.loads(raw.decode())
            if "id" in msg:
                # response to a prior request
                fut = self.pending.pop(msg["id"],
None)
                if fut:
                    if "error" in msg:

fut.set_exception(Exception(msg["error"]["message"]
))
                    else:

fut.set_result(msg["result"])
            else:
                # notification: invoke callback if
registered
                cb =
self.callbacks.get(msg["method"])
                if cb:
                    # run callback in background

asyncio.create_task(cb(msg["params"]))
python

#  Pro Tip: Always wrap callback invocation in
try/except to prevent one bad handler from stopping
the listener.
```

B. Synchronous Streaming Client with Threaded Listener

```python
python

import json
import socket
```

```python
import threading
from queue import Queue, Empty

class SyncStreamingClient:
    def __init__(self, host: str, port: int):
        self.host = host
        self.port = port
        self.sock = None
        self.pending: Dict[int, Queue] = {}
        self.callbacks: Dict[str, Callable] = {}

    def connect(self):
        self.sock =
socket.create_connection((self.host, self.port))
        threading.Thread(target=self._listener,
daemon=True).start()

    def call(self, method: str, params, req_id:
int, timeout=5):
        """Send and wait synchronously for a
response or raise on timeout."""
        payload = json.dumps({
            "jsonrpc":"2.0", "method": method,
"params": params, "id": req_id
        }).encode() + b"\n"
        q: Queue = Queue()
        self.pending[req_id] = q
        self.sock.sendall(payload)
        try:
            return q.get(timeout=timeout)
        finally:
            del self.pending[req_id]

    def on_notification(self, method: str,
callback: Callable):
        self.callbacks[method] = callback

    def _listener(self):
        buffer = b""
        while True:
            data = self.sock.recv(4096)
            if not data:
```

```python
                break
        buffer += data
        while b"\n" in buffer:
            line, buffer = buffer.split(b"\n",
1)
            msg = json.loads(line.decode())
            if "id" in msg:
                self.pending[msg["id"]].put(
                    msg.get("result") if
"result" in msg else
Exception(msg["error"]["message"])
                )
            else:
                cb =
self.callbacks.get(msg["method"])
                if cb:
                    try:
                        cb(msg["params"])
                    except Exception:
                        pass  # swallow errors
in callbacks
python

#  Watch out: In the sync listener, never block in
callback—use threads or queues if you need long
tasks.
```

Deep Dive & Best Practices

- **Callback Safety:**
    - Always guard your callbacks with try/except to avoid crashing the listener.
    - Offload heavy work to separate tasks/threads.
- **Timeout Management:**
    - Use `asyncio.wait_for` or queue timeouts to detect server unresponsiveness.
- **Cleaning Up:**
    - On disconnect, cancel all pending futures/queues with an exception to unblock callers.
- **Thread vs. Async:**

o Async approach scales better for many subscriptions; sync with threads is simpler but costlier.

Aspect	Async	Sync + Thread
Concurrency model	Coroutines on event loop	Worker thread + listener thread
Performance	High throughput, low overhead	Higher resource use per connection
Simplicity	Requires `asyncio` knowledge	Familiar synchronous code
Safety	Exceptions propagate to futures	Must manage queue timeouts/exceptions

Hands-On Exercise

1. Using `StreamingMCPClient`, subscribe to `"alerts"` with a callback that prints `"ALERT:"` plus the params.
2. In parallel, send a `"subscribeAlerts"` notification, then simulate server pushes via your test server.
3. Verify your callback runs without blocking your ability to make further `call(...)` requests.

Section 5.3 Summary & Cheat Sheet

- **Streaming listener**: background task or thread that reads lines and parses JSON.
- **Demultiplex**: route messages with `id` → futures/queues; without `id` → callbacks.
- **Register callbacks**: `on_notification(method, callback)`.
- **Safety**: guard callbacks, enforce timeouts, clean up on disconnect.

Method	Purpose
`client.on_notification(m, cb)`	Register callback `cb` for method `m`
`await client.call(...)`	Send request and await response

109

Method	Purpose
`listener`	Loop reading, parsing, and dispatching

Further Reading / Next Steps

- In **Section 5.4**, we'll implement **Retry Strategies & Circuit Breakers** to make your client more resilient.

5.4 Retry Strategies & Circuit Breakers

Overview & Objectives

By the end of this section you will:

1. Understand why **retries** and **circuit breakers** improve client resilience.
2. Implement a simple **retry decorator** with exponential backoff.
3. Build a **circuit breaker** to stop retries after repeated failures.
4. Integrate these patterns into both sync and async MCP clients.

Motivation & Context

Network glitches and transient server errors are inevitable—think brief database outages or momentary network partitions. Without retries, your client fails immediately. Without a circuit breaker, endless retries can overload a struggling service. Combining retries with a circuit breaker gives you "smart" resilience: retry sensibly, then back off when it's clear the service is down.

Fundamentals

Pattern	Purpose	Key Parameter
Retry	Re-attempt a failed operation up to N times	`max_attempts`, `delay`
Exponential Backoff	Increase wait time between retries (`delay *= factor`)	`factor` (e.g., 2×)
Circuit Breaker	Stop sending requests after M consecutive failures	`failure_threshold`

Pattern	Purpose	Key Parameter
Reset Timeout	After a cooldown, allow new attempt and reset counter	reset_timeout (seconds)

ASCII Flow: Retry + Circuit Breaker

pgsql

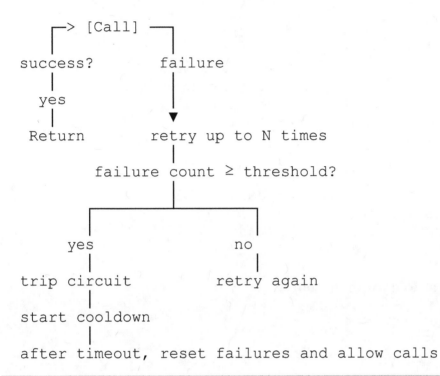

```
       ┌─> [Call] ─┐
       |           |
   success?      failure
       |           |
     yes           |
       |           ▼
    Return    retry up to N times
                   |
            failure count ≥ threshold?
                   |
         ┌─────────┴─────────┐
         |                   |
        yes                  no
         |                   |
    trip circuit        retry again
         |
    start cooldown
         |
    after timeout, reset failures and allow calls
```

Step-by-Step Tutorial

A. Sync Retry Decorator

python

```python
import time
from functools import wraps

def retry(max_attempts=3, delay=1, factor=2):
    """Retry decorator with exponential backoff."""
    def decorator(fn):
        @wraps(fn)
```

```python
        def wrapper(*args, **kwargs):
            attempt = 1
            wait = delay
            while True:
                try:
                    return fn(*args, **kwargs)
                except Exception as e:
                    if attempt >= max_attempts:
                        raise
                    #  Watch out: catch only
transient exceptions
                    time.sleep(wait)
                    wait *= factor
                    attempt += 1
        return wrapper
    return decorator

# Usage
@retry(max_attempts=4, delay=0.5)
def call_add(client, a, b):
    return client.call("add", [a, b],
req_id=42)["result"]
```

B. Async Retry with Backoff

python

```python
import asyncio
from functools import wraps

def async_retry(max_attempts=3, delay=1, factor=2):
    """Async retry decorator with exponential
backoff."""
    def decorator(fn):
        @wraps(fn)
        async def wrapper(*args, **kwargs):
            attempt, wait = 1, delay
            while True:
                try:
                    return await fn(*args,
**kwargs)
                except Exception:
```

```python
                if attempt >= max_attempts:
                    raise
                await asyncio.sleep(wait)
                wait *= factor
                attempt += 1
        return wrapper
    return decorator

# Usage with StreamingMCPClient
@async_retry(max_attempts=5, delay=0.2)
async def safe_call(client, method, params,
req_id):
    return await client.call(method, params,
req_id)
```

C. Simple Circuit Breaker

```python
import time

class CircuitBreaker:
    def __init__(self, failure_threshold=3,
reset_timeout=10):
        self.failure_threshold = failure_threshold
        self.reset_timeout = reset_timeout
        self.failures = 0
        self.tripped_at = None

    def call(self, fn, *args, **kwargs):
        if self.tripped_at:
            # still in cooldown
            if time.time() - self.tripped_at <
self.reset_timeout:
                raise Exception("Circuit is open;
skipping call")
            # reset circuit
            self.failures = 0
            self.tripped_at = None

        try:
            result = fn(*args, **kwargs)
```

```python
            self.failures = 0
            return result
        except Exception as e:
            self.failures += 1
            if self.failures >=
self.failure_threshold:
                self.tripped_at = time.time()
            raise

# Usage
breaker = CircuitBreaker(failure_threshold=2,
reset_timeout=5)

def guarded_call():
    return breaker.call(call_add, client, 1, 2)
```
python

Pro Tip: Expose circuit state (open/closed) via
properties for observability.

Deep Dive & Best Practices

Concern	Recommendation
Which errors to retry?	Retry on network/timeouts; fail fast on validation or client errors.
Max attempts vs. delay	Balance retry count and delay so you don't overwhelm the service or block your app.
Circuit reset strategy	Use fixed reset_timeout or exponential reset after each trip for dynamic cooldown.
Monitoring	Emit metrics on retries and circuit state transitions to a dashboard (e.g., Prometheus).

Hands-On Exercise

1. Wrap your sync `call_sync` function with
   `@retry(max_attempts=4, delay=1)`.
2. Integrate `CircuitBreaker` so after 3 failures your client skips
   calls for 10 s.

3. Simulate a server down scenario and observe retries then circuit open behavior.
4. Log each retry and circuit trip event for analysis.

Section 5.4 Summary & Cheat Sheet

- **Retry decorator**: `@retry(max_attempts, delay, factor)` for sync; `@async_retry` for async.
- **CircuitBreaker**: trips after N failures, holds open for `reset_timeout`.
- **Use cases**: transient network errors vs. persistent downtime.
- **Metrics**: track retry counts and circuit state.

Pattern	Key Params
Retry	`max_attempts, delay, factor`
Circuit Breaker	`failure_threshold, reset_timeout`

Further Reading / Next Steps

- In **Section 5.5**, we'll explore **Embedding Clients into AI Workflows**, including prompt orchestration and multi-request patterns.

5.5 Embedding Clients into AI Workflows

Overview & Objectives

By the end of this section you will:

1. Integrate your MCP client into a simple AI prompt pipeline.
2. Orchestrate multiple tool calls to gather context before invoking an LLM.
3. Handle errors and timeouts gracefully within the workflow.
4. Structure your code so it's easy to extend with new tools or LLM models.

Motivation & Context

Imagine building a virtual assistant that:

1. Fetches a user's calendar events for today.
2. Retrieves the current weather for their location.
3. Feeds both pieces of context to an LLM to generate a personalized morning briefing.

Embedding your MCP client into this workflow lets you stitch together data sources and AI models in a clean, testable way.

Fundamentals

Concept	Description
Orchestration	Sequencing multiple tool calls and aggregating results for a single AI prompt.
Context Gathering	Using MCP calls (`client.call(...)` or `await client.call(...)`) to fetch external data.
Prompt Assembly	Building an LLM prompt string that includes fetched context and a user query.
Error Isolation	Catching individual tool failures to allow fallback or partial context.

ASCII Flow: AI Workflow

```csharp
[Start]
   |
   |──▶ fetch_calendar()        # MCP call
   |
   |──▶ fetch_weather()         # MCP call
   |
   |──▶ assemble_prompt()       # combine data
   |
   └──▶ call_LLM(prompt)        # OpenAI/GPT call
          |
          └──▶ return final reply
```

Step-by--Step Tutorial

python

```python
# ai_workflow.py
import asyncio
import openai
from client import AsyncMCPClient

# 1. Initialize clients
async def setup_clients():
    mcp = AsyncMCPClient(host="127.0.0.1",
port=4000)
    await mcp.connect()
    # Register notification callbacks if needed
(Section 5.3)
    return mcp

# 2. Define your workflow
async def morning_briefing(user_id: int, location:
str):
    mcp = await setup_clients()

    # 3. Gather context via MCP
    cal_resp = await mcp.call("getCalendarEvents",
[user_id], req_id=101)
    weather_resp = await mcp.call("getWeather",
[location], req_id=102)

    # 4. Assemble prompt
    prompt = (
        f"Good morning! Here is the summary for
user {user_id}:\n\n"
        f"Today's events:\n{cal_resp}\n\n"
        f"Weather in
{location}:\n{weather_resp}\n\n"
        "Please generate a concise briefing."
    )

    # 5. Call the LLM (OpenAI as example)
```

```python
    openai.api_key = "YOUR_API_KEY"
    completion = openai.ChatCompletion.create(
        model="gpt-4o-mini",
        messages=[{"role": "user", "content":
prompt}],
    )

    # 6. Return the assistant's reply
    return completion.choices[0].message.content

# 7. Run the workflow
if __name__ == "__main__":
    briefing =
asyncio.run(morning_briefing(user_id=42,
location="Lagos"))
    print("Morning Briefing:\n", briefing)
python
```

```
#  Watch out: If either MCP call fails, wrap in
try/except to provide partial results or a fallback
message.
```

Deep Dive & Best Practices

Concern	Recommendation
Parallel Calls	If context sources are independent, run them concurrently with `asyncio.gather()`.
Timeouts per Call	Use `asyncio.wait_for(mcp.call(...), timeout=5)` to avoid blocking the entire workflow.
Fallback Strategies	On failure, supply default text (e.g., "No events found") rather than aborting.
Prompt Length Control	Truncate or summarize fetched data if it's too long to fit model context window.

Hands-On Exercise

1. Refactor `morning_briefing` to fetch calendar and weather **in parallel** using `asyncio.gather()`.

118

2. Add error handling: if `getWeather` times out, set `weather_resp = "Weather data unavailable"`.
3. Write a test that mocks `mcp.call` to return sample data and verifies the assembled prompt contains both contexts.

Section 5.5 Summary & Cheat Sheet

- **Orchestrate**: chain or parallelize `client.call` invocations to collect context.
- **Assemble**: build an LLM prompt string incorporating all fetched data.
- **Invoke**: call your chosen LLM API and return the model's reply.
- **Resilience**: wrap each tool call in timeouts and fallbacks.

Step	Code Snippet
Parallel calls	`cal, weather = await asyncio.gather(c1, c2)`
Timeout	`await asyncio.wait_for(mcp.call(...), timeout=5)`
Prompt assembly	`prompt = f"...\n{cal}\n{weather}\n..."`
LLM invocation	`openai.ChatCompletion.create(model=..., messages=[...])`

Chapter 6: Hands On Tutorial: Context Aware Chatbot Server

6.1 Use Case Definition & Data Flow Diagram (ASCII)

Overview & Objectives

By the end of this section you will:

1. Define the core use case for a context-aware chatbot powered by MCP.
2. Identify the components involved (client, MCP server, context store, LLM).
3. Visualize the end-to-end message and data flow in an ASCII diagram.

Motivation & Context

A context-aware chatbot enhances user interactions by fetching relevant data before generating its responses. For example:

- **User:** "What's on my calendar today?"
- **Chatbot:** Retrieves events from a calendar tool, then passes them to the LLM for natural-language summarization.
- **User:** "Can you also remind me of my most recent support ticket?"
- **Chatbot:** Fetches ticket details via MCP, merges with calendar context, and replies seamlessly.

This tutorial will guide you through building that server—one that connects to context sources and orchestrates calls to deliver personalized, informed replies.

Fundamentals

Component	Responsibility
AI Client	Receives user input, fetches manifest, forwards requests to the server.
MCP Server	Hosts tools: calendar, ticket lookup, LLM proxy; validates & invokes them.
Context Store	External data sources (e.g., calendar API, support DB).
LLM Tool	Wraps the language model call via MCP for summarization and reply gen.

Data Flow Diagram (ASCII)

pgsql

```
[User]
   |  "What's on my calendar?"
   ▼
[AI Client]
   |──► fetchManifest() ──► [MCP Server]
   |                             |
   |                             |──► invoke
"getCalendarEvents" ──► [Calendar API]
   |                             |
 ◄─ return events                |
   |                             |
   |                             |──► invoke
"getTicketInfo" ──► [Support DB]
   |                             |
 ◄─ return ticket data           |
   |                             |
   |                             |──► invoke
"summarizeContext" ──► [LLM Tool]
   |
 ◄─ return summary
   |
   |──► receive summary reply
   ▼
[User] "Here's today's schedule… plus your latest
ticket status…"
```

- **Step 1:** Client fetches the manifest to discover available tools.
- **Step 2:** Server calls calendar and ticket tools to gather context.
- **Step 3:** Server sends aggregated context to the LLM tool for a natural-language summary.
- **Step 4:** Client returns the chatbot's reply to the user.

6.1.1 How to Read Our ASCII Diagrams

Overview & Objectives

By the end of this section you will:

1. Understand the basic symbols and layout conventions used in our ASCII diagrams.
2. Read arrows, boxes, and labels to follow data and control flow.
3. Annotate a simple diagram to extract the order of operations.

Motivation & Context

We use ASCII diagrams to illustrate complex flows without relying on images. They render everywhere—plain text, terminals, and markdown—so you can grasp architectures quickly, even when you're deep in code.

Fundamentals

Symbol	Meaning
[Box]	Component or actor (e.g., [AI Client], [MCP Server])
| or |	Vertical flow line: shows continuation of the process downward.
→ or →	Directed arrow: shows a request, call, or data moving forward.
← or ←	Reverse arrow: shows a response or return value moving backward.
Indentation	Nesting of steps under a component to show sub-actions or details.

How to Read a Diagram: Step-by-Step

1. **Identify Actors:**
   - Look for lines encapsulated in square brackets, e.g., [User], [AI Client]. These are your participants.

2. **Follow the Arrows:**
   o A forward arrow (→) means "send" or "invoke."
   o A backward arrow (←) means "return" or "respond."
3. **Track the Sequence Top-to-Bottom:**
   o Read from the topmost box and follow each arrow in order.
   o If multiple arrows emanate from one box, read them in the order they appear.
4. **Use Indentation for Context:**
   o Sub-steps appear indented under a main actor.
   o They represent actions that happen inside that actor before the next arrow.
5. **Combine with Textual Steps:**
   o Diagrams often accompany numbered lists. Cross-reference numbers to see details.

Example Annotation

Original snippet:

```scss
[AI Client]
    ├─► fetchManifest()  ──►  [MCP Server]
    └─► receive summary reply ◄──  [MCP Server]
```

Reading it:

- The AI Client first calls `fetchManifest()` on the MCP Server (├─►).
- Later, after the server processes, the AI Client receives a reply (◄── on the second indented line).

Hands-On Exercise

Challenge:
Take this mini-diagram and list each step in plain English:

```scss
[Client]
    │  ├─► login(user, pass) ─► [Auth Service]
    │  └─► fetchData()          ─► [Data Store]
```

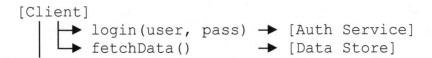

```
|                              ◄─── data
    ◄─── loginResponse(status)
```

1. Which method does `Client` call first?
2. What does the `Data Store` return, and to whom?
3. When does the `Client` get its final response?

Section 6.1.1 Summary & Cheat Sheet

- **Boxes** (`[Name]`) are actors or services.
- ➤ means "invoke" or "send."
- ◄ means "return" or "respond."
- **Indentation** shows nested steps inside an actor.
- **Read top-to-bottom**, left-to-right, following arrows.

Element	Role
`[Component]`	Actor or system module
➤	Forward call or request
◄	Backward response or return
Indent	Sub-actions within an actor

Further Reading / Next Steps

- In **Section 6.2**, we'll design the **User Context Store** and see how data flows from external APIs into our chatbot server.

6.2 Designing the User Context Store

Overview & Objectives

By the end of this section you will:

1. Understand the role of a user context store in a chatbot workflow.
2. Compare in-memory vs. persistent key-value backends.
3. Implement a simple Python context store with `get`, `set`, and `delete` operations.
4. Integrate the store into your MCP server's handlers for stateful conversations.
5. Learn best practices around TTL, serialization, and concurrency.

Motivation & Context

A stateless LLM can't remember earlier messages or user preferences. By adding a **context store**, your chatbot can:

- Recall user data (e.g., name, locale) across turns.
- Accumulate conversation history for richer prompts.
- Persist session state even if your server restarts.

For example, when a user says "What was my last question?" the bot fetches the last query from the context store rather than asking the user to repeat it.

Fundamentals

Concept	Description
Key-Value Store	Maps string keys to JSON-serializable values.
TTL (Time-to-Live)	Optional expiry on entries to limit stale data.
Backend Choices	In-memory (`dict`), Redis, SQLite (via `sqlite3`), or file-based.
Serialization	Convert Python objects to JSON(strings) before storage.
Concurrency	Handle simultaneous reads/writes—use locks or atomic operations.

ASCII Flow: Context Lookup in Handler

```csharp
[ incoming chat request ]
        |
        |-> context = store.get(user_id)        #
retrieve history
        |
        |-> new_response = handler(params, context)
        |
```

```
        ┗▶ store.set(user_id, updated_context)  #
update history
```

Step-by-Step Tutorial

A. Simple In-Memory Store

python

```python
# mcp_server/context_store.py
import threading
import time
import json

class InMemoryContextStore:
    def __init__(self, default_ttl=None):
        self._store = {}
        self._lock = threading.Lock()
        self._default_ttl = default_ttl  # seconds

    def set(self, key: str, value, ttl=None):
        """Store JSON-serializable value under key
with optional TTL."""
        expire_at = time.time() + (ttl or
self._default_ttl) if (ttl or self._default_ttl)
else None
        entry = {"value": json.dumps(value),
"expire_at": expire_at}
        with self._lock:
            self._store[key] = entry

    def get(self, key: str):
        """Retrieve and deserialize value,
respecting TTL."""
        with self._lock:
            entry = self._store.get(key)
            if not entry:
                return None
            if entry["expire_at"] and time.time() >
entry["expire_at"]:
                del self._store[key]
```

```
                return None
            return json.loads(entry["value"])

    def delete(self, key: str):
        """Remove an entry."""
        with self._lock:
            self._store.pop(key, None)
```

B. Integrating into Your MCP Server

python

```
# mcp_server/server.py (excerpt)
from mcp_framework import MCPServer
from mcp_server.context_store import
InMemoryContextStore

server = MCPServer(...)
store = InMemoryContextStore(default_ttl=3600)    #
1-hour sessions

# Example handler using context
def chat_handler(params):
    user_id, message = params
    history = store.get(user_id) or []
    history.append({"user": message})
    # Here you'd call LLM tool with history as
context...
    reply = f"(simulated reply to {message})"
    history.append({"bot": reply})
    store.set(user_id, history)
    return reply

server.register_tool("chat", chat_handler,
description="Chat with context", version="1.0.0")
server.serve()
```

Deep Dive & Best Practices

- **Persistent Backends:**
    - o   Swap in **Redis** (redis-py) for distributed, durable storage.

- o Or use **SQLite** for file-based persistence in low-scale setups.
- **TTL Management:**
  - o Choose sensible defaults (e.g., session length).
  - o Implement periodic cleanup for expired keys in memory stores.
- **Serialization Formats:**
  - o JSON is portable; for complex objects consider **MessagePack** or **Protobuf**.
- **Concurrency Control:**
  - o In-memory: use locks to avoid race conditions.
  - o Redis: operations are atomic; no additional locking needed.
- **Data Size:**
  - o Limit history length (e.g., last 20 messages) to fit LLM context windows.
- **Security:**
  - o Encrypt PII at rest if storing sensitive user data.
  - o Sanitize inputs before storage to prevent injection attacks.

Hands-On Exercise

Challenge:

1. Extend `InMemoryContextStore` to support a `cleanup()` method that removes all expired entries.
2. Replace the in-memory store with **Redis**:
   - o Install `redis` and run a local server.
   - o Write `RedisContextStore` with the same interface (`get`, `set`, `delete`).
3. Modify your `chat_handler` to trim history to the last 10 exchanges before saving.

Section 6.2 Summary & Cheat Sheet

- **Context store** holds per-user conversation state keyed by user ID.
- **Methods:**
  - o `set(key, value, ttl=None)`
  - o `get(key)` → `value or None`

o `delete(key)`
- **Backends:** in-memory (dict + lock), Redis, SQLite.
- **Best practices:** TTL, size limits, serialization, and concurrency.

Method	Description
`set`	Store value under key with optional TTL
`get`	Retrieve deserialized value; returns `None` if expired
`delete`	Remove entry

Further Reading / Next Steps

- **Section 6.3**: Implement chat handlers with context look-up and LLM integration.

6.3 Implementing Chat Handlers with Context Look Up

Overview & Objectives

By the end of this section you will:

1. Write chat handler functions that fetch and update user context from your store.
2. Integrate MCP tool calls (e.g., LLM summarization) within handlers.
3. Handle missing or expired context gracefully.
4. Structure your handlers for clarity, testability, and future extension.

Motivation & Context

A good chatbot remembers past exchanges and weaves them into its replies. Your **chat handler** must:

- Retrieve prior messages (if any) from the context store.
- Append the new user message.
- Call an LLM tool (via MCP) with the full conversation history.
- Save the LLM's reply back into the store.

This pattern ensures continuity across turns and lets the LLM generate richer, context-aware responses.

Fundamentals

Term	Definition
Conversation History	List of alternating user and bot messages for a session (e.g., `[{user:...},{bot:...}]`).
LLM Tool	MCP-registered function that wraps your LLM call (e.g., `summarizeContext`).
Context Lookup	`store.get(user_id)` to fetch existing history or `[]` if none.
State Update	`store.set(user_id, history)` to persist the new conversation state.

Handler Flow (ASCII)

```bash
Incoming request → chat_handler(params):
    ↳ history = store.get(user_id) or []
    ↳ history.append({"user": message})
    ↳ reply = client.call("summarizeContext",
[history], id)
    ↳ history.append({"bot": reply})
    ↳ store.set(user_id, history); return reply
```

Step-by-Step Tutorial

```python
# mcp_server/handlers/chat.py

from mcp_framework import MCPClient, RPCError
from mcp_server.context_store import
InMemoryContextStore
```

```python
# Initialize a shared context store and MCP client
store = InMemoryContextStore(default_ttl=3600)
client =
MCPClient(manifest_url="http://127.0.0.1:4000/manif
est")

def chat_handler(params):
    """
    params: [user_id: str, message: str]
    Returns: the LLM-generated reply string.
    """
    user_id, message = params

    # 1. Load existing conversation history (or
start fresh)
    history = store.get(user_id) or []
# why: avoid NoneType
    history.append({"user": message})
# record user turn

    # 2. Call the LLM summarization tool via MCP
    try:
        # synchronous call; returns a dict with
"result"
        resp = client.call("summarizeContext",
[history], req_id=hash(user_id) & 0xffffffff)
        reply = resp.get("result")
    except RPCError as e:
        # Watch out: handle LLM failures to avoid
crashing the chat
        reply = "Sorry, I'm having trouble
generating a reply right now."

    # 3. Update history with the bot's reply
    history.append({"bot": reply})
    store.set(user_id, history)
# persist for next turn

    return reply
# return raw string
python
```

```
#  Pro Tip: Use a stable hash for req_id or a UUID
to prevent collisions in concurrent sessions.
```

Deep Dive & Best Practices

Concern	Recommendation
History Size	Trim `history` to last N entries (e.g., 20) to fit LLM context windows.
Timeouts on LLM Calls	Wrap `client.call` in a timeout (e.g., via `asyncio.wait_for`) to avoid hanging handlers.
Error Granularity	Distinguish between network errors (`RPCError`) and bad parameters (`-32602`) for tailored fallbacks.
Testability	Inject a mock `client` and `store` when unit-testing `chat_handler`.

Pattern	In-Handler Code Example
Trim History	`history = history[-20:]`
Timeout Handling	`with timeout(5): resp = client.call(...)`
Dependency Injection	`def chat_handler(params, client=client, store=store): ...`

Hands-On Exercise

Challenge:

1. Modify `chat_handler` to **limit** history to the **last 10** exchanges before sending to the LLM.
2. Write a pytest for `chat_handler` that:
    - Uses a **fake store** (in-memory dict) pre-populated with history.
    - Uses a **mock client** returning a known reply.
    - Asserts that the returned reply matches the mock and that `store.set` was called with the updated history.
3. Add handling so that if `message` is empty or whitespace, the handler raises an `RPCError(-32602, "Empty message")`.

Section 6.3 Summary & Cheat Sheet

- **Load history:** `history = store.get(user_id) or []`
- **Record user turn:** `history.append({"user": message})`
- **LLM call:** `resp = client.call("summarizeContext", [history], req_id)`
- **Handle errors:** catch `RPCError` for graceful fallback
- **Persist reply:** `history.append({"bot": reply});` `store.set(user_id, history)`

Step	Code Snippet
Fetch history	`history = store.get(user_id) or []`
Send to LLM	`resp = client.call("summarizeContext",[history],id)`
Update history	`history.append({"bot": reply})`
Save context	`store.set(user_id, history)`

Further Reading / Next Steps

- In **Section 6.4**, we'll **integrate with an LLM via MCP Calls** and explore prompt engineering within handlers.

6.4 Integrating with an LLM via MCP Calls

Overview & Objectives

By the end of this section you will:

1. Define an MCP "LLM tool" that wraps your LLM API (e.g., OpenAI).
2. Register that tool in your server manifest with proper input/output schemas.
3. Implement the `summarizeContext` handler to call the LLM and return its reply.
4. Handle API keys, timeouts, and errors gracefully.

Motivation & Context

Your chatbot needs to transform raw conversation history into a human-friendly message. Rather than embedding LLM calls directly in every handler, MCP lets you expose the LLM as a discrete **tool**. This separation:

- Keeps prompt logic centralized.
- Simplifies error handling and testing.
- Allows AI clients (and even other tools) to reuse the LLM capability.

Fundamentals

Concept	Description
LLM Tool	An MCP capability whose handler invokes an external LLM API.
Prompt Template	A reusable string format that injects conversation history into the LLM call.
Environment Variable	Secure storage for OPENAI_API_KEY or similar credentials.
Timeouts	Maximum wait time for the LLM API call to avoid hanging your server.
Error Handling	Catch API errors (rate limits, network) and return JSON-RPC error codes for client awareness.

Manifest Snippet for `summarizeContext`

jsonc

```
{
  "methods": {
    "summarizeContext": {
      "params": [
        { "name": "history", "type": "array",
"description": "List of user/bot turns" }
      ],
      "result": { "type": "string" },
```

```
      "description": "Generate a natural-language
summary of the conversation history",
      "version": "1.0.0"
    }
  }
}
```

Step-by-Step Tutorial

1. **Install the OpenAI SDK**

   bash

   ```bash
   pip install openai
   ```

2. **Load your API key securely** in `config.py`:

   python

   ```python
   import os
   from dotenv import load_dotenv

   load_dotenv()  # reads .env
   OPENAI_API_KEY = os.getenv("OPENAI_API_KEY")
   if not OPENAI_API_KEY:
       raise ValueError("Missing OPENAI_API_KEY
   in environment")
   ```

3. **Implement the LLM handler** in
   `mcp_server/handlers/llm.py`:

   python

   ```python
   # mcp_server/handlers/llm.py
   import openai
   from mcp_framework import RPCError

   # Load key from config
   from mcp_server.config import OPENAI_API_KEY

   openai.api_key = OPENAI_API_KEY
   ```

```python
PROMPT_TEMPLATE = (
    "You are a helpful assistant. Given the
conversation history:\n\n"
    "{history}\n\n"
    "Provide a concise, friendly reply to
continue the chat."
)

def summarize_context(params):
    """
    params: [history: list of {user:
str}|{bot: str}]
    returns: str (the LLM-generated summary or
reply)
    """
    (history,) = params
    # Build a single string from history list
    formatted = "\n".join(
        f"{turn['user'] if 'user' in turn else
'Assistant'}: {turn.get('user') or
turn.get('bot')}"
        for turn in history
    )
    prompt =
PROMPT_TEMPLATE.format(history=formatted)

    try:
        # Call the OpenAI ChatCompletion API
        resp = openai.ChatCompletion.create(
            model="gpt-4o-mini",
            messages=[{"role":"user",
"content": prompt}],
            timeout=10  # seconds
        )
        return resp.choices[0].message.content
    except openai.error.OpenAIError as e:
        # Convert API errors into JSON-RPC
errors for clients
        raise RPCError(code=-32002,
message="LLM call failed", data={"detail":
str(e)})
```

```python

#  Pro Tip: Use `timeout` to guard against
slow API responses; wrap only the API call.
```

4. **Register the tool** in your server bootstrap (`server.py`):

```python

from mcp_framework import MCPServer
from mcp_server.handlers.llm import
summarize_context

server = MCPServer(host="0.0.0.0", port=4000)
server.register_tool(
    "summarizeContext",
    summarize_context,
    description="Summarize conversation
history with an LLM",
    version="1.0.0"
)
# ... register other handlers ...
server.serve()
```

Deep Dive & Best Practices

Concern	Recommendation
Prompt Engineering	Keep a clear system instruction; test variations to improve output quality.
Token Limits	Truncate `formatted` history if it exceeds model context window (e.g., last 20 turns).
API Key Security	Use a secrets manager (AWS Secrets Manager, Vault) in production instead of `.env`.
Caching Responses	If identical histories recur, cache replies to reduce API costs and latency.
Streaming Outputs	For long summaries, consider `stream=True` and forward chunks as notifications to clients.

Hands-On Exercise

Challenge:

1. Modify `summarize_context` to:
   o Limit history to the last 20 messages.
   o Add a system prompt before the user prompt for role definition.
2. Write a pytest for `summarize_context` that mocks `openai.ChatCompletion.create` to return a fixed reply and asserts the handler returns it correctly.
3. Experiment with a different model (e.g., `"gpt-4o-mini"` → `"gpt-3.5-turbo"`) and note differences in output style.

Section 6.4 Summary & Cheat Sheet

- **Tool Definition:**

python

```python
def summarize_context(params) -> str
server.register_tool("summarizeContext",
summarize_context, …)
```

- **Prompt Template:** Keep system + history clear.
- **API Call:**

python

```python
openai.ChatCompletion.create(
    model="…",
    messages=[{"role":"user","content":
prompt}],
    timeout=10
)
```

- **Error Handling:**

Code	Meaning
-32002	LLM call failed

Further Reading / Next Steps

- OpenAI Chat API docs: https://platform.openai.com/docs/guides/chat
- Prompt design best practices:
  https://platform.openai.com/docs/guides/prompt-design
- In **Section 6.5**, we'll cover **Interactive Testing & Demo Scripts** to validate your chatbot end-to-end.

6.5 Interactive Testing & Demo Script

Overview & Objectives

By the end of this section you will:

1. Build an **interactive demo script** to converse with your context-aware chatbot.
2. Test end-to-end behavior without manual JSON-RPC payload crafting.
3. Verify context persistence across turns in a live session.
4. Automate simple end-to-end smoke checks for your chatbot server.

Motivation & Context

Running isolated unit tests is essential—but nothing beats a live conversation to uncover edge cases in state management, prompt formatting, or network handling. An interactive demo script:

- Speeds up manual QA.
- Serves as a minimal "app" for stakeholders.
- Doubles as an example for users on how to integrate your client library.

Fundamentals

Concept	Description
REPL Loop	Read–Eval–Print loop: prompt user, send to server, print response, repeat.
Session ID	Unique identifier per demo session to scope context storage (e.g., a UUID).
Graceful Shutdown	Handle `Ctrl+C` to cleanly close connections and exit.
Smoke Assertions	Optional inline checks (e.g., non-empty reply) to flag basic failures automatically.

Demo Flow (ASCII Diagram)

pgsql

```
[User types] ──▶ Demo Script ──▶
client.call("chat", [session_id, input], id)
         |                                      |
         ◀── print chatbot reply ───────────────┘
(repeat until user exits)
```

Step-by-Step Tutorial

python

```python
# demo.py
import asyncio
import uuid
from client import AsyncMCPClient  # from Section 5
import signal, sys

async def run_demo():
    # 1. Establish a unique session for context
separation
    session_id = str(uuid.uuid4())
    client = AsyncMCPClient(host="127.0.0.1",
port=4000)
    await client.connect()

    print(f"Starting demo session: {session_id}")
```

```python
    print("Type your message and press Enter
(Ctrl+C to quit):")

    # 2. Graceful shutdown on Ctrl+C
    loop = asyncio.get_event_loop()
    loop.add_signal_handler(signal.SIGINT,
loop.stop)

    # 3. REPL loop
    req_id = 1
    while True:
        try:
            user_input = await
asyncio.get_event_loop().run_in_executor(
                None, sys.stdin.readline
            )
            message = user_input.strip()
            if not message:
                continue  # skip empty lines

            # 4. Send chat request
            resp = await client.call("chat",
[session_id, message], req_id=req_id)
            print(f"Bot: {resp.get('result')}")
            #  Pro Tip: increment req_id to match
each call uniquely
            req_id += 1

        except Exception as e:
            print(f"[Error] {e}")
            break

    # 5. Cleanup
    await client.close()
    print("\nDemo session ended.")

if __name__ == "__main__":
    asyncio.run(run_demo())
python

#  Watch out: ensure your terminal encoding
supports emojis or special characters in replies!
```

141

Deep Dive & Best Practices

- **Concurrent Sessions:**
  - Allow passing a `--session-id` flag to reuse context across multiple demo runs.
- **Automated Smoke Checks:**
  - After each reply, assert `resp.get("result")` is non-empty or matches a regex.
- **Logging:**
  - Add `--verbose` to log raw JSON-RPC payloads for debugging.
- **Dockerized Demo:**
  - Package your client and demo script in a lightweight container for easy sharing.
- **Timeouts:**
  - Wrap `client.call(...)` in `asyncio.wait_for(..., timeout=5)` to avoid hangs.

Hands-On Exercise

1. **Enhance** `demo.py` to accept command-line arguments:
   - `--host`, `--port`, and optional `--session-id`.
2. Add a **smoke test** mode (`--smoke`) where the script:
   - Sends a predefined list of messages,
   - Verifies each reply is non-empty,
   - Exits with code 0 on all passes or 1 on failure.
3. Write a **GitHub Actions** workflow that runs your smoke tests on every push.

Section 6.5 Summary & Cheat Sheet

- **REPL structure:** loop reading `stdin`, calling `client.call("chat", [session_id, msg])`, printing replies.

- **Session management:** use a unique `session_id` to keep context isolated.
- **Shutdown:** trap `SIGINT` to close gracefully.
- **Smoke tests:** inline assertions after each reply.

Step	Code Snippet
Session ID	`session_id = str(uuid.uuid4())`
REPL read	`message = sys.stdin.readline().strip()`
Call chat tool	`resp = await client.call("chat", [session_id, message], req_id=req_id)`
Print bot reply	`print(f"Bot: {resp.get('result')}")`

Further Reading / Next Steps

- In **Chapter 7**, we'll explore **Integrating with OpenAI & Claude** at scale via HTTP and serverless deployments.
- Look into building a simple web UI atop your demo script using **FastAPI** and **WebSockets**: https://fastapi.tiangolo.com/advanced/websockets/

Chapter 7: Integrating MCP with Large Language Models

7.1 OpenAI & Claude Function Calling Overview

Overview & Objectives

By the end of this section you will:

1. Understand how **function calling** works in OpenAI and Claude APIs.
2. Compare differences in defining and handling tool schemas.
3. Implement a basic function-calling example with OpenAI's Python SDK.
4. Parse model responses that request function invocations.
5. Integrate this pattern into your MCP-based handlers for seamless tool orchestration.

Motivation & Context

Large language models can "hallucinate" tool names or param shapes when asked to call external services. Function calling locks down the interface: you provide the exact function schema up front, and the model will emit a structured **function_call** object, ensuring consistent tool invocation. This both simplifies downstream parsing and tightly couples your MCP server's capabilities with the model's reasoning.

Fundamentals

Aspect	OpenAI	Claude (Anthropic)
Schema Definition	`functions=[{name,type,description,parameters: JSON Schema}]`	`tools=[{name,description,parameters: JSON Schema}]`

Aspect	OpenAI	Claude (Anthropic)
Invocation Signal	`message.function _call`	`completion&.tool` or `completion&.tool_inp ut`
Auto Execution	you detect `function_call`, call locally, then re-prompt	similar: detect `tool` field, execute, then re-prompt
Streaming Support	yes, via `stream=True`	yes, via streaming endpoints
Error Handling	model may emit unknown function → handle gracefully	model may skip tool → fallback to default response

ASCII Flow: Function Calling with OpenAI

```csharp
[Your Code]
    ├─ define functions schema
    ├─ send messages + functions → [OpenAI API]
    │                                  ├─ returns message
with function_call
    │                                  │
{name:"getWeather", arguments:"{...}"}
    │                                ◄─
    │
    ├─ parse function_call, invoke local
getWeather(...)
    ├─ send new message with role="function",
content=results
    └─ receive final assistant reply
```

Step-by-Step Tutorial

A. OpenAI Function Calling

1. **Define your function schema**

   ```python
   ```

```python
functions = [
    {
        "name": "getWeather",
        "description": "Get the current
weather for a given location",
        "parameters": {
            "type": "object",
            "properties": {
                "location": {"type": "string",
"description": "City name"},
                "unit": {"type": "string",
"enum": ["celsius","fahrenheit"]}
            },
            "required": ["location"]
        }
    }
]
```

2. Call the ChatCompletion endpoint

python

```python
import openai
openai.api_key = os.environ["OPENAI_API_KEY"]

response = openai.ChatCompletion.create(
    model="gpt-4o-mini",
    messages=[
        {"role":"user", "content":"What's the
weather in Lagos right now?"}
    ],
    functions=functions,
    function_call="auto"  # let the model
decide
)
msg = response.choices[0].message
```

3. Handle the function_call

python

```python
if msg.get("function_call"):
    fn_name = msg.function_call["name"]
    args =
json.loads(msg.function_call["arguments"])
    # Invoke your local tool
    result =
get_weather_tool(args["location"],
args.get("unit"))
    # Send back the function result
    followup = openai.ChatCompletion.create(
        model="gpt-4o-mini",
        messages=[
            {"role":"user", "content":"What's
the weather in Lagos right now?"},
            msg,  # the function_call message
            {"role":"function", "name":
fn_name, "content": json.dumps(result)}
        ]
    )
    final =
followup.choices[0].message["content"]
    print(final)
```

B. Claude Function Calling (Anthropic)

Note: Claude's API may use different parameter names; adjust accordingly.

python

```python
from anthropic import Client, HUMAN_PROMPT,
AI_PROMPT

claude =
Client(api_key=os.environ["ANTHROPIC_API_KEY"])

tools = [
    {
        "name": "getCurrentTime",
        "description": "Get current local time for
a timezone",
        "parameters": {
            "type": "object",
```

```
                "properties": {
                    "timezone": {"type": "string",
"description": "IANA timezone name"}
                },
                "required": ["timezone"]
            }
        }
    ]

response = claude.completions.create(
    model="claude-2",
    prompt=(
        HUMAN_PROMPT
        + "What time is it in London?"
        + AI_PROMPT
    ),
    tools=tools,
    tool_invocation="AUTO"  # let Claude pick
)

# Parse tool invocation
invocation = response.completion.get("tool")
if invocation:
    args = json.loads(invocation["tool_input"])
    time_str =
get_current_time_tool(args["timezone"])
    # Feed back tool result
    followup = claude.completions.create(
        model="claude-2",
        prompt=(
            HUMAN_PROMPT
            + invocation["tool_input"]
            + AI_PROMPT
            + time_str
        )
    )
    print(followup.completion)
```

Deep Dive & Best Practices

Concern	Recommendation
Schema Alignment	Reuse your MCP manifest JSON Schema as the function schema to ensure consistency.
Idempotence	Design tool functions (e.g., `getWeather`) to be idempotent, so re-invocations don't cause side effects.
Argument Validation	Validate `arguments` payload against your JSON Schema before invoking the tool.
Streaming Considerations	When `stream=True`, handle partial `function_call` chunks to assemble full arguments.
Fallback Logic	If model doesn't choose a function, default to code-based processing or a canned response.

Hands-On Exercise

1. **Extend** your MCP server's manifest to include a `getCurrentTime` method with JSON Schema.
2. **Implement** `get_current_time` handler in your server.
3. **Write** a client script that uses OpenAI function calling to request both weather and time in one conversation (two functions available).
4. **Assert** in your test that the model invokes the correct function name and that your final reply includes both pieces of information.

Section 7.1 Summary & Cheat Sheet

- **Enable function calling** by passing `functions` (OpenAI) or `tools` (Claude) schemas to the API call.
- **Check** `message.function_call` (OpenAI) or `completion.tool` (Claude) in the response.
- **Invoke** the corresponding local function, then send its output back as a `role="function"` message.
- **Reuse** your MCP manifest definitions to drive schema consistency.

Step	OpenAI Code Snippet
Define schema	`functions=[{name,description,parameters:` `JSON Schema}]`
Call API	`ChatCompletion.create(...,` `functions=functions, function_call="auto")`
Detect invocation	`if msg.get("function_call"):`
Send back result	Add `{"role":"function", "name":...,` `"content":...}` to `messages` array

Further Reading / Next Steps

- OpenAI function calling docs:
  https://platform.openai.com/docs/guides/function-calling
- Anthropic Claude tools guide:
  https://console.anthropic.com/docs/tools-introduction
- In **Section 7.2**, we'll show how to **wrap LLM calls as MCP tools** for seamless server integration.

7.2 Wrapping LLM Calls as MCP Tools

By the end of this section you will:

1. Understand how to expose your LLM calls as standard MCP tools.
2. Define input/output schemas for your LLM-wrapping tools in the manifest.
3. Implement a Python handler that accepts tool parameters, calls the LLM, and returns structured results.
4. Register your LLM tool with `MCPServer.register_tool` so clients can discover and invoke it.

Motivation & Context

Rather than embedding raw OpenAI or Claude API calls throughout your code, you can centralize them as MCP tools. This keeps your server's capabilities self-documented, discoverable via the manifest, and reusable by any MCP-aware client. Clients simply see "summarizeContext" or "chatWithModel" as another tool—no SDK imports needed.

Fundamentals

Concept	Description
Tool Wrapper	A handler function that maps JSON-RPC params → LLM API call → JSON-serializable result.
Input Schema	JSON Schema for the tool's `params` (e.g., prompt text, model name, max tokens).
Output Schema	JSON Schema for the tool's `result` (e.g., `{"type":"object","properties":{"reply":{"type":"string"}}}`).
Registration	Calling `server.register_tool(name, fn, description, version, params_schema, result_schema)`

ASCII Flow: LLM Tool Invocation

pgsql

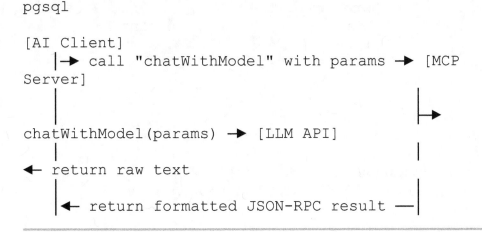

```
[AI Client]
    |→ call "chatWithModel" with params → [MCP
Server]
    |                                        |
    |                                        |→
    |                                        |
chatWithModel(params) → [LLM API]
    |                                        |
 ← return raw text                           |
    |                                        |
    |← return formatted JSON-RPC result —|
```

Step-by-Step Tutorial

1. **Extend your manifest** with an LLM tool entry:

```jsonc
{
  "methods": {
    "chatWithModel": {
      "description": "Send a sequence of
messages to the LLM and get its reply",
      "version": "1.0.0",
      "params": [
        {
          "name": "messages",
          "type": "array",
          "description": "List of {role,
content} dicts for the chat history"
        },
        {
          "name": "model",
          "type": "string",
          "description": "Model name to use
(e.g., gpt-4o-mini)"
        }
      ],
      "result": {
        "type": "object",
        "properties": {
          "reply": { "type": "string" }
        },
        "required": ["reply"]
      }
    }
  }
}
```

2. **Implement the tool handler** in Python
   (mcp_server/handlers/llm_tool.py):

```python
import json
import openai
from mcp_framework import RPCError
```

```python
openai.api_key = os.environ["OPENAI_API_KEY"]

def chat_with_model(params):
    """
    params: [messages: List[dict], model: str]
    returns: {"reply": str}
    """
    messages, model = params
    try:
        resp = openai.ChatCompletion.create(
            model=model,
            messages=messages,
            timeout=10
        )
        text = resp.choices[0].message.content
        return {"reply": text}
    except Exception as e:
        # Wrap any API error in an RPCError so
clients get structured feedback
        raise RPCError(code=-32003,
message="LLM tool failed", data={"detail":
str(e)})
python
```

```
#  Watch out: Validate that `messages` is a
non-empty list before calling the API to avoid
model errors.
```

3. **Register the tool** in your server bootstrap (server.py):

```
python
```

```python
from mcp_framework import MCPServer
from mcp_server.handlers.llm_tool import
chat_with_model

server = MCPServer(host="0.0.0.0", port=4000)
server.register_tool(
    "chatWithModel",
    chat_with_model,
    description="Chat with the LLM given a
message history",
```

```
        version="1.0.0"
)
# ... other registrations ...
server.serve()
```

Deep Dive & Best Practices

Concern	Recommendation
Schema Enforcement	Use `jsonschema` on the server side to validate `params` before invoking the LLM handler.
Prompt Safety	Sanitize user-provided content in `messages` to prevent injection of malicious prompts.
Parameter Defaults	Provide sensible defaults (e.g., default model) when optional params are omitted.
Cost Control	Track token usage per call and expose via `data` in `RPCError` for billing insights.
Caching	Cache identical requests (same `messages` + `model`) to reduce repeated API calls.

Hands-On Exercise

1. **Add a second LLM tool** called `summarizeText` that takes `{"text": string}` and returns `{"summary": string}`.
2. **Write tests** that send invalid `params` (e.g., missing `messages`) and assert you get a `-32602` error for schema violation.
3. **Benchmark** response times for `chatWithModel` versus direct SDK calls to measure overhead.

Section 7.2 Summary & Cheat Sheet

- **Tool manifest entry** defines `params` and `result` schemas for your LLM tool.
- **Handler signature**: `def fn(params: Any)` → JSON-serializable.

- **Register** with `server.register_tool(name, fn, description, version)`.
- **Error wrapping**: raise `RPCError` for API failures.

Step	Code Snippet
Manifest entry	See JSON snippet above
Handler definition	`def chat_with_model(params): ...`
Registration	`server.register_tool("chatWithModel", chat_with_model, ...)`

Further Reading / Next Steps

- In **Section 7.3**, we'll discuss **Managing Streaming & Partial Outputs** from LLMs and forwarding them to clients in real time.

7.3 Managing Streaming & Partial Outputs

Overview & Objectives

By the end of this section you will:

1. Understand how to consume streaming LLM outputs as they arrive.
2. Forward partial results to MCP clients via JSON-RPC **notifications**.
3. Handle message framing and delimiters to reconstruct complete content if needed.
4. Integrate streaming logic into both synchronous and asynchronous MCP server handlers.

Motivation & Context

For long responses (like document summaries or code generation), waiting for the entire LLM reply can introduce unacceptable delays. By **streaming** partial outputs as they arrive, clients can render a progressive—almost real-time—experience, showing users each chunk without waiting for the full response.

Fundamentals

Concept	Description
Streaming	LLM API emits partial content chunks over time instead of a single complete message.
Notification	MCP server → client one-way message (method="streamChunk") to deliver each chunk immediately.
Delimiter/Framing	Strategy (e.g., newline) to indicate end of each JSON-RPC notification payload on the wire.
Backpressure	Managing flow so fast-arriving chunks don't overwhelm slow clients—queue or drop if necessary.
Reassembly	(Optional) Client may concatenate chunks to reconstruct the full reply after streaming ends.

ASCII Flow: Streaming from Server to Client

css

```
[LLM API] —— stream chunks ——▶ [MCP Server]
                                        |
    for each chunk:                     ├▶ send
notification:
    ├ chunk="Hel"                              {
"jsonrpc":"2.0",
    ├ chunk="lo,"
"method":"streamChunk",
    └ chunk=" world!"
"params":["Hel"], "id":null }

                                        ┌ ...
                                        └▶ send

final chunk...
```

Step-by-Step Tutorial

A. Asynchronous Handler with Streaming Notifications

python

```python
# mcp_server/handlers/llm_stream.py
import json
import openai
from mcp_framework import MCPServer

openai.api_key = "<YOUR_KEY>"
server = MCPServer(host="0.0.0.0", port=4000)

@server.tool(name="streamSummary",
description="Stream summary chunks",
version="1.0.0")
async def stream_summary(params, client_writer):
    """
    params: [history: list]
    client_writer: transport to send notifications
directly
    """
    history, = params
    prompt = "Summarize:\n" +
"\n".join(f"{h['user']}: {h['message']}" for h in
history)
    # Call LLM in stream mode
    response = await openai.ChatCompletion.acreate(
        model="gpt-4o-mini",
        messages=[{"role":"user", "content":
prompt}],
        stream=True
    )
    # Iterate over partial chunks
    async for chunk in response:
        text =
chunk.choices[0].delta.get("content")
        if text:
            # Build notification payload
            note = {
                "jsonrpc": "2.0",
                "method": "streamChunk",
                "params": [text]
            }
            # Send with delimiter
```

```python
client_writer.write(json.dumps(note).encode() +
b"\n")
            await client_writer.drain()
    # Optionally send an "end" notification
    end_note = {
        "jsonrpc": "2.0",
        "method": "streamEnd",
        "params": []
    }

client_writer.write(json.dumps(end_note).encode() +
b"\n")
    await client_writer.drain()
python
```

```python
# Pro Tip: Use `stream=True` only for clients that
explicitly support notifications to avoid lost
data.
```

B. Synchronous Variant with Threaded Streaming

```python
python

# mcp_server/handlers/llm_stream_sync.py
import json, openai, threading
from mcp_framework import MCPServer

server = MCPServer(...)

def stream_summary_sync(params, client_writer):
    history, = params
    prompt = "Summarize:\n" +
"\n".join(f"{h['user']}: {h['message']}" for h in
history)
    # Start a thread to consume stream
    def streamer():
        for chunk in openai.ChatCompletion.create(
            model="gpt-4o-mini",

messages=[{"role":"user","content":prompt}],
            stream=True
```

```python
    ):
        text =
chunk.choices[0].delta.get("content")
        if text:
            note =
{"jsonrpc":"2.0","method":"streamChunk","params":[t
ext]}

client_writer.write(json.dumps(note).encode()+b"\n"
)
                client_writer.drain()
        # end marker
        end_note =
{"jsonrpc":"2.0","method":"streamEnd","params":[]}

client_writer.write(json.dumps(end_note).encode()+b
"\n")
        client_writer.drain()

    thread = threading.Thread(target=streamer,
daemon=True)
    thread.start()
    # Return immediately; streaming happens in
background
    return {"status":"streaming_started"}
python

#  Watch out: Ensure `client_writer` remains open
until the background thread finishes streaming.
```

Deep Dive & Best Practices

Concern	Recommendation
Delimiter choice	Newlines work but avoid content with line breaks; length-prefix framing is more robust.
Backpressure	Track client drain times—if await `writer.drain()` blocks too long, consider dropping chunks.
Error in Stream	Catch exceptions in the loop and send a `streamError` notification to the client.

Concern	Recommendation
End-of-Stream Marker	Always send a distinct `"streamEnd"` so clients know when to finalize the reassembly.
Concurrent Streams	Isolate streams per request—use unique writer instances or locks to prevent interleaving.

Hands-On Exercise

1. **Implement** a client callback for `"streamChunk"` that prints each chunk as it arrives, concatenating into a buffer.
2. **Simulate** a slow client by adding `await asyncio.sleep(0.5)` in the callback and observe backpressure.
3. **Extend** the server to send a `"streamError"` notification if the LLM API raises an exception mid-stream.

Section 7.3 Summary & Cheat Sheet

- **Stream mode**: use `stream=True` in LLM API calls to get partial outputs.
- **Notifications**: wrap each chunk in `method="streamChunk"` with no `id`.
- **Delimiter**: send \n (or length prefix) after each JSON payload.
- **End marker**: send a final `streamEnd` notification.
- **Backpressure**: await `drain()` and handle slow clients.

Step	Code Snippet
Invoke LLM streaming	`response = await openai.ChatCompletion.acreate(..., stream=True)`
Send chunk notification	`client_writer.write(json.dumps(note).encode( )+b"\n")`
Send end marker	`method="streamEnd"`

Step	Code Snippet
Error handling	catch and `method="streamError"`

Further Reading / Next Steps

- OpenAI streaming guide:
  https://platform.openai.com/docs/guides/streaming-completions
- Robust framing patterns: https://github.com/user/repo#streaming-patterns
- In **Section 7.4**, we'll explore **Prompt Engineering Best Practices** for function-calling and streaming scenarios.

7.4 Prompt Engineering Best Practices

Overview & Objectives

By the end of this section you will:

1. Understand key prompt engineering principles for reliable tool-calling and streaming.
2. Design clear **system** + **user** messages to guide model behavior.
3. Construct JSON-RPC–compatible prompts that minimize hallucinations.
4. Apply few-shot and template techniques to improve consistency.

Motivation & Context

Even the best tools fail if the model misunderstands your intent. Well-crafted prompts ensure the LLM:

- Chooses the right function.
- Emits arguments that match your JSON Schema.
- Streams useful content rather than gibberish.

Prompt engineering bridges your tool definitions and the model's generative power.

Fundamentals

Principle	Description
Role Definitions	Use a **system** message to set model behavior, then **user** messages for inputs.
Clarity & Specificity	State exactly what you want, referencing your tool names and parameters.
Few-Shot Examples	Provide 1–2 examples of correct function_call outputs to guide the model.
Length Control	Keep prompts within the model's context window; truncate or summarize history.
Validation Hooks	Include "If unable, respond with function_call name 'none'" fallbacks.

Prompt Template (ASCII)

```typescript
SYSTEM: You are a strict JSON-RPC assistant.
You may only reply with a {"function_call":{...}}
object matching provided schemas.

USER: Request: <user question>
```

Step-by-Step Tutorial

1. **Define your system message** to enforce JSON-RPC output:

   ```json
   {
     "role": "system",
     "content": "You are a JSON-RPC agent. "\
                "All outputs must be valid JSON
   with a 'function_call' field "\
                "matching the schema for
   available tools."
   }
   ```

2. **List your functions** with precise descriptions and parameter schemas (see Section 7.1).
3. **Add few-shot examples** showing a typical function_call:

```jsonc
// Example 1
{
  "role":"assistant",
  "function_call": {
    "name":"getWeather",
    "arguments":
{"location":"Lagos","unit":"celsius"}
  }
}
// Example 2...
```

4. **Send the messages** in order: system → examples → user → model.
5. **On streaming calls**, include a note:

```json
{ "role":"system",
  "content":"You may stream chunks via
function_call 'streamChunk' notifications." }
```

Deep Dive & Best Practices

Concern	Recommendation
Hallucinations	Force the model to select from your defined function names only; never free-form.
Parameter Precision	Describe each parameter's purpose and type in your schema description to avoid ambiguity.
Error Handling	Include in your system message: "On error, return {'function_call':{'name':'errorHandler'}}."
Few-Shot Balance	1–2 examples suffice—too many can crowd the context window.
Prompt Reuse	Store templates in code and interpolate only dynamic fields (user input, history).

Hands-On Exercise

1. **Craft a prompt** for a "getNews" tool that fetches the latest headlines:
   o Write a system message enforcing JSON-RPC.
   o Provide one few-shot example of a correct function_call.
   o Formulate the user message asking for "Top 3 AI news today."
2. **Test** with your OpenAI client; verify the model emits the correct function_call JSON.
3. **Adjust** your template if the model wraps the function_call in natural language.

Section 7.4 Summary & Cheat Sheet

- **System vs. User:** System sets rules; user provides input.
- **Function locking:** Model may only reply with defined function names.
- **Few-Shot:** Show 1–2 examples of correct structured outputs.
- **Error fallback:** Instruct the model how to respond when uncertain.
- **Template reuse:** Parameterize only dynamic parts.

Element	Example Snippet
System message	"All replies must be JSON with function_call…"
Few-shot example	Assistant message with `"function_call":{"name":…,"arguments":…}`
User message	"What's the weather in Paris?"

Further Reading / Next Steps

- OpenAI prompt best practices: https://platform.openai.com/docs/guides/chat/prompt-design
- Streaming patterns: see Section 7.3 for real-time chunking.
- In **Section 7.5**, we'll cover **API Key Management & Rate Limiting** to secure and stabilize your LLM integrations.

7.5 API Key Management & Rate Limiting

Overview & Objectives

By the end of this section you will:

1. Securely load your LLM API key without embedding it in code.
2. Implement client-side **rate limiting** to avoid exceeding API quotas.
3. Handle **HTTP 429** ("Too Many Requests") responses with backoff and retries.
4. Compare approaches: environment variables vs. secrets managers, and token bucket vs. fixed-window rate limiting.

Motivation & Context

APIs enforce quotas to protect their infrastructure and control costs. If your client floods the LLM endpoint, you'll get 429 errors—or worse, your key may be throttled or revoked. Proper key management and rate limiting keeps your service reliable, respects your usage plan, and avoids unexpected failures.

Fundamentals

Concern	Environment Variable	Secrets Manager (e.g., AWS Secrets Manager)
Security	Simple, but local files can be leaked	Centralized, auditable, rotated automatically
Ease of Setup	`python-dotenv`, native support	Requires IAM roles, SDK integration
Rotation	Manual updates	Automated via provider policies

Rate Limiting Pattern	Description	Use Case
Fixed Window	Count calls in each minute/hour window	Simple quotas (e.g., 60 calls/minute)

Concern	Environment Variable	Secrets Manager (e.g., AWS Secrets Manager)
Token Bucket	Tokens refill at interval, consume per call	Smooth bursts, steady rate

ASCII Flow: Handling a 429 Response

scss

```
client.call() ──▶ [LLM API]
                   |
                   429 Too Many Requests
                   |
                   retry with backoff
                   |
                   client.call() ──▶ [LLM API]
                   |
                   200 OK
```

Step-by-Step Tutorial

A. Securely Loading the API Key

python

```
# config.py
import os
from dotenv import load_dotenv

load_dotenv()  # loads .env into os.environ

OPENAI_API_KEY = os.getenv("OPENAI_API_KEY")
if not OPENAI_API_KEY:
    raise RuntimeError("Missing OPENAI_API_KEY
environment variable")
```
bash

```
# .env (add to .gitignore!)
OPENAI_API_KEY=sk-...
```

B. Simple Fixed-Window Rate Limiter (Sync)

python

```python
# rate_limiter.py
import time
from threading import Lock

class FixedWindowRateLimiter:
    def __init__(self, max_calls: int,
window_seconds: int):
        self.max_calls = max_calls
        self.window = window_seconds
        self.call_times = []
        self.lock = Lock()

    def acquire(self):
        """Block until a call can be made."""
        with self.lock:
            now = time.time()
            # remove timestamps outside the window
            self.call_times = [t for t in
self.call_times if now - t < self.window]
            if len(self.call_times) >=
self.max_calls:
                # wait until the oldest timestamp
falls out of window
                sleep = self.window - (now -
self.call_times[0])
                time.sleep(sleep)
                now = time.time()
                self.call_times = [t for t in
self.call_times if now - t < self.window]
            self.call_times.append(now)

# Usage in sync client
limiter = FixedWindowRateLimiter(max_calls=60,
window_seconds=60)

def safe_call_add(client, a, b):
    limiter.acquire()  # Watch out: blocks until
under limit
```

```python
    return client.call("add", [a, b], req_id=1)
```

C. Async Token-Bucket Rate Limiter

python

```python
# async_rate_limiter.py
import asyncio
import time

class TokenBucket:
    def __init__(self, rate: float, capacity: int):
        """
        rate: tokens added per second
        capacity: max tokens
        """
        self.rate = rate
        self.capacity = capacity
        self.tokens = capacity
        self.last = time.monotonic()
        self.lock = asyncio.Lock()

    async def acquire(self):
        async with self.lock:
            now = time.monotonic()
            # refill tokens
            delta = (now - self.last) * self.rate
            self.tokens = min(self.capacity,
self.tokens + delta)
            self.last = now
            if self.tokens < 1:
                # need to wait for next token
                await asyncio.sleep((1 -
self.tokens) / self.rate)
                return await self.acquire()
            self.tokens -= 1

# Usage in async client
bucket = TokenBucket(rate=1, capacity=5)  # e.g., 5
calls burst, 1 call/sec
```

```python
async def safe_async_call(client, method, params,
req_id):
    await bucket.acquire()   #  Pro Tip: burst of 5
then steady 1/sec
    return await client.call(method, params,
req_id)
```

D. Handling HTTP 429 with Exponential Backoff

python

```python
# backoff.py
import time
import requests
from requests.exceptions import HTTPError

def call_with_backoff(fn, *args, max_retries=3,
base_delay=1):
    """
    Wrap a function that may raise HTTPError for
status 429.
    """
    attempt, delay = 1, base_delay
    while True:
        try:
            return fn(*args)
        except HTTPError as e:
            if e.response.status_code != 429 or
attempt >= max_retries:
                raise
            time.sleep(delay)
            delay *= 2
            attempt += 1
```

Deep Dive & Best Practices

Concern	Recommendation
Exhaustion Handling	After max_retries, alert or degrade gracefully rather than crash.
Distributed Rate Limits	For multi-instance servers, coordinate limits via Redis or a shared store.

Concern	Recommendation
Monitoring	Emit metrics on 429 rates and limiter wait times to detect plan overuse.
Key Rotation	Rotate keys periodically; integrate secrets manager for automated rotation.

Hands-On Exercise

1. **Add** a `FixedWindowRateLimiter` to your demo script so it never exceeds **30 calls/minute**.
2. **Simulate** 40 rapid calls to `streamSummary` and observe the limiter delaying appropriately.
3. **Implement** a simple backoff wrapper around your HTTP transport in Section 5.1 to retry on 429.
4. **Log** each delay and retry attempt for later analysis.

Section 7.5 Summary & Cheat Sheet

- **API Key**: store in environment or secrets manager; never in code.
- **Fixed-Window vs. Token Bucket**: simple vs. smooth burst control.
- **429 Backoff**: exponential delays on `Too Many Requests`.
- **Distributed Limits**: use Redis or central store for multi-instance coordination.

Pattern	Use Case	Key Code
Env Var Loading	local dev	`os.getenv + dotenv.load_dotenv()`
Fixed Window	simple quotas	`FixedWindowRateLimiter.acquire()`
Token Bucket	bursts + steady rate	`await bucket.acquire()`
429 Backoff	handle HTTP rate limits	`call_with_backoff(fn)`

Further Reading / Next Steps

- Python rate-limiting libraries: https://pypi.org/project/ratelimit/
- Managing secrets with AWS Secrets Manager:
  https://docs.aws.amazon.com/secretsmanager/
- In **Chapter 8**, we'll dive into **Advanced Tool Implementations**, including database connectors and custom data pipelines.

Chapter 8: Advanced Tool Implementations

8.1 File System Tool: Reading/Writing with Path Permissions

Overview & Objectives

By the end of this section you will:

1. Recognize why your file-system tool must enforce path permissions and sandboxing.
2. Define manifest entries for `read_file` and `write_file` methods.
3. Implement `read_file` and `write_file` handlers in Python using `pathlib` and permission checks.
4. Handle errors—missing files, unauthorized paths, I/O exceptions— gracefully.

Motivation & Context

A context-aware agent often needs to load templates, logs, or write reports to disk. Exposing file-system access without controls risks path traversal attacks, data leaks, or corruption. By building a dedicated MCP "File System" tool with explicit read/write methods and path permission checks, you grant needed functionality while keeping your server secure and predictable.

Fundamentals

Method	Purpose	Permissions Check
read_file	Return the contents of a text file.	Path must reside under a configured `BASE_DIR`.
write_file	Write text content to a file (create/overwrite).	Same directory restriction + overwrite flag.

ASCII Flow: Secure File Read

pgsql

```
[AI Client]
    ├─► call "read_file" with
{"path":"notes/todo.txt"} ──► [MCP Server]
    │
│   │
│   │
├─► normalize & validate path under BASE_DIR
    │
├─► open & read file
    │
└─► return content or error
    │
    ◄─ JSON-RPC response ──[MCP Server]
```

Step-by-Step Tutorial

jsonc

```jsonc
// manifest.json snippet
{
  "methods": {
    "read_file": {
      "description": "Read a UTF-8 text file under
the allowed directory",
      "version": "1.0.0",
      "params": [
        { "name": "path", "type": "string",
"description": "Relative file path" }
      ],
      "result": { "type": "string" }
    },
    "write_file": {
      "description": "Write text to a file under
the allowed directory",
      "version": "1.0.0",
      "params": [
```

173

```
        { "name": "path", "type": "string",
"description": "Relative file path" },
        { "name": "content", "type": "string",
"description": "Text to write" }
      ],
      "result": { "type": "object", "properties": {
"success": { "type": "boolean" } } }
    }
  }
}
python

# mcp_server/handlers/files.py

import os
from pathlib import Path
from mcp_framework import RPCError

# Base directory for all file operations
BASE_DIR = Path("/srv/mcp_files").resolve()

def _secure_path(rel_path: str) -> Path:
    """
    Normalize and ensure the given relative path
lives under BASE_DIR.
    Prevents path traversal attacks.
    """
    candidate = (BASE_DIR / rel_path).resolve()
    if not
str(candidate).startswith(str(BASE_DIR)):
        raise RPCError(code=-32010,
message="Unauthorized file path")
    return candidate

def read_file(params):
    """Read and return text content from a file."""
    (rel_path,) = params
    path = _secure_path(rel_path)
    if not path.is_file():
        raise RPCError(code=-32011, message="File
not found", data={"path": rel_path})
    try:
```

```python
        return path.read_text(encoding="utf-8")
    except Exception as e:
        # Wrap any I/O error
        raise RPCError(code=-32012, message="Failed
to read file", data={"detail": str(e)})

def write_file(params):
    """Write text content to a file, creating
parent directories as needed."""
    rel_path, content = params
    path = _secure_path(rel_path)
    try:
        path.parent.mkdir(parents=True,
exist_ok=True)  # create dirs
        path.write_text(content, encoding="utf-8")
# overwrite or create
        return {"success": True}
    except Exception as e:
        raise RPCError(code=-32013, message="Failed
to write file", data={"detail": str(e)})
python
```

```
#  Watch out: Without the `resolve()` check, paths
like "../secret.txt" could escape the sandbox.
```

Deep Dive & Best Practices

Concern	Recommendation
Path Traversal	Always resolve paths and verify they start with BASE_DIR.
Concurrent Writes	Use file locks (e.g., fcntl or flock) if multiple handlers might write the same file.
Large Files	For huge files, stream reads in chunks instead of read_text.
Encoding	Explicitly specify UTF-8 and handle decoding errors with errors="replace".
Permission Errors	Catch PermissionError separately to return a clear Unauthorized error code.

Hands-On Exercise

1. **Implement** a new `delete_file` handler that securely removes a file under `BASE_DIR`, raising an error if the file is missing.
2. **Write pytest tests** for:
   - Reading a small file.
   - Attempting to read `../outside.txt` to verify you get a -`32010` unauthorized error.
   - Writing then reading back content from `notes/example.txt`.
3. **Extend** your `_secure_path` to reject absolute paths outright (`rel_path.startswith("/")`).

Section 8.1 Summary & Cheat Sheet

- **Tool methods:** `read_file(path) → str,`
  `write_file(path, content) → {"success": True}.`
- **Security:**
  - Use `resolve()` to normalize.
  - Ensure resulting path starts with `BASE_DIR`.
- **Error codes:**
  - `-32010` Unauthorized path
  - `-32011` File not found
  - `-32012` Read error
  - `-32013` Write error

Operation	Checkpoints
Path security	`candidate = (BASE_DIR/rel).resolve();` `candidate.startswith(BASE_DIR)`
Read file	`is_file()` before `read_text()`
Write file	`mkdir(parents=True)` then `write_text()`

Further Reading / Next Steps

- Python `pathlib` documentation:
  https://docs.python.org/3/library/pathlib.html

- OWASP file path security guidelines: https://owasp.org/www-community/Path_Traversal
- In **Section 8.2**, we'll build a **Database Tool** for CRUD operations with SQLite and PostgreSQL.

8.2 Database Tool: CRUD Operations (SQLite, PostgreSQL)

Overview & Objectives

By the end of this section you will:

1. Define MCP methods for basic CRUD operations: **dbCreate**, **dbRead**, **dbUpdate**, and **dbDelete**.
2. Understand how to configure connections to **SQLite** and **PostgreSQL** via environment variables.
3. Implement Python handlers that execute parameterized SQL safely and return JSON-serializable results.
4. Handle errors—constraint violations, missing records, connection issues—using `RPCError`.

Motivation & Context

Many real-world agents need to persist and query structured data: user profiles, logs, analytics. A dedicated **Database Tool** lets your MCP server expose CRUD operations in a uniform way, so clients can store and retrieve records without embedding SQL. By building both **SQLite** (file-based) and **PostgreSQL** (server-based) backends, you support lightweight demos and production-grade deployments.

Fundamentals

Method	Params	Result Schema	Description
dbCreate	`[table: string, data: object]`	`{ id: number }`	Insert a new row, return its primary key.
dbRead	`[table: string, id: number]`	`object`	Fetch a row by primary key; error if not found.

177

Method	Params	Result Schema	Description
dbUpdate	[table: string, id: number, data: object]	{ success: boolean }	Update given columns; true on success, error on no match.
dbDelete	[table: string, id: number]	{ success: boolean }	Delete row by key; true if deleted, error if not found.

ASCII Flow: A Simple Read

```pgsql
[Client]
    ├──▶ call "dbRead" params ["users", 42]
    │
[MCP Server]
    ├──▶ connect to DB
    ├──▶ execute: SELECT * FROM users WHERE id=?
    ├──▶ fetch row or no result
    └──▶ return row as JSON or raise error
    ◀── JSON-RPC response
```

Step-by-Step Tutorial

A. Configuration

```python
# mcp_server/config.py
import os
from dotenv import load_dotenv

load_dotenv()

# SQLite file path
SQLITE_PATH = os.getenv("SQLITE_PATH",
"data/app.db")

# PostgreSQL DSN, e.g.
"postgresql://user:pass@host:5432/dbname"
```

```python
POSTGRES_DSN = os.getenv("POSTGRES_DSN")
if not POSTGRES_DSN:
    raise RuntimeError("Missing POSTGRES_DSN
environment variable")
```
bash

```bash
# .env
SQLITE_PATH=./data/app.db
POSTGRES_DSN=postgresql://user:password@localhost:5
432/mcp_db
```

B. Manifest Snippet

jsonc

```jsonc
{
  "methods": {
    "dbCreate": {
      "description": "Insert a record and return
its new id",
      "version": "1.0.0",
      "params": [
        { "name": "table", "type": "string" },
        { "name": "data",  "type": "object" }
      ],
      "result": {
        "type": "object",
        "properties": { "id": { "type": "number" }
},
        "required": ["id"]
      }
    },
    "dbRead": {
      "description": "Fetch a record by its primary
key",
      "version": "1.0.0",
      "params": [
        { "name": "table", "type": "string" },
        { "name": "id",    "type": "number" }
      ],
      "result": { "type": "object" }
    },
```

```
   "dbUpdate": {
     "description": "Update a record by id",
     "version": "1.0.0",
     "params": [
       { "name": "table", "type": "string" },
       { "name": "id",    "type": "number" },
       { "name": "data",  "type": "object" }
     ],
     "result": {
       "type": "object",
       "properties": { "success": { "type":
"boolean" } },
       "required": ["success"]
     }
   },
   "dbDelete": {
     "description": "Delete a record by id",
     "version": "1.0.0",
     "params": [
       { "name": "table", "type": "string" },
       { "name": "id",    "type": "number" }
     ],
     "result": {
       "type": "object",
       "properties": { "success": { "type":
"boolean" } },
       "required": ["success"]
     }
   }
 }
}
```

C. Handler Implementations

python

```python
# mcp_server/handlers/database.py

import sqlite3
import psycopg2
from psycopg2.extras import RealDictCursor
from mcp_framework import RPCError
```

```python
from mcp_server.config import SQLITE_PATH,
POSTGRES_DSN

# -- Helper to prevent SQL injection --
def _validate_identifier(name: str):
    if not name.isidentifier():
        raise RPCError(code=-32020,
message=f"Invalid table name: {name}")

# -- SQLite backend connection --
def _sqlite_conn():
    return sqlite3.connect(SQLITE_PATH,
detect_types=sqlite3.PARSE_DECLTYPES)

# -- PostgreSQL backend connection --
def _pg_conn():
    return psycopg2.connect(POSTGRES_DSN,
cursor_factory=RealDictCursor)

# -- Common create logic --
def dbCreate(params):
    table, data = params
    _validate_identifier(table)
    cols = ", ".join(data.keys())
    placeholders = ", ".join("?" for _ in data)
    values = tuple(data.values())
    try:
        conn = _sqlite_conn()
        cur = conn.cursor()
        sql = f"INSERT INTO {table} ({cols}) VALUES
({placeholders})"
        cur.execute(sql, values)
        conn.commit()
        new_id = cur.lastrowid
        return {"id": new_id}
    except Exception as e:
        raise RPCError(code=-32021, message="SQLite
insert failed", data={"detail": str(e)})
    finally:
        conn.close()

def dbRead(params):
```

```
    table, record_id = params
    _validate_identifier(table)
    try:
        conn = _pg_conn()
        with conn:
            cur = conn.cursor()
            cur.execute(f"SELECT * FROM {table}
WHERE id = %s", (record_id,))
            row = cur.fetchone()
            if row is None:
                raise RPCError(code=-32022,
message="Record not found", data={"id": record_id})
            return row  # RealDictCursor yields
dict
    except RPCError:
        raise
    except Exception as e:
        raise RPCError(code=-32023,
message="PostgreSQL read failed", data={"detail":
str(e)})
    finally:
        conn.close()


def dbUpdate(params):
    table, record_id, data = params
    _validate_identifier(table)
    set_clause = ", ".join(f"{k} = %s" for k in
data.keys())
    values = tuple(data.values()) + (record_id,)
    try:
        conn = _pg_conn()
        with conn:
            cur = conn.cursor()
            cur.execute(f"UPDATE {table} SET
{set_clause} WHERE id = %s", values)
            if cur.rowcount == 0:
                raise RPCError(code=-32024,
message="Update failed; record not found",
data={"id": record_id})
            return {"success": True}
    except RPCError:
        raise
```

```python
    except Exception as e:
        raise RPCError(code=-32025,
message="PostgreSQL update failed", data={"detail":
str(e)})
    finally:
        conn.close()


def dbDelete(params):
    table, record_id = params
    _validate_identifier(table)
    try:
        conn = _sqlite_conn()
        cur = conn.cursor()
        cur.execute(f"DELETE FROM {table} WHERE id
= ?", (record_id,))
        conn.commit()
        if cur.rowcount == 0:
            raise RPCError(code=-32026,
message="Delete failed; record not found",
data={"id": record_id})
        return {"success": True}
    except RPCError:
        raise
    except Exception as e:
        raise RPCError(code=-32027, message="SQLite
delete failed", data={"detail": str(e)})
    finally:
        conn.close()
```
python

Pro Tip: Always use parameterized queries (`?` or `%s`) to prevent SQL injection.

4. **Register these tools** in your server bootstrap:

   python

```python
from mcp_framework import MCPServer
from mcp_server.handlers.database import
dbCreate, dbRead, dbUpdate, dbDelete

server = MCPServer(host="0.0.0.0", port=4000)
```

```
server.register_tool("dbCreate", dbCreate,
description="Insert record", version="1.0.0")
server.register_tool("dbRead",  dbRead,
description="Read record by id",
version="1.0.0")
server.register_tool("dbUpdate", dbUpdate,
description="Update record by id",
version="1.0.0")
server.register_tool("dbDelete", dbDelete,
description="Delete record by id",
version="1.0.0")
server.serve()
```

Deep Dive & Best Practices

- **Connection Pooling:**
  - For PostgreSQL, use
    `psycopg2.pool.ThreadedConnectionPool` or
    switch to `asyncpg` with `asyncio` for high throughput.
- **Transaction Management:**
  - Wrap multi-step operations in explicit transactions to ensure atomicity.
- **Schema Validation:**
  - Validate `data` keys against an allowed column list or JSON Schema to prevent unexpected writes.
- **Error Granularity:**
  - Distinguish constraint violations (duplicate keys) from connection errors for better client feedback.
- **Performance:**
  - Create database indexes on foreign keys or frequently queried columns.
- **Migration Strategy:**
  - Integrate Alembic (for SQLAlchemy) or raw SQL migration scripts to evolve your schema safely.

Hands-On Exercise

1. **Create** a `users` table in both SQLite and PostgreSQL with columns (`id INTEGER PRIMARY KEY`, `name TEXT`, `email TEXT UNIQUE`).
2. **Write pytest** tests for each CRUD method:
   - `dbCreate(["users",` `{"name":"Alice","email":"a@x.com"}])` returns a new `id`.
   - `dbRead(["users", id])` returns `{"id":…,` `"name":"Alice", "email":"a@x.com"}`.
   - Trying to create another user with the same email raises a constraint error code.
3. **Extend** `dbRead` to accept an optional second parameter `fields:` `string[]` to select only specific columns.

Section 8.2 Summary & Cheat Sheet

- **Methods & Signatures:**

Method	Params	Returns
dbCreate	[table, data]	{"id": number}
dbRead	[table, id]	object
dbUpdate	[table, id, data]	{"success": boolean}
dbDelete	[table, id]	{"success": boolean}

- **Key Practices:**
  - **Validate identifiers** before interpolation.
  - **Use parameterized queries** (`?` for SQLite, `%s` for PostgreSQL).
  - **Catch and map** exceptions to `RPCError` with distinct codes.
  - **Close connections** in `finally` blocks or use connection pools.

Further Reading / Next Steps

- SQLite Python guide: https://docs.python.org/3/library/sqlite3.html
- psycopg2 connection pooling:
  https://www.psycopg.org/docs/pool.html
- Schema migrations with Alembic: https://alembic.sqlalchemy.org/
- In **Section 8.3**, we'll build an **HTTP Tool** for invoking REST and GraphQL APIs safely.

8.3 HTTP Tool: REST & GraphQL APIs

Overview & Objectives

By the end of this section you will:

1. Define MCP methods for interacting with REST (`restGet`, `restPost`) and GraphQL (`graphqlQuery`) APIs.
2. Extend your manifest with appropriate JSON Schema for URL, headers, payload, and query.
3. Implement Python handlers using `requests` (sync) or `aiohttp` (async) that perform HTTP calls safely.
4. Handle common HTTP errors (timeouts, non-2xx statuses) and map them to `RPCError`.

Motivation & Context

Agents often need to fetch live data from web services—weather APIs, stock quotes, or custom GraphQL backends. A dedicated **HTTP Tool** in your MCP server standardizes these calls, lets clients discover endpoints via the manifest, and centralizes error handling and retries.

Fundamentals

Method	Params	Result	Description
restGet	{"url":"string","headers": "object","params":"object" }	object	Perform an HTTP GET; return JSON-decoded response.
restPost	{"url":"string","headers": "object","body":"object"}	object	Perform an HTTP POST; return JSON-decoded response.
graphqlQuery	{"url":"string","headers": "object","query":"string", "variables":"object"}	object	Send a GraphQL query; return data or errors.

ASCII Flow: REST GET Tool

```
arduino

[AI Client]
   ├─► call "restGet" params {"url":...,
"params":{...}} ──► [MCP Server]

|

├─► requests.get(url, params, headers, timeout)

├─► resp.raise_for_status()

└─► return resp.json()
```

```
    ← JSON-RPC response —[MCP
Server]————————————► [AI Client]
```

Step-by-Step Tutorial

```jsonc
// manifest.json snippet
{
  "methods": {
    "restGet": {
      "description": "Perform an HTTP GET and
return JSON response",
      "version": "1.0.0",
      "params": [
        { "name": "url",     "type": "string" },
        { "name": "headers", "type": "object" },
        { "name": "params",  "type": "object" }
      ],
      "result": { "type": "object" }
    },
    "graphqlQuery": {
      "description": "Send a GraphQL query and
return the response data",
      "version": "1.0.0",
      "params": [
        { "name": "url",      "type": "string" },
        { "name": "headers",   "type": "object" },
        { "name": "query",     "type": "string" },
        { "name": "variables","type": "object" }
      ],
      "result": { "type": "object" }
    }
  }
}
```
```python
python

# mcp_server/handlers/http_tools.py

import requests
from mcp_framework import RPCError
```

```python
def rest_get(params):
    """Perform HTTP GET; return parsed JSON."""
    url, headers, query = params
    try:
        resp = requests.get(url, headers=headers or
{}, params=query or {}, timeout=5)
        resp.raise_for_status()  # Watch out:
raises HTTPError on 4xx/5xx
        return resp.json()       # May raise
ValueError if non-JSON
    except requests.exceptions.HTTPError as e:
        raise RPCError(code=-32030, message="HTTP
GET failed", data={"status": resp.status_code})
    except requests.exceptions.RequestException as
e:
        raise RPCError(code=-32031, message="HTTP
request error", data={"detail": str(e)})

def graphql_query(params):
    """Perform GraphQL POST; return 'data' or raise
on 'errors'."""
    url, headers, query, variables = params
    payload = {"query": query, "variables":
variables or {}}
    try:
        resp = requests.post(url, json=payload,
headers=headers or {}, timeout=5)
        resp.raise_for_status()
        body = resp.json()
        if "errors" in body:
            raise RPCError(code=-32032,
message="GraphQL errors", data={"errors":
body["errors"]})
        return body.get("data", {})
    except RPCError:
        raise
    except Exception as e:
        raise RPCError(code=-32033,
message="GraphQL request error", data={"detail":
str(e)})
python
```

```
#  Pro Tip: Always validate 'url' with a whitelist
or regex to prevent SSRF attacks.
```

Deep Dive & Best Practices

Concern	Recommendation
Timeouts	Set a sensible `timeout` (e.g., 5 s) to avoid hanging handlers.
Error Mapping	Map 4xx vs. 5xx to distinct `RPCError` codes for client logic.
SSRF Protection	Validate URLs against allowed domains before calling.
Retries	Wrap calls with retry decorator (Section 5.4) for transient errors.
Asynchronous Variant	Use `aiohttp` for non-blocking servers; mirror sync logic with `async`.

Hands-On Exercise

1. **Implement** a `restPost` handler similar to `rest_get`, handling JSON body.
2. **Write pytest** tests that mock `requests.get` to return status 200 with JSON, status 404, and a `Timeout` exception—assert correct `RPCError` codes.
3. **Extend** `graphql_query` to support batching multiple queries in one request.

Section 8.3 Summary & Cheat Sheet

- **Methods & Signatures:**

Method	Params
restGet	[url, headers, params]
graphqlQuery	[url, headers, query, variables]

- **Key Patterns:**
  - Use `resp.raise_for_status()` to catch HTTP errors.
  - Wrap all exceptions in `RPCError` with unique codes.
  - Validate and sanitize URLs to prevent SSRF.

Further Reading / Next Steps

- `requests` documentation: https://docs.python-requests.org/
- `aiohttp` for async: https://docs.aiohttp.org/
- GraphQL spec: https://graphql.org/learn/
- In **Section 8.4**, we'll build a **Custom Data-Processing Tool** (e.g., Pandas pipeline).

8.4 Custom Data Processing Tool

Overview & Objectives

By the end of this section you will:

1. Define an MCP method for custom data processing (e.g., `processData`).
2. Extend your manifest with JSON Schema for specifying a Pandas pipeline (operations, parameters).
3. Implement a Python handler using Pandas to load, transform, and return JSON-serializable results.
4. Handle errors—invalid operations, malformed data, I/O issues— using `RPCError`.

Motivation & Context

Data pipelines power analytics, cleansing, and reporting tasks. Exposing a **Custom Data-Processing Tool** lets your MCP server:

- Read tabular data (CSV, JSON).
- Apply transformations (filter, aggregate, pivot).
- Return results ready for further AI analysis or direct consumption.

For example, an agent could request "compute the monthly average sales from this CSV," and your server would run a Pandas pipeline and return the output.

Fundamentals

Concept	Description
Data Source	File path or raw CSV/JSON string that the pipeline will load.
Operations	A list of transformation steps (e.g., `filter`, `groupby`, `sum`, `pivot`).
Parameters	Operation-specific arguments (column names, conditions).
Result	JSON-serializable object (list of dicts, summary metrics).
Pipeline Schema	JSON Schema defining valid operations and their parameter structure.

Manifest Snippet for `processData`

jsonc

```
{
  "methods": {
    "processData": {
      "description": "Run a Pandas pipeline on
tabular data and return the transformed result",
      "version": "1.0.0",
      "params": [
        {
          "name": "data_source",
          "type": "object",
          "description": "Either
{'csv_text':string} or {'csv_path':string}"
        },
        {
          "name": "pipeline",
          "type": "array",
          "description": "List of operations to
apply",
```

```
        "items": {
          "type": "object",
          "required": ["op"],
          "properties": {
            "op": { "type": "string", "enum":
["filter","groupby","sum","pivot"] },
            "args": { "type": "object" }
          }
        }
      }
    ],
    "result": {
      "type": "array",
      "items": { "type": "object" }
    }
  }
}
}
```

Step-by-Step Tutorial

python

```python
# mcp_server/handlers/data_tool.py

import io
import json
import pandas as pd
from mcp_framework import RPCError

def process_data(params):
    """
    params: [data_source: dict, pipeline: list of
{op:str, args:dict}]
    returns: list of dicts (pipeline result)
    """
    data_source, pipeline = params

    # 1. Load the DataFrame
    try:
        if "csv_text" in data_source:
```

```python
                df =
pd.read_csv(io.StringIO(data_source["csv_text"]))
            elif "csv_path" in data_source:
                df =
pd.read_csv(data_source["csv_path"])
            else:
                raise RPCError(code=-32040,
message="Invalid data_source")
        except FileNotFoundError:
            raise RPCError(code=-32041, message="CSV
file not found", data={"path":
data_source.get("csv_path")})
        except Exception as e:
            raise RPCError(code=-32042, message="Failed
to load DataFrame", data={"detail": str(e)})

        # 2. Apply each pipeline step
        for step in pipeline:
            op = step.get("op")
            args = step.get("args", {})
            try:
                if op == "filter":
                    # args: {"condition": "column > 5"}
                    df = df.query(args["condition"])
                elif op == "groupby":
                    # args: {"by": ["col1"], "agg":
{"col2":"sum"}}
                    df =
df.groupby(args["by"]).agg(args["agg"]).reset_index
()
                elif op == "sum":
                    # args: {"column": "col2"}
                    total = df[args["column"]].sum()
                    return [{"total": total}]
                elif op == "pivot":
                    # args:
{"index":"col1","columns":"col2","values":"col3"}
                    df = df.pivot(index=args["index"],
columns=args["columns"],
values=args["values"]).reset_index()
                else:
```

```python
        raise RPCError(code=-32043,
message=f"Unsupported op '{op}'")
        except KeyError as e:
            raise RPCError(code=-32044,
message="Missing pipeline argument",
data={"detail": str(e)})
        except Exception as e:
            raise RPCError(code=-32045,
message=f"Pipeline step '{op}' failed",
data={"detail": str(e)})

    # 3. Return result as list of dicts
    try:
        return df.to_dict(orient="records")
    except Exception as e:
        raise RPCError(code=-32046, message="Failed
to serialize result", data={"detail": str(e)})
python

#  Pro Tip: Use `df.query()` for expressive filters
but validate the 'condition' to avoid injection
risks.
```

Deep Dive & Best Practices

Concern	Recommendation
Operation Validation	Validate op against allowed list before execution.
Condition Safety	Restrict query conditions to column names and safe operators; avoid raw user input.
Large Data	For very large CSVs, consider chunked reading with pd.read_csv(chunksize=...).
Error Granularity	Map individual step failures to distinct error codes for easier debugging.
Extensibility	Allow custom functions by mapping op to callables registered in a dictionary.

Pattern	Benefit
Chunked Read	Reduces memory footprint for big files
Preflight Checks	Verify columns exist before running heavy operations

Concern	Recommendation
Registered Ops Map	Use `OPS = {"filter":do_filter, ...}` to simplify adding new operations

Hands-On Exercise

1. **Extend** the pipeline with an `"average"` operation that takes `{"column":"col2"}` and returns `[{"average": float}]`.
2. **Write pytest** tests for:
   - Filtering rows (`filter`).
   - Grouping and summing (`groupby`, `"agg"`: `{"value":"sum"}`).
   - Handling a missing column in `filter` to confirm error code `-32044`.
3. **Profile** the handler on a 100 MB CSV to measure processing time and optimize if needed (e.g., using chunksize).

Section 8.4 Summary & Cheat Sheet

- **Method:** `processData(data_source, pipeline)` → `list[dict]`
- **Pipeline Ops:** `filter`, `groupby`, `sum`, `pivot` (+ custom)
- **Key Points:**
  - Load via `io.StringIO` or file path.
  - Loop through steps, apply with Pandas methods.
  - Return `df.to_dict(orient="records")`.
  - Raise `RPCError` on any failure with specific codes.

Operation	Example `args`	Returns
filter	`{"condition":"age>30"}`	filtered rows
groupby	`{"by":["dept"],"agg":{"salary":"mean"}}`	aggregated DataFrame

Operation	Example `args`	Returns
sum	`{"column":"sales"}`	`[{"total": ...}]`
pivot	`{"index":"month","columns":"region","values":"rev"}`	pivoted DataFrame

Further Reading / Next Steps

- Pandas user guide: https://pandas.pydata.org/docs/
- Secure expression evaluation: https://github.com/dantosha/evalfire
- In **Section 8.5**, we'll cover **Dynamic Capability Manifests** for runtime extension of your server's tool set.

8.5 Dynamic Capability Manifests

Overview & Objectives

By the end of this section you will:

1. Understand the concept of **dynamic capability manifests**—how your server advertises tools added at runtime.
2. See how to design a manifest generator that merges static and dynamic tools.
3. Implement Python code to **watch** a plugins directory, **load** new modules, and **update** the manifest on the fly.
4. Handle version conflicts and safely reload capabilities without restarting the server.

Motivation & Context

In a plugin-driven architecture—where new tools can be dropped into a `plugins/` folder—you want your MCP server to automatically pick up and advertise those new capabilities. A **dynamic manifest** ensures clients always fetch the latest list of tools, including those added or removed at runtime, without manual server restarts or hard-coding entries.

Fundamentals

Concept	Description
Static Manifest	A JSON file (`manifest.json`) listing the server's built-in tools at startup.
Dynamic Plugins	Python modules in a watched directory that define additional tools via decorators or registration.
Manifest Generator	Function that inspects `server.tools` registry and builds the current manifest as JSON.
Hot Reload	File-system watcher (e.g., `watchdog`) triggers re-import and re-registration of changed plugins.
Version Resolution	Strategy to handle duplicate tool names or version bumps from dynamic plugins.

ASCII Flow: Dynamic Manifest Reload

scss

```
[ plugins/new_tool.py added ]
             |
   filesystem watcher event
             |
   reload_plugins()  ──▶ import new module
             |              register its tools
             ▼
   regenerate_manifest()  ──▶ write to manifest.json
or cache
             |
  client.fetchManifest()  ◀── updated manifest
```

Step-by-Step Tutorial

python

```python
# mcp_server/manifest_manager.py
import json, os, importlib
from watchdog.observers import Observer
```

```python
from watchdog.events import FileSystemEventHandler

MANIFEST_PATH = "manifest.json"
PLUGINS_DIR = "plugins"

class PluginReloader(FileSystemEventHandler):
    def __init__(self, server):
        self.server = server

    def on_created(self, event):
        if event.src_path.endswith(".py"):
            self.reload_plugin(event.src_path)

    def reload_plugin(self, path):
        module_name =
os.path.splitext(os.path.basename(path))[0]
        spec =
importlib.util.spec_from_file_location(f"plugins.{m
odule_name}", path)
        mod = importlib.util.module_from_spec(spec)
        spec.loader.exec_module(mod)
        # any @server.tool registrations in mod
will have run
        regenerate_manifest(self.server)

def regenerate_manifest(server):
    """Dump current capabilities to
manifest.json."""
    manifest = {
        "version": server.manifest_version,
        "name": server.name,
        "description": server.description,
        "methods": {}
    }
    for tool in server.registered_tools:
        manifest["methods"][tool.name] = {
            "description": tool.description,
            "version": tool.version,
            "params": tool.params_schema,
            "result": tool.result_schema
        }
    with open(MANIFEST_PATH, "w") as f:
```

```python
        json.dump(manifest, f, indent=2)

# In server bootstrap:
from mcp_framework import MCPServer
from mcp_server.manifest_manager import
PluginReloader, regenerate_manifest
import os

server = MCPServer(...)
# register built-ins...
regenerate_manifest(server)

# start filesystem watcher
observer = Observer()
observer.schedule(PluginReloader(server),
PLUGINS_DIR, recursive=False)
observer.start()

server.serve()
observer.stop()
observer.join()
python

#  Pro Tip: Use `Observer(timeout=1)` so your
server shutdown isn't blocked by the watcher.
```

Deep Dive & Best Practices

Concern	Recommendation
Name Collisions	Detect duplicate `tool.name` during regeneration; either reject or auto-suffix version numbers.
Performance	Debounce rapid file events (e.g., copy editors) to avoid repeated imports.
Security	Only load plugins from a trusted directory; consider code signing for production.
State Reset	If a plugin unregisters a tool, you may need to restart the server or implement an unregister API.
Atomic Manifest Writes	Write to a temp file then rename to avoid clients fetching a partially written manifest.

Hands-On Exercise

1. **Create** a new plugin file `plugins/math_tools.py` defining a decorator-registered `square` tool.
2. **Drop** it into the `plugins/` directory while your server is running.
3. **Fetch** `/manifest` and verify that `square` appears with its schema.
4. **Invoke** `square` via your client to confirm dynamic registration worked.

Section 8.5 Summary & Cheat Sheet

- **Dynamic manifest** picks up new tools from a watched plugins directory.
- **Key components:**
  - `PluginReloader` (file-watch handler)
  - `regenerate_manifest(server)` to dump `server.registered_tools`
- **Safety:** debounce events, validate tool names, write manifest atomically.

Step	Code Snippet
Watch plugins folder	`Observer().schedule(PluginReloader, "plugins")`
Import new module	`spec.loader.exec_module(mod)`
Regenerate manifest	`regenerate_manifest(server)`

Further Reading / Next Steps

- `watchdog` documentation: https://github.com/gorakhargosh/watchdog
- Secure plugin architectures: https://12factor.net/codebase
- In **Chapter 9**, we'll explore **Deployment & Scaling**: Docker, Kubernetes, and serverless MCP servers.

Chapter 9: Security & Sandboxing

9.1 Authentication Strategies

Section 9.1 Overview & Objectives

By the end of this section you will:

1. Compare API-key vs. OAuth 2.0 authentication flows for MCP tools.
2. Securely validate incoming requests using header-based API keys.
3. Integrate an OAuth 2.0 client to obtain and refresh tokens for downstream services.
4. Configure your MCP server to enforce per-tool access controls.

Motivation & Context

In production, you don't want just anyone calling your MCP server's powerful tools. API keys are simple to issue and revoke, while OAuth 2.0 provides delegated, scoped access for user-centric flows. Choosing and implementing the right strategy ensures only authorized clients—or end users—can invoke sensitive operations (database writes, file access, LLM calls).

Fundamentals

Strategy	Description	Strengths	Trade-offs
API Key	Static token sent in an HTTP header (e.g., `Authorization: Bearer ...`).	Easy to implement; minimal overhead.	Harder to rotate per user; bearer tokens shared.
OAuth 2.0	Standardized flows (Client Credentials, Authorization Code) to obtain short-lived tokens.	Per-user scopes; token revocation.	More complex setup; needs token store and refresh logic.

Strategy Component	Description API Key Flow	Strengths OAuth 2.0 Client Credentials	Trade-offs OAuth 2.0 Auth Code (User)
Token Issuance	Manual or automated dashboard	`/token` endpoint with client_secret	User login + consent → `/token`
Validation	Match header against server list	Verify JWT signature and claims	Ditto with user scopes
Rotation	Revoke old key, issue new key	Configure token TTL and rotation policy	User revokes grant
Use Case	Machine-to-machine scripts	Service-to-service calls	End-user–driven interactions

Step-by-Step Tutorial

A. API-Key Validation in MCPServer

python

```
# mcp_server/auth/apikey.py
from mcp_framework import RPCError

# In production, load from secure store or env
VALID_KEYS = {"service-a": "sk-abc123", "service-b": "sk-def456"}

def require_api_key(func):
    def wrapper(params, client_writer=None,
context=None):
        api_key =
context.headers.get("Authorization",
"").split("Bearer ")[-1]
        if api_key not in VALID_KEYS.values():
            raise RPCError(code=-32604,
message="Unauthorized: invalid API key")
        return func(params)
```

```
        return wrapper
python

# server.py (excerpt)
from mcp_framework import MCPServer
from mcp_server.handlers.files import read_file
from mcp_server.auth.apikey import require_api_key

server = MCPServer(...)
# Wrap handlers that need protection
server.register_tool("read_file",
require_api_key(read_file), description="...",
version="1.0.0")
```

B. OAuth 2.0 Client Credentials Flow

```python
python

# mcp_server/auth/oauth2.py
import time, requests
from threading import Lock

TOKEN_URL = "https://auth.example.com/oauth2/token"
CLIENT_ID = os.getenv("OAUTH_CLIENT_ID")
CLIENT_SECRET = os.getenv("OAUTH_CLIENT_SECRET")

class OAuth2Client:
    def __init__(self):
        self.token = None
        self.expiry = 0
        self.lock = Lock()

    def get_token(self):
        with self.lock:
            if not self.token or time.time() >=
self.expiry:
                resp = requests.post(TOKEN_URL,
data={
                    "grant_type":
"client_credentials",
                    "client_id": CLIENT_ID,
                    "client_secret": CLIENT_SECRET,
```

```
                }, timeout=5)
                resp.raise_for_status()
                data = resp.json()
                self.token = data["access_token"]
                self.expiry = time.time() +
data.get("expires_in", 300) - 30
                return self.token

oauth_client = OAuth2Client()

def require_service_scope(scope):
    def decorator(func):
        def wrapper(params, client_writer=None,
context=None):
            token = oauth_client.get_token()
            # validate token has required scope
(JWT decode or /introspect)
            # omitted for brevity...
            return func(params)
        return wrapper
    return decorator
```

Deep Dive & Best Practices

Concern	API Key	OAuth 2.0
Key Distribution	Distribute manually to clients.	Automate via CI/CD and provider dashboards.
Revocation	Track valid keys list; remove compromised.	Use token introspection and short TTLs.
Scope Enforcement	Coarse (all-or-nothing per key).	Fine-grained scopes in tokens.
Audit Logging	Log key usage with timestamps.	Include sub claim and scopes in logs.

- **Token Stores:** For OAuth 2.0, back your server with a secure token cache (in-memory or Redis).
- **Introspection vs. JWT:** If your provider uses opaque tokens, call the introspection endpoint; with JWT, verify signature and claims locally.

- **Header Parsing:** Standardize header names (`Authorization`) and handle missing or malformed headers gracefully.

Hands-On Exercise

1. **Issue** a new API key (e.g., `sk-xyz789`), add it to `VALID_KEYS`, and test a protected tool with and without the key.
2. **Configure** a mock OAuth 2.0 server (e.g., using `oauthlib`'s testing utilities) and integrate the client credentials flow.
3. **Write pytest** fixtures to simulate both valid and expired tokens, asserting that expired tokens are refreshed.

Section 9.1 Summary & Cheat Sheet

- **API Keys:** simple header-based tokens; easy but coarse-grained.
- **OAuth 2.0:** standardized flows with scopes and token expiry.
- **Implementation:** use decorators (`require_api_key`, `require_service_scope`) to guard handlers.
- **Token Refresh:** cache tokens with expiry buffer; thread-safe.

Pattern	Code Snippet
API-Key decorator	`@require_api_key` wrapping handler
OAuth2 client	`token = oauth_client.get_token()`
Require scope	`@require_service_scope("read:files")`

Further Reading / Next Steps

- RFC 6749 (OAuth 2.0): https://tools.ietf.org/html/rfc6749
- OWASP API Security Top 10: https://owasp.org/www-project-api-security/
- In **Section 9.2**, we'll cover **Input Sanitization & Injection Prevention** to harden your MCP tools.

9.2 Input Validation & Sanitization

Section 9.2 Overview & Objectives

By the end of this section you will:

1. Know why validating and sanitizing inputs is critical to prevent injection attacks and runtime errors.
2. Use **JSON Schema** and `jsonschema` to enforce parameter shapes before handler execution.
3. Apply custom checks (regex, type casting, range checks) for stronger guarantees.
4. Return clear JSON-RPC errors (-32602) when validation fails.

Motivation & Context

Untrusted inputs can exploit your tools—SQL injection on your Database Tool, path traversal in your File System Tool, or malformed JSON crashing your server. By validating with JSON Schema and sanitizing values (escaping, whitelisting), you ensure only well-formed, safe data reaches business logic.

Fundamentals

Concept	Description
JSON Schema Validation	Declaratively enforce types, required fields, formats (e.g., `"format": "email"`).
Type Coercion	Convert strings $\rightarrow$ ints/floats with explicit checks, rejecting non-numeric values.
Range & Enum Checks	Ensure numeric values fall within safe limits or strings belong to a predefined set.
Regex Sanitization	Validate free-form inputs (e.g., file names) against an allow-list pattern like `^[\w\-.]+$`.
Escape/Encode	For HTML or shell contexts, escape characters (<, >, &, ;) to prevent XSS or shell injection.

ASCII Flow: Request Validation

pgsql

```
Client Request ──▶ MCP Server ──▶
jsonschema.validate() ──▶ passes? ──▶ invoke
handler
                                              └▶

fails? ──▶ return {-32602, "Invalid params", data}
```

Step-by-Step Tutorial

1. **Define your JSON Schema** for a tool (e.g., dbRead):

   jsonc

   ```jsonc
   {
     "type": "object",
     "required": ["table", "id"],
     "properties": {
       "table": { "type": "string", "pattern":
   "^[A-Za-z_][A-Za-z0-9_]*$" },
       "id":    { "type": "integer", "minimum": 1
   }
     },
     "additionalProperties": false
   }
   ```

2. **Integrate validation in your server:**

   python

   ```python
   # mcp_server/validation.py
   import jsonschema
   from mcp_framework import RPCError

   # Example schema registry
   SCHEMAS = {
       "dbRead": {
         "type": "object",
         "required": ["table", "id"],
         "properties": {
           "table": { "type": "string",
   "pattern": "^[A-Za-z_][A-Za-z0-9_]*$" },
   ```

208

```python
        "id":    { "type": "integer",
"minimum": 1 }
        },
        "additionalProperties": False
    },
    # add other method schemas...
}

def validate_params(method: str, params:
dict):
    schema = SCHEMAS.get(method)
    if not schema:
        return  # no schema defined
    try:
        jsonschema.validate(instance=params,
schema=schema)
    except jsonschema.ValidationError as e:
        # Wrap into JSON-RPC invalid params
error
        raise RPCError(
          code=-32602,
          message="Invalid params",
          data={"method": method, "error":
e.message}
        )
```

3. **Invoke validation in a handler wrapper**:

python

```python
# mcp_server/auth/validate_wrapper.py
from mcp_framework import RPCError

def with_validation(method_name):
    def decorator(fn):
        def wrapper(params):
            # params arrives as list, convert
to dict if needed
            # here we assume handlers expect
dicts
```

```
            params_dict = params[0] if
isinstance(params, list) and len(params)==1
else {}
            from mcp_server.validation import
validate_params
            validate_params(method_name,
params_dict)
            return fn(params_dict)
        return wrapper
    return decorator
```

4. **Sanitize free-form strings** inside handlers:

python

```python
import re
from mcp_framework import RPCError

FILE_NAME_RE = re.compile(r'^[\w\-. ]+$')  #
allow letters, digits, dash, dot, space

def safe_filename(name: str) -> str:
    if not FILE_NAME_RE.match(name):
        raise RPCError(code=-32602,
message="Invalid filename", data={"filename":
name})
    return name
```

Deep Dive & Best Practices

Concern	Recommendation
Schema Coverage	Define schemas for every method's params; disallow extra fields with `"additionalProperties": false`.
Performance	Cache compiled schemas (`jsonschema.Draft7Validator`) for high-throughput servers.
Custom Formats	Register JSON Schema formats (e.g., `"format":"email"`) via `jsonschema.FormatChecker`.

Concern	Recommendation
Layered Sanitization	After schema validation, perform context-specific sanitization (e.g., HTML escaping).
Error Transparency	Return `data` with the specific validation message so clients can correct inputs.

Hands-On Exercise

1. **Add JSON Schema** for the `read_file` tool to enforce `path` matches `^[\w\-/\.]+$`.
2. **Wrap** your `read_file` handler with `with_validation("read_file")` to auto-validate.
3. **Write pytest** that sends invalid paths (`"../etc/passwd"`, `"/abs.txt"`) and asserts a `-32602` error with the correct `data`.

Section 9.2 Summary & Cheat Sheet

- **Validate early:** use JSON Schema to ensure correct shapes and types.
- **Sanitize strings:** use regex whitelists for file paths, table names, and user input.
- **Disallow extras:** set `"additionalProperties": false` to catch typos.
- **Return clear errors:** code `-32602`, include `data` with the validation failure.

Technique	JSON Schema Property / Code
Type check	`"type": "integer"`
Pattern match	`"pattern": "^[A-Za-z_][A-Za-z0-9_]*$"`
Minimum/Maximum	`"minimum": 1, "maximum": 1000`
Disallow extra fields	`"additionalProperties": false`
Custom sanitization	`if not re.match(...): raise RPCError(code=-32602, ...)`

Further Reading / Next Steps

- JSON Schema Validation: https://json-schema.org/understanding-json-schema/
- jsonschema Python docs: https://python-jsonschema.readthedocs.io/
- OWASP Input Validation Cheat Sheet: https://owasp.org/www-project-top-ten/2017/A1_2017-Injection
- In **Section 9.3**, we'll cover **Sandboxing & Execution Isolation** to further harden your MCP server.

9.3 Rate Limiting & Quotas

Section 9.3 Overview & Objectives

By the end of this section you will:

1. Distinguish **rate limiting** (throttling over time) from **quotas** (hard caps over a billing period).
2. Configure per-client and per-tool limits to protect your server.
3. Implement both **fixed-window** and **token-bucket** rate-limiters in your MCP server.
4. Return a clear JSON-RPC error (-32050) when clients exceed their allowed usage.

Motivation & Context

Uncontrolled usage—whether accidental loops or malicious scripts—can overwhelm your MCP server, degrade performance, and drive up API costs (e.g., LLM calls). By enforcing rate limits and quotas you:

- Ensure fair usage across clients.
- Protect downstream services (databases, third-party APIs) from spikes.
- Provide predictable cost and capacity planning.

Fundamentals

Concept	Description
Fixed-Window Limit	Count calls in discrete time windows (e.g., 100 calls/minute).
Token-Bucket	Tokens refill continuously; allows bursts up to capacity then steady rate.
Quota	Hard cap over a longer period (e.g., 10 000 calls/month); once consumed, block until reset.
Per-Client vs. Global	Limits can apply per API key / user or across all usage to protect shared resources.
Error Handling	Return an RPCError with code −32050 ("Rate limit exceeded") and include retry-after info in `data`.

Step-by-Step Tutorial

A. Per-Client Fixed-Window in MCPServer

python

```
# mcp_server/rate_limit.py
import time
from threading import Lock
from mcp_framework import RPCError

# Track counts per client_key
REQUEST_COUNTS = {}
LOCK = Lock()
WINDOW = 60        # seconds
MAX_CALLS = 100    # per window

def enforce_fixed_window(client_key):
    now = time.time()
    window_start, count =
REQUEST_COUNTS.get(client_key, (now, 0))
    # reset if window expired
    if now - window_start >= WINDOW:
        window_start, count = now, 0
    if count >= MAX_CALLS:
        retry_after = WINDOW - (now - window_start)
        raise RPCError(
            code=-32050,
```

```
            message="Rate limit exceeded",
            data={"retry_after":
round(retry_after)}
        )
    REQUEST_COUNTS[client_key] = (window_start,
count + 1)


def rate_limited(fn):
    def wrapper(params, client_writer=None,
context=None):
        client_key = context.headers.get("X-API-
Key", "")
        enforce_fixed_window(client_key)
        return fn(params)
    return wrapper
python


# server.py excerpt
from mcp_server.handlers.chat import chat_handler
from mcp_server.rate_limit import rate_limited

# Protect the chat tool at 100 calls/minute per
client
server.register_tool("chat",
rate_limited(chat_handler), description="Chat with
context", version="1.0.0")
```

B. Token-Bucket for Steadier Flow (Async)

```
python


# mcp_server/async_rate_limit.py
import asyncio, time
from mcp_framework import RPCError


class TokenBucket:
    def __init__(self, rate, capacity):
        self.rate = rate
        self.capacity = capacity
        self.tokens = capacity
        self.last = time.monotonic()
        self.lock = asyncio.Lock()
```

```python
    async def consume(self, client_key):
        async with self.lock:
            now = time.monotonic()
            # refill tokens
            delta = (now - self.last) * self.rate
            self.tokens = min(self.capacity,
self.tokens + delta)
            self.last = now
            if self.tokens < 1:
                # calculate wait
                wait = (1 - self.tokens) /
self.rate
                raise RPCError(
                    code=-32050,
                    message="Rate limit exceeded",
                    data={"retry_after":
round(wait, 2)}
                )
            self.tokens -= 1

bucket = TokenBucket(rate=1, capacity=5)  # 5-
request burst, 1/sec refill

def async_rate_limited(fn):
    async def wrapper(params, client_writer=None,
context=None):
        await
bucket.consume(context.headers.get("X-API-Key",""))
        return await fn(params, client_writer)
    return wrapper
python

# server.py excerpt (async server)
from mcp_server.handlers.llm import
summarize_context
from mcp_server.async_rate_limit import
async_rate_limited

server.register_tool(
    "summarizeContext",
    async_rate_limited(summarize_context),
```

```python
        description="Summarize conversation history",
        version="1.0.0"
)
```

C. Enforcing Monthly Quotas

python

```python
# mcp_server/quota.py
import time
from threading import Lock
from mcp_framework import import RPCError

QUOTAS = {}        # client_key → (period_start,
used_calls)
LOCK = Lock()
PERIOD = 30 * 24 * 3600    # 30 days
MAX_MONTHLY = 10000

def enforce_monthly_quota(client_key):
    now = time.time()
    period_start, used = QUOTAS.get(client_key,
(now, 0))
    if now - period_start >= PERIOD:
        period_start, used = now, 0
    if used >= MAX_MONTHLY:
        raise RPCError(
            code=-32050,
            message="Monthly quota exceeded",
            data={"reset_in_days": int((PERIOD -
(now - period_start)) // 86400)}
        )
    QUOTAS[client_key] = (period_start, used + 1)
```

Register quota checks alongside rate limits in your decorator chain.

Deep Dive & Best Practices

Concern	Recommendation
Synchronizing State	For multi-instance servers, store counters in Redis or a distributed cache rather than in-memory dicts.
Dynamic Limits	Allow per-client customization via a config file or database (e.g., `client → {rate:…, quota:…}`).
Combined Enforcement	Layer a token-bucket for smooth flow inside a fixed-window or quota guard for gross usage caps.
Backoff Handling	On RPCError `-32050`, clients should respect `retry_after` and use exponential backoff for retrials.
Monitoring & Alerts	Emit metrics on limit hits to detect abusive or misbehaving clients.

Hands-On Exercise

1. **Configure** two client keys with different limits:
   - `key-A`: 200 calls/minute, 20 000 calls/month
   - `key-B`: 50 calls/minute, 5 000 calls/month
2. **Simulate** rapid calls in a loop and verify the correct `retry_after` values in the RPCError `data`.
3. **Switch** to a Redis-backed counter and observe that state persists across server restarts.

Section 9.3 Summary & Cheat Sheet

- **Fixed-Window:** simple counters per time window; can cause spikes at boundaries.
- **Token-Bucket:** smoother rate control, allows bursts up to capacity.
- **Quota:** hard cap over a longer period; block once exceeded.
- **Error Code:** use `-32050` for "Rate limit exceeded" and include `retry_after` or `reset_in_days`.

Pattern	Params	Error Data
Fixed-Window	`MAX_CALLS,` `WINDOW_SEC`	`retry_after` (seconds)

Pattern	Params	Error Data
Token-Bucket	`rate, capacity`	`retry_after` (seconds float)
Monthly Quota	`MAX_MONTHLY, PERIOD`	`reset_in_days`

Further Reading / Next Steps

- Distributed rate limiting:
  https://redis.io/docs/manual/policies/ratelimit/
- Token bucket design: https://en.wikipedia.org/wiki/Token_bucket
- In **Section 9.4**, we'll explore **Sandboxing & Execution Isolation** to securely run untrusted code snippets.

9.4 Sandboxing Untrusted Code (Process Isolation)

Section 9.4 Overview & Objectives

By the end of this section you will:

1. Grasp why running untrusted code inside your MCP server requires strict isolation.
2. Learn techniques for **process-level sandboxing** using OS primitives (RLIMIT, chroot) or containers.
3. Implement a Python handler that executes user-supplied code in a subprocess with resource limits.
4. Handle timeouts, resource exhaustion, and capture stdout/stderr safely.

Motivation & Context

Allowing users or agents to run arbitrary Python snippets (for data transformations, custom logic, etc.) can open your server to denial-of-service, data leaks, or host compromise. By sandboxing in a separate process with tightly controlled permissions and resource limits, you protect the main MCP server while still offering flexible "code execution" tools.

Fundamentals

Technique	Description
Subprocess with RLIMIT	Launch a child process and apply CPU/memory/file-descriptor limits via the `resource` module.
chroot Jail	Restrict filesystem view by changing the root directory of the subprocess.
User Namespace	Drop privileges by running the process under an unprivileged UID/GID.
Docker/gVisor	Containerize execution with an immutable image and cgroup limits for CPU/memory.
Timeouts	Enforce a maximum wall-clock time to prevent endless loops.

ASCII Flow: Sandboxed Code Execution

csharp

```
[Client]
    ├─► call "runCode" params {"code": "..."}
    │
[MCP Server]
    ├─► spawn subprocess with:
    │       - new UID/GID
    │       - resource.setrlimit(CPU, MEMORY)
    │       - chroot or container
    ├─► send code via stdin or temp file
    ├─► wait for completion or timeout
    └─► capture output/errors → return as result or
RPCError
    ◄─ JSON-RPC response
```

Step-by-Step Tutorial

python

```
# mcp_server/handlers/sandbox.py
```

```python
import subprocess
import tempfile
import os
import shlex
from mcp_framework import RPCError

def run_code(params):
    """
    Execute a user-supplied Python snippet in a
sandboxed subprocess.
    Params: [code: str]
    Returns: {"stdout": str, "stderr": str}
    """
    (code,) = params

    # 1. Write code to a temporary file
    with tempfile.NamedTemporaryFile("w",
suffix=".py", delete=False) as tmp:
        tmp_path = tmp.name
        tmp.write(code)

    # 2. Build the sandboxed command
    #    - `python3` interpreter must be available
    #    - `preexec_fn` will drop privileges and
set resource limits
    def preexec():
        import resource, pwd, grp
        # Drop to nobody user
        nobody = pwd.getpwnam("nobody")
        os.setgid(nobody.pw_gid)
        os.setuid(nobody.pw_uid)
        # CPU time limit: 2 seconds
        resource.setrlimit(resource.RLIMIT_CPU, (2,
2))
        # Memory limit: 100 MB
        mem_bytes = 100 * 1024 * 1024
        resource.setrlimit(resource.RLIMIT_AS,
(mem_bytes, mem_bytes))
        # No file creation beyond scratch
        resource.setrlimit(resource.RLIMIT_FSIZE,
(10*1024*1024, 10*1024*1024))
```

```python
    cmd = ["python3", tmp_path]

    try:
        # 3. Run subprocess with timeout
        proc = subprocess.run(
            cmd,
            stdin=subprocess.DEVNULL,
            stdout=subprocess.PIPE,
            stderr=subprocess.PIPE,
            preexec_fn=preexec,
            timeout=3,  # wall-clock seconds
            cwd="/tmp"  # confinement to /tmp
        )
    except subprocess.TimeoutExpired:
        raise RPCError(code=-32050, message="Code
execution timed out")
    finally:
        # 4. Clean up temp file
        try:
            os.remove(tmp_path)
        except OSError:
            pass

    # 5. Check exit code
    if proc.returncode != 0:
        raise RPCError(
            code=-32051,
            message="Error during code execution",
            data={"stderr":
proc.stderr.decode(errors="replace")}
        )

    # 6. Return output
    return {
        "stdout":
proc.stdout.decode(errors="replace"),
        "stderr":
proc.stderr.decode(errors="replace")
    }
python
```

```
#  Pro Tip: Use a dedicated, empty directory (e.g.,
a tmpfs mount) as cwd to prevent file leakage.
```

Deep Dive & Best Practices

Concern	Recommendation
Privilege Dropping	Run under a non-root UID/GID; use Linux user namespaces for extra isolation.
Filesystem Isolation	Use `chroot` or mount a minimal directory (e.g., tmpfs) so the process can't see your server files.
Resource Limits	Enforce CPU, memory, and file-size RLIMITs; consider RLIMIT_NPROC to prevent forking bombs.
Containerization	For stronger guarantees, launch code inside a minimal Docker container with cgroup limits.
Logging & Auditing	Capture and log each executed snippet and its outcome for post-mortem analysis.
Security Updates	Keep the interpreter and base images patched; untrusted code may exploit interpreter vulnerabilities.

Hands-On Exercise

1. **Test** `run_code` with:
   - A simple `print("Hello")` snippet
   - A malicious `while True: pass` (should time out)
   - A memory-hogging snippet ($x = [0]*10**8$) (should hit memory limit)
2. **Extend** the sandbox to disable network by removing socket capabilities in the child (e.g., unshare or seccomp).
3. **Compare** performance of this pure-Python sandbox vs. a Docker-based approach.

Section 9.4 Summary & Cheat Sheet

- **Process isolation:** use subprocess with `preexec_fn` to drop privileges and set RLIMITs.

- **Key limits:** CPU time (RLIMIT_CPU), memory (RLIMIT_AS), file size (RLIMIT_FSIZE).
- **Timeout:** use `subprocess.run(..., timeout)`.
- **Error codes:**
  - `-32050` execution timed out
  - `-32051` runtime error in snippet

Step	Code Snippet
Write temp file	`tmp = NamedTemporaryFile(...);` `tmp.write(code)`
Drop privileges	`os.setuid(nobody_uid)` inside `preexec_fn`
Set RLIMITs	`resource.setrlimit(resource.RLIMIT_CPU,` `(2,2))`
Run subprocess	`subprocess.run(cmd, preexec_fn=preexec,` `timeout=3)`
Handle errors	Check `returncode`, catch `TimeoutExpired`

Further Reading / Next Steps

- `resource` module docs: https://docs.python.org/3/library/resource.html
- Linux namespaces & seccomp: https://man7.org/linux/man-pages/man7/user_namespaces.7.html
- Docker security best practices: https://docs.docker.com/engine/security/security/
- In **Section 9.5**, we'll discuss **Audit Logging & Monitoring** to track and alert on tool usage.

9.5 Secure Logging of Sensitive Data

Section 9.5 Overview & Objectives

By the end of this section you will:

1. Understand why unfiltered logs can expose sensitive data (PII, API keys, secrets).

2. Configure your logging framework to **mask**, **redact**, or **omit** sensitive fields.
3. Implement structured logging with contextual metadata (request IDs, user IDs) without leaking secrets.
4. Use log filters or handlers (e.g., `logging.Filter`, `structlog`) to enforce policies.

Motivation & Context

Logs are invaluable for debugging and audit trails—but can become a liability if they contain passwords, tokens, or personal information. A secure logging strategy ensures you capture enough context to trace issues while protecting user privacy and compliance (e.g., GDPR, HIPAA).

Fundamentals

Concept	Description
Structured Logging	Emit logs as JSON or key-value pairs to enable parsing and filtering.
Masking	Replace sensitive values with placeholders (e.g., $****$) before writing to log.
Redaction	Programmatically remove or scramble PII fields (names, emails, credit cards).
Log Levels	Use appropriate levels (`DEBUG`, `INFO`, `WARN`, `ERROR`) and avoid logging secrets at lower thresholds.
Filters & Handlers	Leverage `logging.Filter` or middleware in frameworks to inspect and sanitize log records.

Step-by-Step Tutorial

A. Configure Structured Logging with Sensitive-Field Masking

python

```
# logging_config.py
```

```python
import logging
import re
import json

SENSITIVE_KEYS = {"password", "token", "api_key",
"authorization"}

class SensitiveFilter(logging.Filter):
    """Redacts sensitive values in structured JSON
logs."""
    def filter(self, record):
        try:
            payload =
json.loads(record.getMessage())
            for key in list(payload):
                if key.lower() in SENSITIVE_KEYS:
                    payload[key] = "****"
            record.msg = json.dumps(payload)
        except Exception:
            # Non-JSON payloads: simple regex mask
            msg = record.getMessage()
            record.msg =
re.sub(r"(?:password|token)=\S+", r"\1=****", msg,
flags=re.IGNORECASE)
        return True

def setup_logging():
    handler = logging.StreamHandler()

handler.setFormatter(logging.Formatter("%(asctime)s
%(levelname)s %(message)s"))
    handler.addFilter(SensitiveFilter())
    root = logging.getLogger()
    root.setLevel(logging.INFO)
    root.addHandler(handler)
```

- **Watch out:** Always attach your filter *before* any handler to ensure all loggers inherit it.

B. Using Contextual, Per-Request Logging

```
python
```

```python
# request_logger.py
import logging
import uuid

logger = logging.getLogger("mcp")

def log_request_start(context):
    request_id = str(uuid.uuid4())
    context.request_id = request_id
    logger.info({
        "event": "request_start",
        "request_id": request_id,
        "method": context.method,
        "user_id": context.user_id
    })

def log_request_end(context, status="success"):
    logger.info({
        "event": "request_end",
        "request_id": context.request_id,
        "status": status,
        # omit params for sensitive methods
    })
```

- Here, `context` is an object passed to handlers
  (`context.headers`, `context.params`).

Deep Dive & Best Practices

Concern	Recommendation
Accidental Logging	Review all `logger.debug/info` calls—never pass raw `params` or `headers` without filtering.
PII Compliance	Identify data classes as PII (emails, phone numbers) and scrub them via regex or schema before logging.
Log Retention & Access	Store logs in a secure, access-controlled system (e.g., ELK with RBAC). Expire old logs per policy.

Concern	Recommendation
Exception Logging	Avoid logging stack traces that include locals—use `logger.exception()` sparingly and scrub exception data.
Audit Trails	Emit high-level events (`request_start`, `tool_invoked`) with IDs for traceability without payloads.

Hands-On Exercise

1. **Extend** `SensitiveFilter` to redact email addresses (`\S+@\S+`).
2. **Instrument** a sample handler to call `log_request_start/end` and test that logs include `request_id` but not the full payload.
3. **Simulate** a login attempt logging `{"user":"alice","password":"secret"}` and confirm output shows `"password":"****"` only.

Section 9.5 Summary & Cheat Sheet

- **Structured logs** (JSON/key-values) make filtering and alerting easier.
- **Mask/Redact** any fields in your `SENSITIVE_KEYS` set before writing logs.
- **Use filters** to centralize sanitization logic rather than sprinkling it across code.
- **Include context** (request IDs, user IDs) but never raw secret values.

Technique	Code Snippet
Sensitive Filter	`handler.addFilter(SensitiveFilter())`
Structured Entry	`logger.info({"event":"x","request_id":id, "user_id":uid})`
Regex Masking	`re.sub(r"\S+@\S+", "****", msg)`

Further Reading / Next Steps

- OWASP Logging Cheat Sheet: https://cheatsheetseries.owasp.org/cheatsheets/Logging_Cheat_Sheet.html
- Python `logging` docs: https://docs.python.org/3/library/logging.html
- GDPR best practices for logs: https://gdpr.eu/logging/
- In **Chapter 10**, we'll discuss **Deployment & Scaling** strategies for your MCP server.

9.6 Managing Manifest & Protocol Versioning

Section 9.6 Overview & Objectives

By the end of this section you will:

1. Apply **semantic versioning** to your manifest and tool definitions.
2. Expose and consume a **protocol version** for JSON-RPC compatibility.
3. Manage **backward-compatible changes** vs. breaking changes.
4. Automate version bumps and deprecation notices in your manifest.

Motivation & Context

As your MCP server evolves—adding new methods, changing parameter shapes, or upgrading JSON-RPC behavior—you need a clear, systematic way to communicate compatibility guarantees to clients. Proper versioning lets clients detect when they must upgrade or can safely continue using older functionality.

Fundamentals

Version Field	Scope	Change Type
`manifest.version`	Entire manifest (all methods)	MAJOR.MINOR.PATCH

Version Field	Scope	Change Type
`methods.<m>.version`	Individual tool/method	MAJOR.MINOR.PATCH
`jsonrpc`	Protocol version in each message (always `"2.0"`)	Fixed by spec
`protocol_version`	Custom field to signal MCP protocol changes	Increment on breaking changes

Semantic Versioning Rules (SemVer)

- **MAJOR**: incompatible API changes (e.g., removed params).
- **MINOR**: added functionality in a backward-compatible manner.
- **PATCH**: backward-compatible bug fixes.

Step-by-Step Tutorial

1. **Initial Manifest with Versioning**

   jsonc

```
{
  "protocol_version": "1.0.0",
  "version": "1.2.3",          // manifest
version
  "methods": {
    "echo": {
      "version": "1.0.0",      // method
version
      "params": [...],
      "result": {...}
    }
  }
}
```

2. **Bumping a PATCH Release**
   o Fix a typo in method `echo`'s description.
   o Update only the PATCH segment:

```bash
bash

semver bump patch manifest.json  # from
1.2.3 → 1.2.4
```

- o No client changes required.

3. **Adding a New Method (MINOR Release)**
   - o Introduce `reverse` method.
   - o Increment MINOR and reset PATCH:

```jsonc
jsonc

{
  "version": "1.3.0",        // was 1.2.4
  "methods": {
    "echo": { ... },
    "reverse": {
      "version": "1.0.0",
      "params": [...],
      "result": {...}
    }
  }
}
```

4. **Removing a Parameter (MAJOR Release)**
   - o Drop optional `unit` param from `getWeather`.
   - o Increment MAJOR and reset MINOR/PATCH:

```jsonc
jsonc

{
  "version": "2.0.0",
  "protocol_version": "2.0.0",
  "methods": { ... }       // clients
must upgrade
}
```

5. **Exposing Protocol Version**

```python
python

# server.py excerpt
```

```python
@server.notification("getProtocolVersion")
def get_protocol(params):
    return {"protocol_version":
server.manifest["protocol_version"]}
```

6. **Client-Side Compatibility Check**

python

```python
manifest = client.fetch_manifest()
if manifest["protocol_version"].split(".")[0]
!= "2":
    raise Exception("Incompatible protocol
version; please upgrade client.")
```

Deep Dive & Best Practices

Concern	Recommendation
Deprecation Policy	Mark methods "deprecated": true" in manifest; clients can warn but continue using for a cycle.
Version Locking	Allow clients to pin to a specific manifest version in `pyproject.toml` or config.
Automated Releases	Use CI to run `semver bump` and commit version changes when merging feature/fix branches.
Changelog Maintenance	Keep a `CHANGELOG.md` documenting each MAJOR, MINOR, and PATCH change with dates and details.
Dual-Versioning During Migrations	Serve multiple manifests (e.g., `/manifest/v1`, `/manifest/v2`) during a transition period.

Hands-On Exercise

1. **Simulate a breaking change** by removing a method param in your manifest and issuing a MAJOR bump.
2. **Implement** a `deprecated` flag on an old method and have your client emit a console warning when it's detected.

3. **Write a small script** that reads your `manifest.json`, bumps the MINOR version, and adds a changelog entry automatically.

Section 9.6 Summary & Cheat Sheet

- **Semantic Versioning:** MAJOR.MINOR.PATCH for manifest and methods.
- **protocol_version:** signal breaking protocol changes.
- **Deprecation:** use `"deprecated": true` to phase out methods.
- **Compatibility Check:** clients should verify `protocol_version` before calls.

Action	Version Bump Command / JSON Update
PATCH (bugfix)	`semver bump patch` → `"1.2.4"`
MINOR (new method)	`semver bump minor` → `"1.3.0"`
MAJOR (breaking change)	`semver bump major` → `"2.0.0"`
Deprecate method	Add `"deprecated": true` to method entry

Further Reading / Next Steps

- SemVer specification: https://semver.org/
- JSON-RPC versioning guidelines: https://www.jsonrpc.org/specification
- In **Chapter 10**, we'll cover **Deployment & Scaling**: containerization, orchestration, and serverless strategies.

Chapter 10: Testing & Debugging Strategies

10.1 Unit Testing with pytest & MCP Mocks

Section 10.1 Overview & Objectives

By the end of this section you will:

1. Write **pytest** unit tests for your MCP handlers and clients.
2. Use **fixtures** to set up common test state (e.g., in-memory context store, temp databases).
3. **Mock** MCP framework classes (e.g., `MCPServer`, `MCPClient`) and external dependencies (LLM, HTTP).
4. Assert correct JSON-RPC responses, error-raising, and side effects without running a live server.

Motivation & Context

Automated unit tests catch regressions early, document expected behavior, and speed up refactoring. By mocking out the MCP transport and external systems, you can test each handler's logic in isolation—ensuring your file-system, database, and LLM tools behave correctly under both normal and error conditions.

Fundamentals

Concept	Description
pytest	A lightweight test framework using `assert` statements, fixtures, and parameterization.
Fixture	A reusable setup/teardown function supplying test data or objects (e.g., `tmp_path`, `monkeypatch`).
Monkeypatch	Built-in pytest fixture for dynamically replacing attributes, env vars, or modules during a test.

Concept	Description
MCP Mocks	Fake or stub implementations of `server.register_tool`, `client.call`, or handler context objects.
Parametrize	Mark tests to run multiple input/output combinations via `@pytest.mark.parametrize`.

Step-by-Step Tutorial

1. **Install pytest**

   bash

   ```
   pip install pytest pytest-mock
   ```

2. **Test a simple handler** (add) in `tests/test_basic_handlers.py`:

   python

   ```python
   # tests/test_basic_handlers.py
   import pytest
   from mcp_server.handlers.basic import add,
   echo
   from mcp_framework import RPCError

   @pytest.mark.parametrize("a,b,expected", [
       (1, 2, 3),
       (-5, 5, 0),
       (0, 0, 0),
   ])
   def test_add(a, b, expected):
       assert add([a, b]) == expected

   def test_echo():
       assert echo(["hello"]) == "hello"

   def test_add_invalid_params():
       with pytest.raises(TypeError):
           add(["not", "numbers"])
   ```

3. **Mocking an MCPClient call** in
   tests/test_chat_handler.py:

python

```python
# tests/test_chat_handler.py
import pytest
from mcp_server.handlers.chat import
chat_handler, store
from mcp_framework import RPCError

class DummyClient:
    def __init__(self, reply):
        self.reply = reply
    def call(self, method, params, req_id):
        assert method == "summarizeContext"
        return {"result": self.reply}

@pytest.fixture(autouse=True)
def clear_store():
    # Ensure context store is empty each test
    store._store.clear()
    yield
    store._store.clear()

def test_chat_handler_happy_path(monkeypatch):
    # Arrange
    dummy = DummyClient("ok")

monkeypatch.setattr("mcp_server.handlers.chat.
client", dummy)
    user_id = "user1"
    # Act
    reply = chat_handler([user_id, "hi"])
    # Assert
    assert reply == "ok"
    # Context should have two turns
    history = store.get(user_id)
    assert history == [
        {"user": "hi"},
        {"bot": "ok"}
    ]
```

```python
def test_chat_handler_llm_error(monkeypatch):
    # Simulate RPCError in client.call
    class BadClient:
        def call(self, *args, **kwargs):
            raise RPCError(code=-32002,
message="LLM failure")

monkeypatch.setattr("mcp_server.handlers.chat.
client", BadClient())
    reply = chat_handler(["u","msg"])
    assert "trouble" in reply.lower()
```

4. **Mocking external services** (e.g., HTTP GET) in tests/test_http_tools.py:

python

```python
# tests/test_http_tools.py
import pytest
import requests
from mcp_server.handlers.http_tools import
rest_get
from mcp_framework import RPCError

def test_rest_get_success(monkeypatch):
    fake = type("R", (), {})()
    fake.status_code = 200
    fake.json = lambda: {"data": 123}
    def fake_get(url, headers, params,
timeout):
        return fake
    monkeypatch.setattr(requests, "get",
fake_get)
    result = rest_get(["http://api", {},
{"q":1}])
    assert result == {"data": 123}

def test_rest_get_404(monkeypatch):
    class Resp:
        status_code = 404
        def raise_for_status(self):
```

```
                raise
requests.HTTPError(response=self)
        def json(self):
            return {}
    monkeypatch.setattr(requests, "get",
lambda *a,**k: Resp())
    with pytest.raises(RPCError) as exc:
        rest_get(["url", {}, {}])
    assert exc.value.code == -32030
```

Deep Dive & Best Practices

Concern	Recommendation
Fixture Scope	Use `function` scope for isolated tests; `module` or `session` for expensive setup you don't modify.
Monkeypatch vs. pytest-mock	Use built-in `monkeypatch` for simple replaces; `pytest-mock` for auto-cleanup and spy assertions.
Parametrization	Cover edge cases (empty inputs, invalid types) via `@pytest.mark.parametrize`.
Coverage	Measure with `pytest --cov`; aim for $\geq 80\%$ on critical modules.
Test Naming	Prefix test files `test_*.py` and functions `test_`; use descriptive names to document intent.

Hands-On Exercise

1. **Write tests** for your **database handlers** (`dbCreate`, `dbRead`, etc.) using a temporary SQLite file (`tmp_path` fixture).
2. **Mock** the OpenAI SDK in `tests/test_llm.py` to return a canned response, and verify your `summarize_context` handler propagates it.
3. **Add a test** for your **sandbox** code execution tool to confirm it times out on an infinite loop snippet.

Section 10.1 Summary & Cheat Sheet

- **pytest fixtures**: `monkeypatch`, `tmp_path`, and custom fixtures for context.
- **MCP mocks**: replace `client.call`, `requests.get`, or `subprocess.run` to isolate logic.
- **Assertions**: use `with pytest.raises(...)` for error cases and direct `assert` for results.
- **Parameterize** tests to cover multiple scenarios succinctly.

Tool	Usage Example
`monkeypatch`	`monkeypatch.setattr(module, "attr", fake_fn)`
`tmp_path`	`def test_db(tmp_path): db = tmp_path/"app.db"; …`
`pytest.mark.parametrize`	`@pytest.mark.parametrize("input, expected", [...])`
`pytest-cov`	`pytest --cov=mcp_server --cov-report=term-missing`

Further Reading / Next Steps

- pytest documentation: https://docs.pytest.org/
- pytest-mock plugin: https://github.com/pytest-dev/pytest-mock
- Testing async code: https://docs.pytest.org/en/stable/reference.html#pytest-asyncio

10.2 Integration Tests with Real Clients

Section 10.2 Overview & Objectives

By the end of this section you will:

1. Write **integration tests** that spin up a real MCP server instance.
2. Use the real `MCPClient` (sync or async) to exercise end-to-end tool calls.
3. Leverage pytest fixtures to start and stop the server in a subprocess or thread.

4. Assert on actual JSON-RPC responses, notifications, and side effects (e.g., database writes) to validate your full stack.

Motivation & Context

Unit tests verify isolated logic, but only full integration tests confirm that your server, transport, and client all work together under real-world conditions. They catch mis-configurations in networking, manifest loading, dependency wiring, and resource initialization that unit tests can't.

Fundamentals

Concept	Description
Server Fixture	A pytest fixture that launches your MCP server (e.g., via `subprocess.Popen` or a background thread).
Client Invocation	Use the real `MCPClient` to connect over TCP or HTTP and call your registered tools.
Cleanup	Ensure the server process is terminated and any temp resources (DB files, ports) are cleaned up.
Side-Effect Verification	After calls (e.g., `write_file`, `dbCreate`), inspect the filesystem or database to confirm changes.

Step-by-Step Tutorial

```python
# tests/conftest.py
import subprocess, time, os, signal, tempfile
import pytest

# Path to your server bootstrap script
SERVER_CMD = ["python", "-m", "mcp_server.server"]

@pytest.fixture(scope="session")
def mcp_server():
```

```python
    # Use a dedicated temp directory for any state
(DBs, files)
    temp_dir = tempfile.TemporaryDirectory()
    env = os.environ.copy()
    env["SQLITE_PATH"] =
os.path.join(temp_dir.name, "test.db")
    env["POSTGRES_DSN"] = ""  # if unused in tests

    proc = subprocess.Popen(
        SERVER_CMD,
        env=env,
        stdout=subprocess.DEVNULL,
        stderr=subprocess.DEVNULL
    )
    # Wait for the server to start listening
    time.sleep(1)
    yield
    # Teardown: terminate server
    proc.send_signal(signal.SIGINT)
    proc.wait(timeout=5)
    temp_dir.cleanup()
```
python

```python
# tests/test_integration_chat.py
import pytest
from mcp_framework import MCPClient, RPCError

@pytest.mark.usefixtures("mcp_server")
def test_chat_end_to_end(tmp_path):
    client =
MCPClient(manifest_url="http://127.0.0.1:4000/manif
est")
    # 1st turn
    res1 = client.call("chat", ["session123",
"Hello"], req_id=1)
    assert "result" in res1
    # 2nd turn
    res2 = client.call("chat", ["session123", "How
are you?"], req_id=2)
    history = client.call("dbRead",
["conversation_history", 1], req_id=3)  # example
side-effect
```

```python
    assert isinstance(history, dict)
python

# tests/test_integration_db.py
import pytest
import sqlite3
from mcp_framework import MCPClient

@pytest.mark.usefixtures("mcp_server")
def test_db_crud(tmp_path):
    # point SQLite path at the same as server uses
    db_path = tmp_path / "test.db"
    conn = sqlite3.connect(str(db_path))
    conn.execute("CREATE TABLE users (id INTEGER
PRIMARY KEY, name TEXT)")
    conn.commit()
    conn.close()

    client =
MCPClient(manifest_url="http://127.0.0.1:4000/manif
est")
    # Create
    cr = client.call("dbCreate", ["users", {"name":
"Alice"}], req_id=10)
    assert "result" in cr and cr["result"]["id"] ==
1
    # Read
    rd = client.call("dbRead", ["users", 1],
req_id=11)
    assert rd["name"] == "Alice"
    # Update
    up = client.call("dbUpdate", ["users", 1,
{"name": "Bob"}], req_id=12)
    assert up["result"]["success"]
    # Delete
    dl = client.call("dbDelete", ["users", 1],
req_id=13)
    assert dl["result"]["success"]
```

Deep Dive & Best Practices

Concern	Recommendation
Port Conflicts	Allow your server to pick a random free port (e.g., `port=0`) and communicate it to the test via stdout or temp file.
Health Checks	After startup, poll a `/health` or `/manifest` endpoint before proceeding with tests.
Parallel Tests	Use session-scoped server for speed, but isolate state per test (different sessions or temp dirs).
Flaky Teardown	Catch and ignore termination errors, but fail the test if the server doesn't exit within timeout.

Hands-On Exercise

1. **Add** a `/health` HTTP endpoint to your server that returns 200 OK when ready.
2. **Update** the `mcp_server` fixture to poll `/health` rather than `sleep(1)`.
3. **Write** an integration test for your **HTTP Tool** (`restGet`) by mocking an external HTTP server (e.g., with `pytest-httpserver`) and invoking `restGet` end to end.

Section 10.2 Summary & Cheat Sheet

- **Server fixture:** launch with `subprocess.Popen`, yield, then terminate in teardown.
- **Client calls:** use real `MCPClient` against actual TCP/HTTP endpoint.
- **State verification:** inspect file, DB, or HTTP mocks to confirm side effects.
- **Health checks & ports:** ensure readiness and avoid collisions.

Component	Code Snippet
Server startup	`proc = subprocess.Popen(SERVER_CMD, env=env)`

Component	Code Snippet
Readiness probe	`assert client.fetch_manifest() or HTTP /health`
Client invocation	`client.call("tool", params, req_id)`
Teardown	`proc.send_signal(signal.SIGINT); proc.wait()`

Further Reading / Next Steps

- pytest-subprocess plugin: https://pypi.org/project/pytest-subprocess/
- Testcontainers for Python: https://github.com/testcontainers/testcontainers-python
- In **Section 10.3**, we'll examine **Live Debugging Techniques**, including logging breakpoints and interactive REPLs.

10.3 Mocking External Dependencies

Section 10.3 Overview & Objectives

By the end of this section you will:

1. Recognize external dependencies in your handlers (LLM APIs, HTTP calls, DB connectors, subprocesses).
2. Use **unittest.mock** (or `pytest-mock`) to stub out those dependencies and control their behavior.
3. Simulate both **success** and **failure** scenarios (timeouts, exceptions, bad data) without hitting real services.
4. Write focused tests that verify your logic in isolation, ensuring fast, deterministic CI runs.

Motivation & Context

Real APIs can be slow, flaky, cost money, or modify real data. By mocking external calls, your tests become:

- **Fast:** no network round-trips

- **Deterministic:** always the same response
- **Safe:** no accidental LLM billing or database corruption
- **Comprehensive:** you can simulate edge cases that are hard to reproduce in production

---

Fundamentals

Technique	Description
`patch()`	Temporarily replace a target attribute or function with a mock object.
`return_value`	Configure the mock to return a specific value when called.
`side_effect`	Make the mock raise an exception or return different values on successive calls.
Autospeccing	Use `patch(..., autospec=True)` to ensure the mock matches the real signature.
Context Manager	Use `with patch(...) as m:` instead of decorators when you need fine-grained control.
Fixture-Based	Leverage `pytest` fixtures (e.g., `mocker` or built-in `monkeypatch`) for setup/teardown.

Step-by-Step Tutorial

A. Mocking an LLM API Call

python

```python
# tests/test_llm_tool.py
import pytest
import openai
from mcp_server.handlers.llm import
summarize_context
from mcp_framework import RPCError

@pytest.fixture(autouse=True)
def fake_openai_create(monkeypatch):
    # Create a dummy response object
```

```python
class DummyChoice:
    def __init__(self, content):
        self.message = type("M", (),
{"content": content})
    class DummyResponse:
        choices = [DummyChoice("mocked reply")]

    # Stub ChatCompletion.create to always return
DummyResponse
    monkeypatch.setattr(openai.ChatCompletion,
"create", lambda *args, **kwargs: DummyResponse())
    yield

def test_summarize_success():
    history = [{"user":"Hi"}]
    resp = summarize_context([history])
    assert resp == "mocked reply"

def test_summarize_api_error(monkeypatch):
    # Simulate an OpenAIError
    def bad_create(*args, **kwargs):
        raise openai.error.OpenAIError("rate
limit")
    monkeypatch.setattr(openai.ChatCompletion,
"create", bad_create)
    with pytest.raises(RPCError) as exc:
        summarize_context([[{"user":"Hi"}]])
    assert exc.value.code == -32002
```

B. Mocking HTTP Calls with `requests`

python

```python
# tests/test_http_tools_responses.py
import pytest
import responses
from mcp_server.handlers.http_tools import
rest_get, graphql_query

@responses.activate
def test_rest_get_status_code_200():
    responses.add(
```

```python
        responses.GET,
        "https://api.example.com/data",
        json={"foo": "bar"},
        status=200
    )
    result =
rest_get(["https://api.example.com/data", {}, {}])
    assert result == {"foo": "bar"}

@responses.activate
def test_rest_get_timeout():
    # Simulate a timeout by raising a
requests.Timeout
    def request_callback(request):
        raise requests.Timeout("timed out")
    responses.add_callback(
        responses.GET,
        "https://api.example.com/data",
        callback=request_callback
    )
    with pytest.raises(RPCError) as exc:
        rest_get(["https://api.example.com/data",
{}, {}])
    assert exc.value.code == -32031
```

C. Mocking Subprocess for Sandboxed Code

python

```python
# tests/test_sandbox.py
import pytest, subprocess
from mcp_server.handlers.sandbox import run_code
from mcp_framework import RPCError

def test_run_code_timeout(monkeypatch):
    # Simulate subprocess.run raising
TimeoutExpired
    def fake_run(*args, **kwargs):
        raise
subprocess.TimeoutExpired(cmd=args[0],
timeout=kwargs.get("timeout",0))
```

```
    monkeypatch.setattr(subprocess, "run",
fake_run)
    with pytest.raises(RPCError) as exc:
        run_code(['print("hi")'])
    assert exc.value.code == -32050

def test_run_code_runtime_error(monkeypatch):
    # Simulate a nonzero exit code with stderr
    class FakeProc: returncode=1; stdout=b"";
stderr=b"error"
    monkeypatch.setattr(subprocess, "run", lambda
*a, **k: FakeProc())
    with pytest.raises(RPCError) as exc:
        run_code(['print("hi")'])
    assert exc.value.code == -32051
    assert "error" in exc.value.data["stderr"]
```

Deep Dive & Best Practices

Concern	Recommendation
Patching Targets	Patch the symbol **where it's looked up**, not where it's defined. E.g., `mcp_server.handlers.llm.openai`.
Restoring State	Mocks applied via fixtures or context managers auto-cleanup—avoid global side effects.
Testing Edge Cases	Use `side_effect` to simulate sequences (e.g., first call ok, second call fails).
Combining Mocks	Chain multiple `patch()` decorators or use `with ExitStack():` for complex setups.
Avoid Over-Mocking	Only mock external behavior—let your own business logic execute unmodified to test true behavior.

Hands-On Exercise

1. **Identify** three more external calls in your codebase (e.g., DB connector, file I/O) and write mocks for them.

2. **Simulate** a network partition by having your HTTP mock raise `ConnectionError` and assert your handler returns the correct RPC error code.
3. **Use `side_effect`** to simulate an LLM API call that returns two different replies on successive calls, and write a test that exercises both.

Section 10.3 Summary & Cheat Sheet

- **`patch()`**: replace functions/attributes with mocks.
- **`return_value`** vs. **`side_effect`**: static vs. dynamic mock behavior.
- **`responses`** library**: ideal for HTTP mocking without actual network.
- **`monkeypatch`** fixture**: simple and powerful for pytest.
- **Autospec**: keeps mocks aligned with real signatures.

Technique	Code Snippet
Patch function	`with patch("module.fn", return_value=42): ...`
Fixture monkeypatch	`monkeypatch.setattr(obj, "attr", fake_fn)`
`side_effect`	`mocked_fn.side_effect = [1, 2, Exception()]`
HTTP mock (responses)	`responses.add(responses.GET, url, json=..., status=200)`

10.4 Structured Logging for Traceability

Section 10.4 Overview & Objectives

By the end of this section you will:

1. Emit **structured logs** (JSON or key-value) for every request and handler invocation.
2. **Correlate** logs across distributed components using a shared **request_id**.

3. Use Python's `logging` (or `structlog`) to attach contextual metadata (method, user, timing).
4. Query and filter logs by fields to reconstruct end-to-end traces.

Motivation & Context

When debugging complex MCP workflows, free-form text logs are brittle: you can't easily stitch together which handler processed which request, or how a particular error bubbled through. Structured logs let you query by `request_id`, `tool`, or `user_id`, reconstructing the full sequence of events—from client call, through server registration, to handler success or failure.

Fundamentals

Term	Description
Structured Log	A log entry encoded as JSON or key-value pairs, enabling machine parsing and field filtering.
Correlated ID	A UUID or unique token (e.g., `request_id`) added to every log so all entries for one request can be joined.
Logger Context	Additional metadata (e.g., `method`, `user_id`, `duration_ms`) attached per log entry.
Log Formatter	Component that serializes log records into JSON or other structured formats.
Log Aggregator	External system (e.g., ELK, Splunk) that ingests structured logs and provides querying.

ASCII Flow: Traceable Request

css

```
[Client] ──► log:
{"event":"call","request_id":"abc","method":"add"}
  |
[Server]
```

```
    ├─► log:
{"event":"receive","request_id":"abc","tool":"add"}
    ├─► handler executes
    └─► log:
{"event":"complete","request_id":"abc","result":5,"
duration_ms":2}
```

Step-by-Step Tutorial

A. Configure a JSON Formatter

```python
python

# logging_config.py
import logging, json

class JSONFormatter(logging.Formatter):
    def format(self, record):
        # Build a dict from record attributes
        log_record = {
            "timestamp": self.formatTime(record,
self.datefmt),
            "level": record.levelname,
            "message": record.getMessage(),
        }
        # Include any extra fields attached to
record
        if hasattr(record, "extra"):
            log_record.update(record.extra)
        return json.dumps(log_record)

def setup_structured_logging():
    handler = logging.StreamHandler()
    handler.setFormatter(JSONFormatter())
    root = logging.getLogger()
    root.setLevel(logging.INFO)
    root.handlers.clear()
    root.addHandler(handler)
```

B. Correlate with a `request_id`

python

```python
# request_logger.py
import logging, uuid

logger = logging.getLogger("mcp")

def new_request_context(method, user_id=None):
    """
    Returns a dict of context fields for this request.
    """
    return {
        "request_id": str(uuid.uuid4()),
        "method": method,
        "user_id": user_id
    }

def log_event(event, context, **kwargs):
    """
    Emit a structured log with context and event-specific data.
    """
    data = {"event": event}
    data.update(context)
    data.update(kwargs)
    # Attach to record via `extra`
    logger.info(event, extra={"extra": data})
```

C. Instrumenting a Handler

python

```python
# mcp_server/handlers/basic.py (excerpt)
from request_logger import new_request_context,
log_event

def add(params, context=None):
    """
```

```
    params: [a, b], context: dict from
new_request_context
    """
    log_event("handler_start", context,
params=params)
    a, b = params
    result = a + b
    log_event("handler_end", context,
result=result)
    return result
```

D. Propagate Context from Client to Server

1. **Client** generates `request_id` and passes it in metadata (e.g., in headers or a dedicated RPC param).
2. **Server** extracts it in `context.headers` and passes into each handler.
3. All logs share the same `request_id`, enabling full-stack correlation.

Deep Dive & Best Practices

Concern	Recommendation
Immutable Context	Create a fresh context dict per request; avoid mutating it across async tasks.
Performance	Keep log payloads small—only include essential fields.
Sampling	For high-throughput systems, sample 1% of requests at DEBUG level but always log ERRORs.
Log Levels	Use INFO for normal events, DEBUG for detailed state, ERROR for failures.
Sensitive Data	Never include PII or secrets in any structured field—mask or omit them.

Hands-On Exercise

1. **Implement** `setup_structured_logging()` in your server's startup sequence.

2. **Wrap** your TCP handler to build a `context = new_request_context(method, user_id)` and pass it to every tool.
3. **Run** a few calls (e.g., `add`, `chat`) and verify logs look like:

```json
{"timestamp":"…","level":"INFO","message":"handler_start",

"request_id":"…","method":"add","event":"handler_start","params":[1,2]}
```

4. **Query** your log file (e.g., `grep '"request_id":"<value>"' logs.json`) to reconstruct the full flow.

Section 10.4 Summary & Cheat Sheet

- **Structured logs:** JSON format with consistent keys: `timestamp`, `level`, `message`, plus `extra`.
- **Correlation:** generate a `request_id` and include it in every log for a request.
- **Contextual fields:** `method`, `user_id`, `params`, `result`, `duration_ms`.
- **Implementation:** use a custom `Formatter` and pass `extra` to `logger`.

Task	Code Snippet
JSON Formatter setup	`handler.setFormatter(JSONFormatter())`
New request context	`ctx = new_request_context("add", user_id)`
Log event	`log_event("handler_end", ctx, result=5)`
Correlate logs	`grep '"request_id":"…"' logs.json`

253

Further Reading / Next Steps

- structlog documentation: https://www.structlog.org/
- "Logging SOAP" by Ben Sigelman on structured tracing patterns
- In **Chapter 11**, we'll explore **Deployment & Scaling**: containerization, orchestration, and load testing.

10.5 Fault Injection & Resilience Testing

Section 10.5 Overview & Objectives

By the end of this section you will:

1. Understand why fault injection is essential to uncover hidden failure modes.
2. Apply techniques to simulate failures in dependencies (network, disk, CPU).
3. Implement resilience tests that verify graceful degradation (retries, fallbacks).
4. Automate fault injection in CI to catch regressions early.

Motivation & Context

Complex distributed systems rarely fail in perfectly predictable ways. Network partitions, slow disks, overloaded CPUs, and downstream service timeouts happen in production. By proactively injecting faults into your MCP server and client workflows, you validate that your retry logic, circuit breakers, and error handling actually protect end users from cascading failures.

Fundamentals

Fault Type	Simulation Technique	Expected Resilience Pattern
Network errors	Drop or delay TCP packets; mock timeouts	Retries with backoff, error return after max attempts

Fault Type	Simulation Technique	Expected Resilience Pattern
Dependency failures	Inject exceptions in DB/HTTP/LLM calls	Circuit breakers open, fallback logic executed
Resource exhaustion	Throttle CPU/memory limits in sandbox tests	Timeouts, graceful failure, resource cleanup
Latency spikes	Sleep in mocks to simulate slowness	Timeouts at client level, degraded but responsive

Step-by-Step Tutorial

1. **Injecting Network Timeouts**
   o Use your HTTP mocking library (e.g., `responses`, `pytest-httpserver`) to delay responses beyond your client timeout.
   o Verify that your client raises the expected `RPCError` code (e.g., `-32031`) and does not hang.
2. **Simulating Downstream Service Errors**

```python
# In a pytest test for your LLM tool
import pytest, openai
from mcp_server.handlers.llm import
summarize_context
from mcp_framework import RPCError

@pytest.fixture(autouse=True)
def slow_create(monkeypatch):
    def delayed_create(*args, **kwargs):
        import time; time.sleep(15)  # exceeds
handler timeout
    monkeypatch.setattr(openai.ChatCompletion,
"create", delayed_create)
    yield

def test_llm_timeout():
    with pytest.raises(RPCError) as exc:
        summarize_context([[{"user":"Hi"}]])
```

```
assert exc.value.code == -32002  # or your
designated timeout error
```

3. **Fault-Injecting Database Errors**
   o Monkeypatch your DB connection factory to raise
      `OperationalError` on connect.
   o Run a small batch of CRUD calls and assert your circuit
      breaker opens and subsequent calls fail fast with a clear error.
4. **Stress Testing Resource Limits in Sandbox**

```python
# In a test for run_code sandbox
import pytest, subprocess
from mcp_server.handlers.sandbox import
run_code
from mcp_framework import RPCError

def test_sandbox_memory_limit(monkeypatch):
    code = "a=[0]*10**9; print(len(a))"
    # no monkeypatch: let real limits apply
    with pytest.raises(RPCError) as e:
        run_code([code])
    assert e.value.code == -32051  #
memory-exhaustion code
```

5. **Chaos Monkey-Style Integration**
   o In your integration fixture, randomly kill or restart the server
      process mid-test.
   o Verify your client reconnect logic and retry decorators
      recover without propagating unhandled exceptions.

Deep Dive & Best Practices

Concern	Recommendation
Controlled vs. Randomized	Start with reproducible fault scenarios, then introduce randomized chaos tests for robustness.
Scope Limitation	Limit fault duration (e.g., single request) so tests remain deterministic and fast.

Concern	Recommendation
Automated in CI	Integrate fault-injection tests in nightly pipelines, not every PR, to balance speed vs. coverage.
Observability	Emit clear logs or metrics when a fault is injected to trace its impact in test runs.
Cleanup and Isolation	Ensure each test resets mocks and restores original behavior to avoid cross-test contamination.

Hands-On Exercise

1. **Write a pytest** that randomly chooses one tool (e.g., `dbRead`, `restGet`, `summarizeContext`) and injects a failure on the first call, then verifies your retry logic succeeds on a subsequent call.
2. **Implement an integration "chaos" test** that, during a batch request, forcibly closes the server's socket mid-payload; assert your client handles the disconnect gracefully.
3. **Measure your resilience** by running a suite of fault-injection tests and recording which scenarios cause unhandled failures—then prioritize fixes.

Section 10.5 Summary & Cheat Sheet

- **Fault injections** validate your error-handling: simulate timeouts, exceptions, resource caps.
- **Tools:** use mocks, HTTP stubs, subprocess resource limits, and chaos tests.
- **Patterns:** retries, backoff, circuit breakers, graceful degradation.
- **CI Integration:** run reproducible fault tests nightly; add randomized chaos tests judiciously.

Fault Type	Injection Method	Expected Behavior
Network timeout	Delay mock HTTP beyond timeout	Client raises timeout RPCError
Dependency exception	Monkeypatch DB/LLM factory to raise	Circuit breaker trips, fast-fail
Resource exhaustion	Run sandbox code exceeding CPU/memory limits	Sandbox handler raises resource RPCError

Fault Type	Injection Method	Expected Behavior
Server crash	Kill server mid-request	Client reconnect logic kicks in

Further Reading / Next Steps

- "Chaos Engineering" by Netflix: https://netflix.github.io/chaosmonkey/
- Gremlin's fault injection patterns: https://www.gremlin.com/
- Resilience patterns in distributed systems: https://martinfowler.com/articles/patterns-of-distributed-systems/

10.6 Advanced Error Injection & Graceful Degradation

Section 10.6 Overview & Objectives

By the end of this section you will:

1. Apply **targeted error injection** at various layers (transport, handler, tool) to simulate complex failure modes.
2. Design and implement **graceful degradation** strategies so your MCP server continues to serve partial functionality under failure.
3. Build **fallback handlers** that return safe defaults, cached data, or call secondary services when primary tools fail.
4. Verify your degradation pathways with automated tests and fault-injection scenarios.

Motivation & Context

Real systems rarely fail cleanly: a database may be up but slow, an LLM API might intermittently reject requests, or a downstream service could suddenly go offline. Without graceful degradation, one tool's failure can bring down the entire MCP server. By injecting advanced faults and baking in fallbacks, you ensure your system remains responsive and predictable—even under partial outages.

Fundamentals

Aspect	Description
Error Domains	Network timeouts, service exceptions, resource exhaustion, data corruption.
Fallback Strategies	Default values, cached responses, secondary APIs, feature disabling.
Bulkhead Isolation	Partition tools into separate execution pools so one failure cannot cascade to others.
Canary vs. All-or-Nothing	Gradually route a small percentage of traffic to new/fallback code before rolling out broadly.

Degradation Strategies at a Glance

Strategy	When to Use	Example
Default Value	Non-critical data or UX	Return `"Unavailable"` for weather instead of error.
Cached Data	Stale data acceptable for short periods	Return last-known calendar events from context store.
Secondary API	Alternate provider available	If primary stock API fails, call backup endpoint.
Disable Feature	Optional tools that can be turned off safely	Skip real-time analytics, log the event, and proceed.

Step-by-Step Tutorial

1. **Inject a Tool Failure**

   python

```
# In tests or fault-injection mode, wrap the
primary handler:
from mcp_server.handlers.weather import
get_weather_tool
def flaky_weather(params):
    raise Exception("Simulated API failure")
```

```
server.register_tool("getWeather",
flaky_weather, description="Flaky weather",
version="1.0.0")
```

2. **Implement a Fallback Handler**

python

```
from cachetools import TTLCache
# Simple in-memory cache for last successful
weather
weather_cache = TTLCache(maxsize=100, ttl=300)

def get_weather_with_fallback(params):
    try:
        result = get_weather_tool(params)
        weather_cache[params[0]] = result
        return result
    except Exception:
        # Graceful fallback: return cached or
default
        return weather_cache.get(params[0],
{"status":"Unavailable"})
```

3. **Register the Fallback**

python

```
server.register_tool(
    "getWeather",
    get_weather_with_fallback,
    description="Get weather with cache
fallback",
    version="1.1.0"
)
```

4. **Integrate Bulkhead Isolation**

python

```
# Use a ThreadPool or asyncio.Semaphore per
tool
```

```
from concurrent.futures import
ThreadPoolExecutor
weather_executor =
ThreadPoolExecutor(max_workers=2)

def get_weather_bulkhead(params):
    future =
weather_executor.submit(get_weather_with_fallb
ack, params)
    return future.result(timeout=2)  # fast
fail if execution pool is saturated
server.register_tool("getWeather",
get_weather_bulkhead, …)
```

Deep Dive & Best Practices

- **Circuit Breaker Integration:**
  Wrap your fallback in a circuit breaker so repeated errors switch to fallback mode automatically for a cooldown period.
- **Cache TTL Tuning:**
  Choose a TTL that balances data freshness against API load.

Concern	Recommendation
Silent Failures	Log each fallback invocation with `event="fallback_used"` and details for post-mortem analysis.
Error Transparency	Include an optional `warning` field in your JSON-RPC result to inform clients a fallback occurred.
Gradual Roll-out	Use feature flags or canary deployments to test new fallback logic on a subset of traffic first.
Bulkhead Parameters	Configure pool sizes or semaphores based on expected load to avoid resource starvation.

Hands-On Exercise

1. **Extend** your `chat_handler` to fallback to a simple rule-based reply (e.g., echo) if the LLM tool fails twice in a row.
2. **Write tests** that inject two successive LLM failures and assert that the second call returns the fallback response.

3. **Simulate** a full dependency outage by having both primary and secondary APIs fail; verify your server skips only the faulty tools and still serves other endpoints.

Section 10.6 Summary & Cheat Sheet

- **Inject faults** at the tool registration layer to test degradation.
- **Fallback patterns:** default, cache, secondary API, feature disable.
- **Bulkhead isolation:** separate execution pools to contain failures.
- **Logging:** emit clear events when fallbacks are used.

Pattern	Code Snippet
Fallback Cache	`try...except: return cache.get(key, default)`
Bulkhead	`executor.submit(fn).result(timeout)`
Circuit Breaker	Wrap fallback logic in a breaker with thresholds and timers
Feature Toggle	Use flags to enable/disable fallbacks per environment

---

Further Reading / Next Steps

- "Release It!" by Michael T. Nygard (Resilience Patterns)
- Netflix OSS Hystrix for circuit breakers: https://github.com/Netflix/Hystrix
- Cache-Aside pattern: https://docs.microsoft.com/azure/architecture/patterns/cache-aside

In **Chapter 11**, we'll explore **Deployment & Scaling**: containerization, orchestration, and load testing.

Chapter 11: Deployment & Scaling

11.1 Dockerizing Your MCP Server

Section 11.1 Overview & Objectives

By the end of this section you will:

1. Containerize your MCP server using Docker for consistent environments.
2. Write a **Dockerfile** that installs dependencies, copies code, and exposes the appropriate port.
3. Build and run the Docker image locally, mounting config or secrets as needed.
4. Understand best practices for small images, multi-stage builds, and secret management.

Motivation & Context

Docker ensures that "it works on my machine" becomes "it works everywhere." By packaging your MCP server into a container, you:

- Eliminate host-specific quirks (Python version, library versions).
- Simplify deployment to Kubernetes, ECS, or any Docker-capable platform.
- Enable scaling replicas behind a load-balancer without worrying about system setup.

Fundamentals

Layer	Responsibility
Base Image	Provides OS and Python runtime (e.g., `python:3.10-slim`).
Dependency Layer	Installs `requirements.txt` or Poetry lock file to pin library versions.

Layer	Responsibility
Application Layer	Copies your MCP server code and sets entrypoint/command.
Ports & Volumes	Exposes TCP port (e.g., 4000) and mounts config/secret volumes.

Multi-Stage Build Pattern

pgsql

```
# builder stage
FROM python:3.10-slim AS builder
WORKDIR /app
COPY pyproject.toml poetry.lock /app/
RUN pip install poetry && poetry install --no-dev

# final stage
FROM python:3.10-slim
WORKDIR /app
COPY --from=builder /root/.cache /root/.cache
COPY . /app
EXPOSE 4000
CMD ["python", "-m", "mcp_server.server"]
```

Step-by-Step Tutorial

1. **Create a Dockerfile at your project root:**

    dockerfile

    ```
    # Use official Python slim image
    FROM python:3.10-slim AS base

    # Install build dependencies
    RUN apt-get update && apt-get install -y --no-
    install-recommends \
        build-essential \
        && rm -rf /var/lib/apt/lists/*

    WORKDIR /app
    ```

```
# Install Python dependencies
COPY requirements.txt /app/
RUN pip install --no-cache-dir -r
requirements.txt

# Copy application code
COPY . /app

# Expose MCP server port
EXPOSE 4000

# Default command
CMD ["python", "-m", "mcp_server.server"]
```

2. **Build the Docker image**:

   bash

   ```bash
   docker build -t mcp-server:1.0 .
   ```

3. **Run a container** mounting a .env for secrets and binding port:

   bash

   ```bash
   docker run -d \
     --name mcp-server \
     --env-file .env \
     -p 4000:4000 \
     mcp-server:1.0
   ```

4. **Verify it's running**:

   bash

   ```bash
   curl http://localhost:4000/manifest
   ```

5. **Iterate on code** with a bind mount for live development:

   bash

   ```bash
   docker run -it --rm \
   ```

```
-v "$(pwd)":/app \
--env-file .env \
-p 4000:4000 \
mcp-server:1.0
```

Deep Dive & Best Practices

Concern	Recommendation
Image Size	Use slim images; remove build-time deps in a multi-stage build to keep final image minimal.
Layer Caching	COPY only `requirements.txt` before installing to leverage Docker cache when code changes but deps don't.
Secret Management	Don't bake secrets into the image; use `--env-file`, Docker secrets, or a secret store at runtime.
Health Checks	Add a HEALTHCHECK instruction to probe your `/health` endpoint.
Non-Root User	Create and switch to a non-root user within the container for security.

dockerfile

```
# Example healthcheck
HEALTHCHECK --interval=30s --timeout=5s \
  CMD curl -f http://localhost:4000/health || exit
1
```

Hands-On Exercise

1. **Add a non-root user** in your Dockerfile:

   dockerfile

   ```
   RUN useradd -m appuser
   USER appuser
   ```

2. **Implement a HEALTHCHECK** that calls `/health` and fails if the server is unresponsive.
3. **Push your image** to Docker Hub or your registry:

```bash
bash

docker tag mcp-server:1.0 myrepo/mcp-
server:1.0
docker push myrepo/mcp-server:1.0
```

4. **Run multiple replicas** locally with Docker Compose: define a `docker-compose.yml` exposing the service.

Section 11.1 Summary & Cheat Sheet

- **Base Image**: `python:3.10-slim` (or multi-stage build).
- **Dependency install**: COPY `requirements.txt` → `pip install` for caching.
- **Code copy & CMD**: COPY app code → CMD `["python","-m","mcp_server.server"]`.
- **Runtime**: `docker run -d --env-file .env -p 4000:4000 mcp-server:1.0`.
- **Best Practices**: slim images, health checks, non-root, secret injection at runtime.

Task	Code Snippet
Build image	`docker build -t mcp-server:1.0 .`
Run container	`docker run -d --env-file .env -p 4000:4000 mcp-server`
Healthcheck	`HEALTHCHECK CMD curl -f http://localhost:4000/health`
Non-root user	`RUN useradd -m appuser && USER appuser`

Further Reading / Next Steps

- Docker best practices: https://docs.docker.com/develop/dev-best-practices/
- Multi-stage builds: https://docs.docker.com/develop/develop-images/multistage-build/

- In **Section 11.2**, we'll cover **Kubernetes Deployment & Autoscaling** including manifests and ingress.

11.2 Kubernetes Basics (Deployments, Services)

Section 11.2 Overview & Objectives

By the end of this section you will:

1. Define a Kubernetes **Deployment** for your MCP server to manage replicas and rolling updates.
2. Expose your Deployment via a **Service** so clients can discover and connect.
3. Configure **ConfigMaps** and **Secrets** to inject environment variables (e.g., API keys) into pods.
4. Understand basic **Horizontal Pod Autoscaler** (HPA) setup for scaling based on CPU usage.

Motivation & Context

Running your containerized MCP server on a single host works for testing, but production requires resilience, self-healing, and load balancing. Kubernetes provides:

- **Deployments** to ensure the desired number of replicas are always running.
- **Services** to provide stable networking and load-distribution.
- **ConfigMaps/Secrets** to decouple configuration and sensitive data from images.
- **Autoscaling** to handle variable traffic without manual intervention.

Fundamentals

Object Type	Purpose	Key Fields
Deployment	Manages replica sets, rolling updates, and pod lifecycles	`spec.replicas`, `spec.template`, `strategy`

Object Type	Purpose	Key Fields
Service	Stable network endpoint for pods; load balances traffic	`spec.type` (ClusterIP/LoadBalancer), `spec.ports`, `selector`
ConfigMap	Stores non-sensitive configuration as key-value pairs	`data`, mounted as env or volume
Secret	Stores sensitive data (API keys, credentials)	`stringData` or base64-encoded `data`
HorizontalPodAutosc aler	Automatically scales Deployment based on metrics (CPU/memory)	`spec.minReplicas`, `spec.maxReplicas`, `metrics`

Step-by-Step Tutorial

A. Create a Deployment

yaml

```
# k8s/deployment.yaml
apiVersion: apps/v1
kind: Deployment
metadata:
  name: mcp-server
  labels:
    app: mcp
spec:
  replicas: 3
  strategy:
    type: RollingUpdate
    rollingUpdate:
      maxSurge: 1
      maxUnavailable: 1
  selector:
    matchLabels:
      app: mcp
  template:
    metadata:
```

```yaml
    labels:
      app: mcp
  spec:
    containers:
    - name: mcp-server
      image: myrepo/mcp-server:1.0
      ports:
      - containerPort: 4000
      env:
      - name: OPENAI_API_KEY
        valueFrom:
          secretKeyRef:
            name: mcp-secrets
            key: OPENAI_API_KEY
      - name: CONFIG_MODE
        valueFrom:
          configMapKeyRef:
            name: mcp-config
            key: MODE
      resources:
        requests:
          cpu: "100m"
          memory: "128Mi"
        limits:
          cpu: "500m"
          memory: "512Mi"
```

B. Expose via a Service

yaml

```yaml
# k8s/service.yaml
apiVersion: v1
kind: Service
metadata:
  name: mcp-service
spec:
  type: LoadBalancer    # Or ClusterIP for internal
only
  selector:
    app: mcp
  ports:
```

```yaml
    - port: 80
      targetPort: 4000
      protocol: TCP
```

C. Add ConfigMap and Secret

yaml

```yaml
# k8s/configmap.yaml
apiVersion: v1
kind: ConfigMap
metadata:
  name: mcp-config
data:
  MODE: "production"
  LOG_LEVEL: "info"
---
# k8s/secret.yaml
apiVersion: v1
kind: Secret
metadata:
  name: mcp-secrets
type: Opaque
stringData:
  OPENAI_API_KEY: "sk-REPLACE_WITH_REAL_KEY"
```

Apply all manifests:

bash

```bash
kubectl apply -f k8s/configmap.yaml \
              -f k8s/secret.yaml \
              -f k8s/deployment.yaml \
              -f k8s/service.yaml
```

D. (Optional) Horizontal Pod Autoscaler

yaml

```yaml
# k8s/hpa.yaml
apiVersion: autoscaling/v2beta2
kind: HorizontalPodAutoscaler
```

```
metadata:
  name: mcp-hpa
spec:
  scaleTargetRef:
    apiVersion: apps/v1
    kind: Deployment
    name: mcp-server
  minReplicas: 3
  maxReplicas: 10
  metrics:
  - type: Resource
    resource:
      name: cpu
      target:
        type: Utilization
        averageUtilization: 60
```
bash

```
kubectl apply -f k8s/hpa.yaml
```

Deep Dive & Best Practices

Concern	Recommendation
Rolling Updates	Use `maxSurge`/`maxUnavailable` to minimize downtime and avoid traffic disruption.
Resource Requests/Limits	Always specify to enable proper scheduling and prevent noisy-neighbor issues.
Secrets Management	Integrate with a secret store (e.g., Vault, AWS Secrets Manager) for automated rotation.
Health Probes	Add `livenessProbe` and `readinessProbe` to detect unhealthy pods and prevent traffic to them.
Namespace Isolation	Deploy to a dedicated namespace (`mcp-production`) to separate from other workloads.

Example of readiness probe in Deployment:

yaml

```
readinessProbe:
```

```
httpGet:
  path: /health
  port: 4000
initialDelaySeconds: 5
periodSeconds: 10
```

Hands-On Exercise

1. **Add health checks** to your Deployment for `/health`.
2. **Deploy** to a Kubernetes cluster (minikube, Kind, or cloud).
3. **Scale** the Deployment manually:

```bash

kubectl scale deployment/mcp-server --
replicas=5
```

Verify pods spin up and the Service load-balances traffic.

4. **Trigger autoscaling** by generating CPU load (e.g., `stress-ng`) inside a pod and observe HPA increasing replicas.

Section 11.2 Summary & Cheat Sheet

- **Deployment**: manages pod replicas, rolling updates, and resource specs.
- **Service**: provides stable network endpoint and load-balancing.
- **ConfigMap/Secret**: decouple config and sensitive data from images.
- **HPA**: auto-scales pods based on CPU or custom metrics.

Object	Key Snippet
Deployment replicas	`spec.replicas: 3`
Container env from Secret	`valueFrom.secretKeyRef`
Service type	`spec.type: LoadBalancer`
ConfigMap	`kind: ConfigMap → data`

Object	Key Snippet
HPA rules	`metrics.resource.name: cpu,` `averageUtilization: 60`

Further Reading / Next Steps

- Kubernetes official docs: https://kubernetes.io/docs/concepts/
- Kustomize for manifest templating: https://kustomize.io/
- Helm charts for packaging: https://helm.sh/
- In **Section 11.3**, we'll explore **Ingress & TLS** to expose your service securely to the internet.

11.3 CI/CD Pipelines with GitHub Actions

Section 11.3 Overview & Objectives

By the end of this section you will:

1. Define a GitHub Actions **workflow** that builds, tests, and deploys your MCP server.
2. Use **CI jobs** to run linting, unit tests, and integration tests on each pull request.
3. Configure **CD jobs** to build Docker images and push to a registry when changes are merged to `main`.
4. Securely manage **secrets** (API keys, registry credentials) in GitHub and inject them into workflows.

Motivation & Context

A robust CI/CD pipeline catches errors early and automates repetitive tasks—ensuring code quality, consistency, and rapid delivery. By integrating GitHub Actions you can:

- Run tests on every PR to prevent regressions.
- Automatically publish container images on merge.
- Deploy to Kubernetes (or other targets) with zero-downtime updates.

Fundamentals

Concept	Description
Workflow	A YAML file under `.github/workflows/` defining events (push, pull_request) and jobs.
Job	A set of **steps** that run on a specific runner (e.g., `ubuntu-latest`).
Step	A shell command or action (pre-built logic) executed sequentially.
Matrix	Run the same job across multiple configurations (e.g., Python versions).
Secrets	Encrypted variables stored in GitHub settings, injected at runtime.
Artifacts	Persisted files (e.g., test reports, coverage data) between jobs or downloadable from the UI.

Step-by-Step Tutorial

1. **Create the workflow file**
   `.github/workflows/ci-cd.yml`

   ```yaml
   name: CI/CD Pipeline

   on:
     pull_request:
       branches: [ main ]
     push:
       branches: [ main ]

   jobs:
     # Lint, unit tests, integration tests
     test:
       runs-on: ubuntu-latest
       strategy:
         matrix:
           python-version: [3.9, 3.10, 3.11]
       steps:
   ```

```yaml
      - uses: actions/checkout@v3

      - name: Set up Python ${{ matrix.python-
version }}
        uses: actions/setup-python@v4
        with:
          python-version: ${{ matrix.python-
version }}

      - name: Install dependencies
        run: |
          python -m pip install --upgrade pip
          pip install -r requirements.txt
          pip install pytest pytest-cov

      - name: Lint with flake8
        run: |
          pip install flake8
          flake8 mcp_server tests

      - name: Run pytest
        run: |
          pytest --cov=mcp_server --cov-
report=xml
        # Upload coverage report for Codecov
or similar
      - uses: actions/upload-artifact@v3
        with:
          name: coverage-report
          path: coverage.xml

  # Build & push Docker image
  build-and-push:
    needs: test
    runs-on: ubuntu-latest
    if: github.event_name == 'push' &&
github.ref == 'refs/heads/main'
    steps:
      - uses: actions/checkout@v3

      - name: Log in to Docker registry
        uses: docker/login-action@v2
```

```yaml
      with:
        registry: ghcr.io
        username: ${{ github.actor }}
        password: ${{ secrets.GITHUB_TOKEN
}}

    - name: Build and push image
      uses: docker/build-push-action@v3
      with:
        context: .
        push: true
        tags: |
          ghcr.io/${{
github.repository_owner }}/mcp-server:latest
          ghcr.io/${{
github.repository_owner }}/mcp-server:${{
github.sha }}

  # Deploy to Kubernetes
  deploy:
    needs: build-and-push
    runs-on: ubuntu-latest
    if: github.event_name == 'push' &&
github.ref == 'refs/heads/main'
    steps:
      - name: Set up kubectl
        uses: azure/setup-kubectl@v3
        with:
          version: 'latest'

      - name: Configure Kubeconfig
        run: echo "${{ secrets.KUBE_CONFIG }}"
> $HOME/.kube/config

      - name: Update deployment image
        run: |
          kubectl set image deployment/mcp-
server \
            mcp-server=ghcr.io/${{
github.repository_owner }}/mcp-server:${{
github.sha }} \
            --record
```

```
    - name: Rollout status
      run: kubectl rollout status
deployment/mcp-server
```

2. **Store secrets** in GitHub:
   - `GITHUB_TOKEN` (provided by default) for registry login.
   - `KUBE_CONFIG` (base64-encoded kubeconfig) to access your cluster.
   - Any API keys your server needs (e.g., `OPENAI_API_KEY`).
3. **Triggering**
   - **Pull requests** run the `test` job only.
   - **Push to main** runs `test`, then `build-and-push`, then `deploy`.

Deep Dive & Best Practices

Concern	Recommendation
Job Isolation	Use `needs:` to express dependencies so failures short-circuit later jobs.
Caching	Cache pip dependencies (`actions/cache`) to speed up installs.
Secret Rotation	Rotate registry and cluster credentials regularly; use least-privilege service accounts.
Environment Promotion	For multi-stage environments (dev/staging/prod), gate deploys on branch or tags (e.g., `v*`).
Notifications	Integrate Slack or email via `actions/slack` to alert on failures or successful deployments.

Hands-On Exercise

1. **Add a caching step** to your `test` job:

yaml

```
- name: Cache pip
  uses: actions/cache@v3
```

```
with:
  path: ~/.cache/pip
  key: ${{ runner.os }}-pip-${{
hashFiles('requirements.txt') }}
  restore-keys: |
    ${{ runner.os }}-pip-
```

2. **Protect your `main` branch** so only PRs can merge and pipelines must pass before merge.
3. **Verify** on merge: open your repository's Actions tab, observe the workflow run, and confirm the Docker image appears in GitHub Container Registry.

Section 11.3 Summary & Cheat Sheet

- **Workflows** triggered on `pull_request` and `push` events.
- **Jobs:** `test` (lint/tests), `build-and-push` (Docker), `deploy` (Kubernetes).
- **Secrets:** define under GitHub Settings → Secrets for registry and cluster access.
- **Best practices:** cache dependencies, use `needs:`, enforce branch protections.

Task	Code Snippet / Action
Lint & tests	`jobs.test.steps` with `flake8` and `pytest`
Docker build & push	`docker/build-push-action@v3`
K8s deploy	`kubectl set image` … and `kubectl rollout status` …
Cache dependencies	`actions/cache@v3` for pip cache

Further Reading / Next Steps

- GitHub Actions docs: https://docs.github.com/actions
- Reusable workflows: https://docs.github.com/actions/using-workflows/reusing-workflows

- Advanced deployment patterns: canary, blue-green:
  https://martinfowler.com/bliki/BlueGreenDeployment.html
- In **Section 11.4**, we'll cover **Load Testing & Performance Tuning** to ensure your MCP server meets SLAs.

11.4 Environment Configuration & Secrets Management

Section 11.4 Overview & Objectives

By the end of this section you will:

1. Understand patterns for configuring applications via environment variables and files.
2. Securely supply secrets (API keys, database credentials) in local dev, CI, Docker, and Kubernetes.
3. Leverage Docker secrets, Kubernetes Secrets, and external vaults (e.g., HashiCorp Vault).
4. Implement automatic secret rotation and access controls for production deployments.

Motivation & Context

Hard-coding credentials or checking them into source control is a common source of breaches and leaks. A robust secrets management strategy keeps sensitive data out of your codebase, limits blast radius when a secret is compromised, and supports automated rotation without downtime. Environment configuration patterns also let you tailor your MCP server's behavior across dev, staging, and production.

Fundamentals

Concept	Description
12-Factor Config	Store config in environment variables, not code.
.env Files	Local development convenience, loaded by tools like `python-dotenv`.

Concept	Description
Docker Secrets	Modeled as files in `/run/secrets/...`, only available at container runtime.
Kubernetes Secrets	Base64-encoded `Secret` objects, injected as env vars or mounted volumes.
Vault Integration	Centralized secret store with dynamic secrets, accessed via agent or SDK, with leasing and rotation.
Access Controls	Use RBAC/policies to restrict which pods or applications can retrieve which secrets.

Step-by-Step Tutorial

A. Local Development with `.env`

```bash
bash

# .env (do NOT commit to git; add to .gitignore)
OPENAI_API_KEY=sk-…
DATABASE_URL=postgresql://user:pass@host:5432/db
python

# config.py
from dotenv import load_dotenv
import os

load_dotenv()   # Read .env into environment

OPENAI_API_KEY = os.getenv("OPENAI_API_KEY")
DATABASE_URL    = os.getenv("DATABASE_URL")
if not (OPENAI_API_KEY and DATABASE_URL):
    raise RuntimeError("Missing required
environment variables")
```

B. Docker Secrets

1. **Create a secret** from the host:

   ```bash
   bash
   ```

```
echo "$OPENAI_API_KEY" | docker secret create
openai_api_key -
```

2. **Use secret in a service** (Docker Swarm example):

```yaml
yaml

version: '3.7'
services:
  mcp-server:
    image: myrepo/mcp-server:1.0
    secrets:
      - openai_api_key
    env_file:
      - .env              # for non-sensitive
vars
secrets:
  openai_api_key:
    external: true
```

3. **Access in container**: Docker mounts
   `/run/secrets/openai_api_key`.

```python
python

# config.py override for Docker
if
os.path.exists("/run/secrets/openai_api_key"):
    OPENAI_API_KEY =
Path("/run/secrets/openai_api_key").read_text(
).strip()
```

C. Kubernetes Secrets & ConfigMaps

1. **Define Secret**:

```yaml
yaml

apiVersion: v1
kind: Secret
metadata: { name: mcp-secrets }
type: Opaque
```

```yaml
stringData:
  OPENAI_API_KEY: "sk-…"
  DATABASE_URL:    "postgresql://…"
```

2. **Mount as env vars** in Deployment:

yaml

```yaml
env:
  - name: OPENAI_API_KEY
    valueFrom: { secretKeyRef: { name: mcp-secrets, key: OPENAI_API_KEY }}
  - name: DATABASE_URL
    valueFrom: { secretKeyRef: { name: mcp-secrets, key: DATABASE_URL }}
```

3. **Use ConfigMap** for non-sensitive flags:

yaml

```yaml
apiVersion: v1
kind: ConfigMap
metadata: { name: mcp-config }
data:
  LOG_LEVEL: "info"
  MODE:      "production"
```

D. HashiCorp Vault Integration

1. **Run Vault Agent** as a sidecar that renders secrets to a shared volume:

hcl

```hcl
# vault-agent.hcl
auto_auth {
  method "kubernetes" { … }
  sink "file" { path = "/vault/secrets/.mcp" }
}
template {
  source     = "/vault/templates/mcp-config.tpl"
```

```
    destination = "/vault/secrets/.env"
}
```

2. **Deployment snippet** mounts sidecar:

```yaml
yaml

volumeMounts:
  - name: vault-secrets
    mountPath: /vault/secrets
volumes:
  - name: vault-secrets
    emptyDir: {}
```

3. **Load generated .env** in your app:

```python
python

load_dotenv(dotenv_path="/vault/secrets/.env")
```

Deep Dive & Best Practices

Concern	Recommendation
Secret Rotation	Automate rotation (Vault leases, Kubernetes TTL) and handle reloading in your application gracefully.
Least Privilege	Grant only necessary roles/policies to each service account or Vault role.
Audit & Encryption	Enable audit logging in Vault/Kubernetes and encrypt secrets at rest and in transit.
Avoid Env Leakages	Don't echo env in logs; use minimal privilege shells and filters to prevent accidental dumps.
Fallback on Missing Secrets	Fail fast on startup if critical secrets are absent; degrade non-critical features safely.

Hands-On Exercise

1. **Migrate** your .env local setup to use Docker secrets in your docker-compose.yml.

2. **Create** Kubernetes Secret and ConfigMap YAMLs, apply them, and verify your pod logs show the server started with correct values.
3. **Configure** a Vault Agent sidecar to inject a dynamically rotated token and update your app to reload secrets without restart.

Section 11.4 Summary & Cheat Sheet

- **12-Factor**: always read config from environment, never code.
- **Local dev**: use `.env` + `python-dotenv`, but don't commit it.
- **Docker**: use `docker secret` and mount at `/run/secrets/...`.
- **Kubernetes**: Secrets for sensitive, ConfigMaps for config; inject via `envFrom` or volumes.
- **Vault**: dynamic secrets with leases; sidecar agent writes to file for your app to consume.

Environment	Management Tool	Injection Method
Local dev	`.env` + dotenv	`load_dotenv()`
Docker Swarm	Docker Secrets	`docker secret →` `/run/secrets/*`
Kubernetes	K8s Secret/ConfigMap	`valueFrom.secretKeyRef/` `configMap`
Vault	Vault Agent & Kubernetes	Sidecar writes file → `load_dotenv()`

Further Reading / Next Steps

- Twelve-Factor App: https://12factor.net/config
- Docker secrets: https://docs.docker.com/engine/swarm/secrets/
- Kubernetes Secrets: https://kubernetes.io/docs/concepts/configuration/secret/
- Vault Kubernetes auth: https://www.vaultproject.io/docs/auth/kubernetes
- In **Section 11.5**, we'll dive into **Load Testing & Performance Tuning** for your MCP server.

11.5 Horizontal Scaling & Load Balancing

Section 11.5 Overview & Objectives

By the end of this section you will:

1. Architect your MCP deployment for **horizontal scaling**, adding more instances to handle increased load.
2. Configure **load balancers** (at L4 and L7) to distribute traffic evenly across replicas.
3. Understand **session affinity**, **health probes**, and **graceful connection draining** to minimize user disruption.
4. Leverage **service meshes** or **Ingress controllers** for advanced traffic routing, retries, and observability.

Motivation & Context

As usage of your context-aware agents grows, a single server instance becomes a bottleneck. Horizontal scaling—running multiple replicas behind a load balancer—lets you:

- Increase throughput by handling more concurrent connections.
- Improve availability: one pod or VM can fail without downtime.
- Perform rolling updates or maintenance without dropping in-flight requests.

A well-configured load-balancing layer ensures that each client request is routed to a healthy instance, and that traffic spikes are smoothed out automatically.

Fundamentals

Concept	Description
L4 Load Balancer	Routes TCP connections across endpoints without inspecting HTTP payload.
L7 Load Balancer (Ingress)	Terminates HTTP(S), can do path- or host-based routing, TLS offload, retries, and rate limits.

Concept	Description
Session Affinity	"Sticky sessions" ensure subsequent requests from the same client go to the same pod for stateful interactions.
Connection Draining	Gracefully shift traffic off a pod before shutting it down to avoid dropped requests.
Service Mesh	Sidecar proxies (e.g., Istio) provide fine-grained traffic control, mutual TLS, and metrics.

Step-by-Step Tutorial

A. Kubernetes Service + Horizontal Pod Autoscaler

1. **Ensure your Deployment** (from Section 11.2) has resource requests/limits set so HPA can scale based on CPU or custom metrics.
2. **Apply an HPA** (example below) to scale between 3 and 10 replicas when CPU > 60%:

yaml

```
apiVersion: autoscaling/v2
kind: HorizontalPodAutoscaler
metadata:
  name: mcp-hpa
spec:
  scaleTargetRef:
    apiVersion: apps/v1
    kind: Deployment
    name: mcp-server
  minReplicas: 3
  maxReplicas: 10
  metrics:
    - type: Resource
      resource:
        name: cpu
        target:
          type: Utilization
          averageUtilization: 60
```

3. **Verify scaling** by generating load:

```
bash
```

```
# e.g., bombard with curl in a loop
while true; do curl -s http://<service-
ip>/health; done
```

Then monitor pods:

```
bash
```

```
kubectl get hpa mcp-hpa --watch
kubectl get pods -l app=mcp
```

B. Ingress Controller for L7 Load Balancing

1. **Install** an Ingress controller (e.g., NGINX, Traefik):

```
bash
```

```
kubectl apply -f
https://raw.githubusercontent.com/kubernetes/i
ngress-
nginx/main/deploy/static/provider/cloud/deploy
.yaml
```

2. **Define an Ingress** resource to route mcp.example.com to your Service:

```
yaml
```

```
apiVersion: networking.k8s.io/v1
kind: Ingress
metadata:
  name: mcp-ingress
  annotations:
    nginx.ingress.kubernetes.io/affinity:
"cookie"
    nginx.ingress.kubernetes.io/session-
cookie-name: "MCPSESSION"
    nginx.ingress.kubernetes.io/session-
cookie-hash: "sha1"
spec:
```

```
    rules:
      - host: mcp.example.com
        http:
          paths:
            - path: /
              pathType: Prefix
              backend:
                service:
                  name: mcp-service
                  port: { number: 80 }
    tls:
      - hosts: ["mcp.example.com"]
        secretName: mcp-tls
```

3. **Enable health checks and draining**: ensure your Service's endpoint readinessProbe is used by Ingress to route only to ready pods, and that pod terminationGracePeriodSeconds ≥ readiness probe period for draining.

C. Linux-Level L4 Load Balancing (e.g., HAProxy/Nginx)

1. **Install HAProxy** on a VM to proxy TCP port 4000:

```
cfg

global
  daemon
  maxconn 256

defaults
  mode tcp
  timeout connect 5s
  timeout client  50s
  timeout server  50s

frontend mcp_front
  bind *:4000
  default_backend mcp_back

backend mcp_back
  balance roundrobin
  server mcp1 10.0.0.1:4000 check
```

```
server mcp2 10.0.0.2:4000 check
server mcp3 10.0.0.3:4000 check
```

2. **Reload** HAProxy config without dropping connections using `service haproxy reload` for near zero-downtime.

Deep Dive & Best Practices

Concern	Recommendation
Even Load Distribution	Prefer round-robin for stateless tools; use least-connections if some requests are heavier.
Session Affinity Trade-off	Sticky sessions simplify stateful workloads but can cause uneven load; use sparingly.
Connection Idle Timeouts	Align load-balancer timeouts with your server's keepalive settings to avoid unexpected disconnects.
Pod Draining	Set `preStop` hook to delay shutdown until in-flight calls complete:

`yaml`

```
lifecycle:
  preStop:
    exec:
      command: ["/bin/sleep","10"]
```

| **Service Mesh Benefits** | Use Istio or Linkerd for circuit-breaking, retries, canary deployments, and fine-grained metrics. |

Hands-On Exercise

1. **Deploy** the HPA and generate synthetic CPU load (`stress-ng --cpu 2`) inside one of the pods to trigger autoscaling; observe replica count changes.
2. **Configure** session affinity in your Ingress and verify that subsequent requests with the same cookie stick to the same pod (check logs or pod names).

3. **Test rolling upgrades** by updating your Deployment image tag, and verify zero-downtime by maintaining open connections (e.g., via `ab` or `hey` load test).

Section 11.5 Summary & Cheat Sheet

- **Horizontal scaling**: use Kubernetes HPA or an external autoscaler (e.g., AWS ALB Target Group).
- **L4 vs. L7 load balancing**: TCP vs. HTTP features—choose based on protocol needs.
- **Session affinity**: use sparingly; cookie or IP-hash based.
- **Graceful draining**: readinessProbe + `terminationGracePeriodSeconds` + `preStop` hook.
- **Service mesh**: for advanced routing, retries, and metrics.

Pattern	Key Config Snippet
HPA CPU scaling	`metrics.resource.name: cpu, averageUtilization`
Ingress affinity	`nginx.ingress.kubernetes.io/affinity: cookie`
L4 HAProxy check	`backend ... check`
Pod draining	`preStop: exec: sleep 10`

Further Reading / Next Steps

- Kubernetes Autoscaling: https://kubernetes.io/docs/tasks/run-application/horizontal-pod-autoscale/
- NGINX Ingress docs: https://kubernetes.github.io/ingress-nginx/
- HAProxy TCP load balancing: https://www.haproxy.com/documentation/

In **Chapter 12**, we'll explore **Monitoring & Observability**: metrics, tracing, and alerting for your MCP platform.

Chapter 12: Monitoring, Metrics & Observability

12.1 Structured Logging Formats (JSON)

Section 12.1 Overview & Objectives

By the end of this section you will:

1. Explain the benefits of emitting logs in **JSON** rather than free-form text.
2. Configure Python's `logging` module to output **structured JSON** records.
3. Include essential fields—`timestamp`, `level`, `message`, and custom `extra` metadata—in every log entry.
4. Verify that your JSON logs can be **parsed** and **filtered** by downstream tools (e.g., `jq`, ELK).
5. Ensure performance and readability by keeping log records concise and consistent.

Motivation & Context

Traditional text logs are difficult to query and prone to parsing errors. By adopting **structured JSON** logging, you enable:

- **Machine-readable** entries for automated processing.
- **Field-based filtering** (e.g., find all errors where `user_id=123`).
- **Indexing and aggregation** in log stores like Elasticsearch or CloudWatch Logs.
- **Consistency** across services, making cross-component tracing simpler.

Fundamentals

Field	Description
`timestamp`	ISO 8601 string (e.g., `"2025-04-18T15:04:05Z"`) indicating when the event occurred.
`level`	Log severity (`DEBUG`, `INFO`, `WARN`, `ERROR`).
`logger`	Name of the logger (`module.submodule`), useful for identifying the source.
`message`	Human-readable summary of the event.
`extra`	Object containing **structured metadata** (e.g., `request_id`, `method`, `user_id`, `duration_ms`).

Step-by-Step Tutorial

1. **Implement a JSON Formatter**

   ```python
   python

   import logging, json
   from datetime import datetime

   class JSONFormatter(logging.Formatter):
       def format(self, record):
           log = {
               "timestamp":
   datetime.utcfromtimestamp(record.created).isof
   ormat() + "Z",
               "level": record.levelname,
               "logger": record.name,
               "message": record.getMessage(),
           }
           # Attach any extra metadata passed via
   'extra'
           extras = getattr(record, "extra", {})
           if isinstance(extras, dict):
               log.update(extras)
           return json.dumps(log)
   ```

2. **Configure the Root Logger**

```python
python
```

```python
def setup_json_logging():
    handler = logging.StreamHandler()
    handler.setFormatter(JSONFormatter())
    root = logging.getLogger()
    root.setLevel(logging.INFO)
    root.handlers.clear()
    root.addHandler(handler)
```

3. **Emit Structured Logs with Extra Metadata**

```python
python

import logging

logger = logging.getLogger("mcp")

def process_request(request_id, user_id,
method):
    context = {"request_id": request_id,
"user_id": user_id, "method": method}
    logger.info("Received request",
extra={"extra": context})
    # ... do work ...
    logger.info("Completed request",
extra={"extra": {**context, "duration_ms":
42}})
```

4. **Parse & Filter with jq**

```bash
bash

# Show only ERROR logs:
cat logs.json | jq 'select(.level=="ERROR")'
# Count requests per method:
cat logs.json | jq -r '.method' | sort | uniq
-c
```

Deep Dive & Best Practices

Concern	Recommendation
Field Consistency	Always include the same set of core fields; avoid typos in `extra` keys.
Payload Size	Keep `message` concise and avoid embedding large objects; use identifiers instead.
Parsing Performance	Emit one JSON object per line (newline-delimited JSON) for high-throughput ingestion.
Error Details	For exceptions, capture minimal context (e.g., `error_type`, `error_message`) rather than full stack.
Time Precision	Use UTC and ISO 8601 to avoid timezone ambiguities.

Hands-On Exercise

1. **Integrate** the `JSONFormatter` into your MCP server's startup routine.
2. **Add** a log entry in one handler that includes dynamic fields (e.g., `tool`, `params`).
3. **Generate** sample logs and write two `jq` queries:
   - Extract all logs where `method == "chat"`.
   - Compute the **average** of `duration_ms` across all entries.

Section 12.1 Summary & Cheat Sheet

- **Why JSON?** Enables machine parsing, filtering, and indexing.
- **Core fields:** `timestamp`, `level`, `logger`, `message`, plus an `extra` object.
- **Implementation:**
  1. Define `JSONFormatter`.
  2. Configure `StreamHandler` with the formatter.
  3. Use `logger.info(..., extra={"extra": {...}})`.
- **Downstream use:** Process logs with tools like `jq`, ELK, or Splunk.

Task	Code Snippet
JSON Formatter	`class JSONFormatter(logging.Formatter): …`
Logger setup	`handler.setFormatter(JSONFormatter())`
Emitting a log	`logger.info("msg", extra={"extra": context})`
jq filtering	`jq 'select(.level=="ERROR")'`

Further Reading / Next Steps

- ndjson format: https://github.com/ndjson/ndjson-spec
- Elastic Common Schema for logs: https://www.elastic.co/guide/en/ecs/current/ecs-base.html
- Fluentd & Logstash for log aggregation: https://www.fluentd.org/, https://www.elastic.co/logstash/
- In **Section 12.2**, we'll cover **Metrics Collection** with Prometheus and client libraries.

12.2 Exposing Health Check & Metrics Endpoints

Section 12.2 Overview & Objectives

By the end of this section you will:

1. Implement a **health check** endpoint (`/health`) that reports service readiness and liveness.
2. Expose a **metrics** endpoint (`/metrics`) compatible with Prometheus scraping.
3. Instrument your MCP server with basic **counters**, **histograms**, and **gauges** for key operations.
4. Verify that your endpoints work locally and can be scraped by a Prometheus instance.

Motivation & Context

Health and metrics endpoints are critical for production services.

- **Health checks** let orchestration layers (Kubernetes, load balancers) know when your server is up or needs replacing.
- **Metrics** provide visibility into request rates, latencies, and errors. Together they enable alerting, autoscaling, and capacity planning.

Fundamentals

Endpoint	Purpose	Typical Response
`/health`	Readiness (ready to serve) & liveness (alive)	HTTP 200 `{"status":"ok"}` or HTTP 500 `{"status":"fail"}`
`/metrics`	Prometheus-formatted metrics for scrape	Plain-text with `# HELP`/`# TYPE` lines and `metric_name value`

Metric Type	Description	Example Use
Counter	Monotonic incrementing value	`requests_total` per method
Histogram	Buckets of observed durations	`request_duration_seconds`
Gauge	Arbitrary value that can go up/down	`in_flight_requests`

ASCII Flow: Health & Metrics

```pgsql
[LoadBalancer] ──▶ GET /health ──▶ [MCP Server]
responds 200
[Prometheus] ──▶ GET /metrics ──▶ [MCP Server]
responds text/plain metrics
```

Step-by-Step Tutorial

1. **Install Prometheus client**

```bash
pip install prometheus-client
```

2. **Add health check handler** (`mcp_server/server.py`):

```python
from http.server import
BaseHTTPRequestHandler, HTTPServer
import json

class HealthHandler(BaseHTTPRequestHandler):
    def do_GET(self):
        if self.path == "/health":
            # Perform any readiness checks
here (DB, dependencies)
            status = {"status": "ok"}
            self.send_response(200)
            self.send_header("Content-Type",
"application/json")
            self.end_headers()

self.wfile.write(json.dumps(status).encode())
        else:
            self.send_response(404)
            self.end_headers()
```

3. **Initialize Prometheus metrics** (`mcp_server/metrics.py`):

```python
from prometheus_client import Counter,
Histogram, Gauge, generate_latest,
CONTENT_TYPE_LATEST

# Counters per tool invocation
REQUEST_COUNTER = Counter(
    "mcp_requests_total",
    "Total number of MCP requests received",
    ["method", "status"]
)
```

```
# Histogram of request durations in seconds
REQUEST_LATENCY = Histogram(
    "mcp_request_duration_seconds",
    "Latency of MCP request handling",
    ["method"]
)

# Gauge of current in-flight requests
IN_FLIGHT = Gauge(
    "mcp_in_flight_requests",
    "Number of MCP requests in progress"
)
```

4. **Wrap each request** to record metrics (pseudo-code integration):

python

```
from mcp_server.metrics import
REQUEST_COUNTER, REQUEST_LATENCY, IN_FLIGHT

def handle_request(method, params):
    IN_FLIGHT.inc()
    with
REQUEST_LATENCY.labels(method=method).time():
        try:
            result =
dispatch_to_handler(method, params)

REQUEST_COUNTER.labels(method=method,
status="success").inc()
            return result
        except Exception:

REQUEST_COUNTER.labels(method=method,
status="error").inc()
            raise
        finally:
            IN_FLIGHT.dec()
```

5. **Expose /metrics endpoint** (mcp_server/server.py):

```python

class MetricsHandler(BaseHTTPRequestHandler):
    def do_GET(self):
        if self.path == "/metrics":
            data = generate_latest()
            self.send_response(200)
            self.send_header("Content-Type",
CONTENT_TYPE_LATEST)
            self.end_headers()
            self.wfile.write(data)
        else:
            self.send_response(404)
            self.end_headers()
```

6. **Run combined server**: start your MCP JSON-RPC server and mount the two HTTP handlers on separate ports or integrate into your existing HTTP loop as multiplexed paths.

Deep Dive & Best Practices

Concern	Recommendation
Health check depth	For readiness, include dependency checks (DB, context store); keep liveness lightweight.
Metrics cardinality	Limit label values (e.g., methods) to prevent high cardinality explosion in Prometheus.
Endpoint security	Expose /health publicly; restrict /metrics to internal or scraped only to your monitoring VPC.
Performance impact	Recording metrics adds minimal overhead; use batch reporting or async if needed at high QPS.
Autoscaling tie-in	Configure HPA on a custom metric (e.g., requests_total rate) via Prometheus adapter.

Hands-On Exercise

1. **Implement** the /health and /metrics handlers in your MCP server bootstrap.

2. **Write a script** to curl both endpoints and verify responses:

```bash
bash

curl http://localhost:4001/health
curl http://localhost:4001/metrics | head -n
20
```

3. **Configure** Prometheus locally with a `prometheus.yml` scrape config:

```yaml
yaml

scrape_configs:
  - job_name: 'mcp-server'
    static_configs:
      - targets: ['localhost:4001']
```

Run Prometheus and view metrics in the UI.

Section 12.2 Summary & Cheat Sheet

- **Health endpoint**: HTTP 200 JSON at `/health`; liveness vs. readiness checks.
- **Metrics endpoint**: Prometheus format at `/metrics`.
- **Core metrics**:
  - Counter: `mcp_requests_total{method, status}`
  - Histogram: `mcp_request_duration_seconds_bucket{method}`
  - Gauge: `mcp_in_flight_requests`
- **Instrument**: wrap request dispatch with counters, histograms, and gauges.

Task	Code Snippet
Install client	`pip install prometheus-client`
Define Counter	`Counter("mcp_requests_total",...,["method","status"])`

Task	Code Snippet
Define Histogram	`Histogram("mcp_request_duration_seconds",...,["method"])`
Health handler	`GET /health` JSON response
Metrics handler	`GET /metrics` using `generate_latest()`

Further Reading / Next Steps

- Prometheus Python client docs:
  https://github.com/prometheus/client_python
- Kubernetes metrics server and Prometheus adapter:
  https://github.com/kubernetes-sigs/prometheus-adapter
- Grafana dashboard examples for MCP metrics:
  https://grafana.com/grafana/dashboards/
- In **Section 12.3**, we'll explore **Distributed Tracing** with OpenTelemetry and Jaeger.

12.3 Integrating with Prometheus & Grafana

Section 12.3 Overview & Objectives

By the end of this section you will:

1. Configure **Prometheus** to scrape your MCP server's `/metrics` endpoint.
2. Stand up a **Grafana** instance and add Prometheus as a data source.
3. Import or build a Grafana **dashboard** to visualize request rates, latencies, and in-flight counts.
4. Define a simple **alert** in Prometheus for high error rates.

Motivation & Context

Prometheus and Grafana form the de facto open-source stack for metrics and visualization.

- **Prometheus** pulls time-series metrics from your services.

- **Grafana** queries Prometheus and renders dashboards and alerts. Together they give you real-time insight into MCP server performance and reliability.

ASCII Flow: Metrics Pipeline

```bash
[ MCP Server ] — exposes ──▶ /metrics endpoint
       |
   Prometheus — scrapes ──▶ MCP /metrics
       |
     time-series store
       |
     Grafana — queries ──▶ Prometheus
       |
     dashboards & alerts
```

Fundamentals

Component	Role
Scrape Job	A `scrape_configs` entry in `prometheus.yml`.
Data Source	Grafana configuration pointing to Prometheus URL.
Dashboard	JSON-defined panels visualizing metrics.
Alert Rule	Prometheus rule that fires when a metric crosses a threshold.

Step-by-Step Tutorial

1. **Install Prometheus** (Docker-compose example)

   ```yaml
   # docker-prometheus.yml
   version: "3"
   services:
     prometheus:
       image: prom/prometheus:latest
       volumes:
   ```

303

```
        -
./prometheus.yml:/etc/prometheus/prometheus.ym
l:ro
    ports:
      - "9090:9090"
```

2. **Configure `prometheus.yml`**

```yaml
yaml

global:
  scrape_interval: 15s

scrape_configs:
  - job_name: 'mcp-server'
    static_configs:
      - targets: ['mcp-server:4000']
```

> Ensure your MCP container is on the same Docker network as Prometheus under the hostname `mcp-server`.

3. **Run Grafana**

```bash
bash

docker run -d \
  --name=grafana \
  -p 3000:3000 \
  grafana/grafana:latest
```

   o   Default login: `admin` / `admin`.
4. **Add Prometheus Data Source**
   o   In Grafana UI → **Configuration** → **Data Sources** → **Add Prometheus**.
   o   URL: `http://prometheus:9090` (or `http://localhost:9090` if running locally).
   o   Click **Save & Test**.
5. **Import a Dashboard**
   o   Grafana UI → **Create** → **Import**.
   o   Paste this minimal JSON (or load from a file):

```
jsonc
```

```json
{
  "title": "MCP Server Metrics",
  "panels": [
    {
      "type": "graph",
      "title": "Request Rate",
      "targets": [
        {
          "expr":
"sum(rate(mcp_requests_total[1m])) by
(method)",
          "legendFormat": "{{method}}"
        }
      ]
    },
    {
      "type": "graph",
      "title": "Request Latency (p95)",
      "targets": [
        {
          "expr": "histogram_quantile(0.95,
sum(rate(mcp_request_duration_seconds_bucket[5
m])) by (le, method))",
          "legendFormat": "{{method}}"
        }
      ]
    },
    {
      "type": "singlestat",
      "title": "In-Flight Requests",
      "targets": [
        { "expr": "mcp_in_flight_requests" }
      ]
    }
  ],
  "schemaVersion": 16,
  "version": 0
}
```

o   Click **Import** and select your Prometheus data source.
6. **Add an Alert Rule**

```yaml
yaml

# alert_rules.yml
groups:
  - name: mcp_alerts
    rules:
      - alert: HighErrorRate
        expr:
rate(mcp_requests_total{status="error"}[5m]) >
1
        for: 2m
        labels:
          severity: critical
        annotations:
          summary: "High MCP error rate
detected"
          description: "More than 1 error/sec
over 5m for MCP server."
```

- o Mount this into Prometheus via `--config.file` or include
  in `prometheus.yml` under `rule_files:`.
- o Reload Prometheus: `curl -X POST`
  `http://localhost:9090/-/reload`.

Deep Dive & Best Practices

Concern	Recommendation
Scrape Cardinality	Avoid high-cardinality labels (e.g., user_id) in Prometheus metrics to prevent performance issues.
Dashboard Layout	Group panels by function (e.g., errors, latency, throughput) and use consistent colors/legends.
Alert Tuning	Set appropriate thresholds and `for:` durations to avoid alert storms on transient glitches.
Secure Access	Protect Grafana with strong credentials or integrate with OAuth/LDAP in production.
Dashboard as Code	Store your JSON dashboards in Git and deploy via Grafana's provisioning API for reproducibility.

Hands-On Exercise

1. **Extend** `prometheus.yml` with a second job scraping your
   Kubernetes Ingress or load balancer metrics.
2. **Modify** the imported dashboard to add a panel showing error rate per
   status code:

```promql
sum(rate(http_requests_total[1m])) by (code)
```

3. **Test** your alert rule by artificially causing errors (e.g., call a
   non-existent method) and confirm that Prometheus triggers
   HighErrorRate.

Section 12.3 Summary & Cheat Sheet

- **Prometheus setup**: `scrape_configs` → scrape your
  `/metrics`.
- **Grafana**: add Prometheus data source, import dashboard JSON.
- **Key panels**: request rate, p95 latency, in-flight gauge.
- **Alerts**: define in Prometheus rule files, reload config to activate.

Task	Code Snippet / UI Path
Scrape config	`prometheus.yml` → `job_name: 'mcp-server'`
Grafana data source	**Configuration → Data Sources → Prometheus**
Dashboard import	**Create → Import** → paste JSON
Alert rule	`alert_rules.yml` + `rule_files:` in `prometheus.yml` + reload endpoint

Further Reading / Next Steps

- Prometheus docs: https://prometheus.io/docs/introduction/overview/
- Grafana dashboards: https://grafana.com/grafana/dashboards

- Alertmanager for notifications:
  https://prometheus.io/docs/alerting/latest/alertmanager/
- In **Section 12.4**, we'll explore **Distributed Tracing** with
  OpenTelemetry and Jaeger.

12.4 Alerting Strategies & SLAs

Section 12.4 Overview & Objectives

By the end of this section you will:

1. Design **alerting rules** that surface critical issues (high error rates, latency, resource exhaustion).
2. Define **Service Level Objectives (SLOs)** and map them to concrete **Service Level Indicators (SLIs)** from your metrics.
3. Configure **alert routing** and **notification channels** (email, Slack, PagerDuty) via Prometheus Alertmanager.
4. Establish **on-call rotations** and **runbooks** to respond to incidents in alignment with your SLAs.

Motivation & Context

Alerts are your first line of defense when production systems deviate from expected behavior. Without clear SLIs/SLOs and actionable alerts, teams either miss critical failures or drown in noise. By codifying your availability and performance targets—and tying them to alert rules and on-call processes—you ensure reliability commitments are met and incidents are handled efficiently.

Fundamentals

Term	Definition
SLI (Service Level Indicator)	A quantitative measure of some aspect of the service (e.g., error rate, request latency p95).
SLO (Service Level Objective)	The target value or range for an SLI over a given period (e.g., "99.9% of requests must succeed").

Term	Definition
SLA (Service Level Agreement)	A contractual agreement that often includes SLOs plus penalties or credits if targets are missed.
Alert	A notification emitted when an SLI breaches its SLO threshold for a defined duration.
Alertmanager	Prometheus component that deduplicates, groups, and routes alerts to notification channels.

Step-by-Step Tutorial

1. **Define Your SLIs & SLOs**

   text

   ```
   SLI:  request_success_rate = 1 - (errors_total
   / requests_total)
   SLO:  request_success_rate ≥ 99.9% over 30d
   SLI:  request_latency_p95 =
   histogram_quantile(0.95,
   rate(request_duration_seconds_bucket[5m]))
   SLO:  request_latency_p95 ≤ 0.5s over 1h
   ```

2. **Write Prometheus Alerting Rules**

   yaml

   ```
   groups:
     - name: mcp_slo_alerts
       rules:
         - alert: HighErrorRate
           expr: |
   (sum(rate(mcp_requests_total{status="error"}[3
   0m]))
           /
           sum(rate(mcp_requests_total[30m])))
           > 0.001
         for: 15m
         labels:
           severity: page
   ```

```
        annotations:
          summary: "MCP error rate > 0.1% for
30m"
          description: "Error rate is {{
printf \"%.2f\" (100 *
(sum(rate(mcp_requests_total{status=\"error\"}
[30m])) / sum(rate(mcp_requests_total[30m])))
) }}%"

      - alert: HighLatencyP95
        expr: histogram_quantile(0.95,
sum(rate(mcp_request_duration_seconds_bucket[5
m])) by (le))
            > 0.5
        for: 10m
        labels:
          severity: ticket
        annotations:
          summary: "MCP p95 latency > 500ms"
          description: "p95 latency is {{
printf \"%.2f\" (histogram_quantile(0.95,
sum(rate(mcp_request_duration_seconds_bucket[5
m])) by (le))) }}s"
```

3. Configure Alertmanager

yaml

```
route:
  group_by: ['alertname', 'severity']
  group_wait: 30s
  group_interval: 5m
  repeat_interval: 2h
  receiver: 'team-slack'

receivers:
  - name: 'team-slack'
    slack_configs:
      - channel: '#alerts'
        send_resolved: true
  - name: 'oncall-email'
    email_configs:
```

```
- to: 'oncall@example.com'
  send_resolved: true
```

   o Map `severity: page` → PagerDuty receiver,
     `severity: ticket` → Email.
4. **Define Runbooks & On-Call**
   o Document steps for each alert in a shared runbook (e.g.,
     Confluence or Git repo).
   o Set up an on-call rotation in PagerDuty or Opsgenie matching
     your team's working hours.
   o Link alert `annotations.runbook_url` to the relevant
     document.

Deep Dive & Best Practices

Concern	Recommendation
Noise Reduction	Use `for:` durations to suppress transient blips; tune thresholds to balance sensitivity and noise.
Grouping & Deduplication	Leverage Alertmanager's `group_by` to coalesce related alerts into single notifications.
Alert Severity	Classify alerts (`critical`, `warning`, `info`) to drive appropriate on-call response.
SLO Monitoring	Continuously evaluate SLO compliance with tools like Prometheus SLO.
Post-Incident Reviews	Conduct blameless retrospectives for outages, updating SLOs, runbooks, and monitoring as needed.

Hands-On Exercise

1. **Calculate** your current 30-day error rate SLI via the Prometheus
   expression in the UI; compare to your target SLO.
2. **Trigger** each alert by temporarily lowering thresholds (e.g., set SLO
   breach at 0.01%) and verify notifications arrive in Slack/email.
3. **Write a runbook** section for "HighErrorRate" that guides responders
   through log analysis, quick rollback, and post-mortem steps.

Section 12.4 Summary & Cheat Sheet

- **SLI/SLO/SLA**: measure, target, and agree on service quality metrics.
- **Alert Rules**: use PromQL to detect SLO breaches over sliding windows.
- **Alertmanager**: configure routing, grouping, and notification receivers.
- **Runbooks**: link alerts to documented response procedures.

Item	Snippet / Location
SLI Calculation (error)	`(sum(rate(...errors...)) / sum(rate(...requests...)))`
Alert rule (error rate)	in `mcp_slo_alerts` group under `alert: HighErrorRate`
Alertmanager receiver	`receivers: - name: team-slack,` `severity: ticket` mapping
Runbook annotation	`annotations.runbook_url:` `https://.../HighErrorRate`

Further Reading / Next Steps

- Prometheus SLO library: https://github.com/prometheus/slo
- Google SRE book: https://landing.google.com/sre/book.html
- "Four Golden Signals" of monitoring: latency, traffic, errors, saturation
- In **Section 12.5**, we'll explore **Distributed Tracing** with OpenTelemetry and Jaeger for full-stack request visibility.

12.5 Performance Profiling & Tuning

Section 12.5 Overview & Objectives

By the end of this section you will:

1. Use Python profilers (CPU and memory) to identify hotspots in your MCP server.
2. Interpret profiler outputs (cProfile, pstats) and flame graphs.

3. Apply tuning techniques—algorithmic improvements, caching, concurrency tweaks—to reduce latency and resource use.
4. Establish a continuous profiling workflow for ongoing performance monitoring.

Motivation & Context

As your MCP server evolves, new features can introduce unseen performance regressions. Without profiling, you might optimize the wrong code path or miss memory leaks. Systematic profiling and tuning ensures that your context-aware tools stay responsive under load and make efficient use of CPU and memory.

Fundamentals

Tool	Purpose	Output Format
cProfile	Built-in CPU profiler	Call statistics (`calls`, `time`)
pstats	Sort and query cProfile dumps	Text tables
pyinstrument	Sampling profiler with text/flame output	Flame graph or text summary
line_profiler	Line-by-line timing for specific functions	Annotated source lines
memory_profiler	Line-by-line memory usage	Console report
Flame Graphs	Visual call stack time breakdown	SVG/HTML

Step-by-Step Tutorial

1. **Profile with cProfile**

   bash

   ```
   python -m cProfile -o profile.raw
   mcp_server/server.py
   ```

Then inspect with pstats:

```python
import pstats
p = pstats.Stats("profile.raw")
p.sort_stats("cumtime").print_stats(20)
```

  o   **Pro Tip:** Sort by `"tottime"` to find self-time hot spots.
2. **Generate a Flame Graph**

```bash
pip install py-spy
py-spy record -o profile.svg -- python
mcp_server/server.py
```

Open `profile.svg` in your browser to visually spot expensive call stacks.

3. **Line-Level Timing**

```bash
pip install line_profiler
kernprof -l -v mcp_server/handlers/chat.py
```

Add the `@profile` decorator to functions you want to analyze:

```python
@profile
def chat_handler(params):
    ...
```

4. **Memory Profiling**

```bash
pip install memory_profiler
mprof run mcp_server/server.py
mprof plot
```

Or decorate:

```python
python

from memory_profiler import profile

@profile
def handle_request(...):
    ...
```

5. **Benchmark Critical Paths**
   Use `timeit` in a REPL or micro-benchmark script:

```python
python

import timeit
setup = "from mcp_server.handlers.chat import
chat_handler; params=['u','hi']"
print(timeit.timeit("chat_handler(params)",
setup=setup, number=1000))
```

Deep Dive & Best Practices

Concern	Recommendation
Sampling vs. Tracing	Use sampling profilers (pyinstrument, py-spy) in production-like environments to minimize overhead.
Isolate Benchmarks	Run benchmarks on dedicated hardware or containers to avoid noisy neighbors skewing results.
Cache Results	Memoize expensive computations (e.g., manifest parsing) where possible to avoid repeated work.
Avoid Premature Optimizations	Focus on top 2–3 hotspots; algorithmic changes often yield the biggest gains.
Continuous Profiling	Integrate lightweight profilers (e.g., py-spy's Agent) in staging to catch regressions early.

Hands-On Exercise

1. **Profile** your `chat_handler` under simulated load and identify the top three slowest functions.
2. **Optimize** the manifest loader by caching the parsed JSON schema—measure latency before and after.
3. **Implement** a decorator to memoize tool manifest fetches for each client and validate its effect via benchmarks.

Section 12.5 Summary & Cheat Sheet

- **cProfile + pstats:** quick CPU profiling; sort by cumulative/self-time.
- **Flame graphs (py-spy):** visual hotspots without code changes.
- **Line profiler:** pinpoint slow lines in critical functions.
- **Memory profiling:** catch leaks or heavy allocations.
- **Benchmarking:** use `timeit` for repeatable micro-benchmarks.

Tool	Command / Usage
cProfile	`python -m cProfile -o prof.raw server.py`
pstats	`Stats("prof.raw").sort_stats("tottime").print_stats(10)`
py-spy Flame	`py-spy record -o flame.svg -- python server.py`
line_profiler	`kernprof -l -v module.py` + `@profile`
memory_profiler	`mprof run server.py` → `mprof plot`

Further Reading / Next Steps

- "High Performance Python" by Micha Gorelick & Ian Ozsvald
- py-spy documentation: https://github.com/benfred/py-spy
- Prometheus profiling with `prometheus_client`'s `ProcessCollector`

In **Chapter 13**, we'll dive into **Extending MCP Protocol** for custom transport layers and authentication schemes.

Chapter13 Real World Projects & Case Studies

13.1 Business Report Agent (CSV → PDF → Email)

Section 13.1 Overview & Objectives

By the end of this section you will:

1. Define MCP tools for loading CSV data, generating a PDF report, and emailing it.
2. Implement a **CSV→PDF→Email** pipeline in Python.
3. Handle file I/O, PDF formatting, and SMTP attachment logic.
4. Securely manage email credentials and error-handle each step.

Motivation & Context

Many businesses need scheduled reports—sales figures, inventory levels, financial summaries—delivered automatically. A **Business Report Agent** can:

- Ingest raw CSV exports from databases or spreadsheets.
- Format the data into a polished PDF report.
- Email the report to stakeholders without human intervention.

For example, every Monday morning your sales manager receives a PDF showing last week's top-selling products and revenue trends.

Fundamentals

Concept	Description
Pandas	Load and preprocess CSV data into a DataFrame.
ReportLab	Library for programmatic PDF generation in Python.
SMTP	Protocol for sending email; use `smtplib` and `email` modules in Python.

Concept	Description
Attachments	Encode PDF as MIME attachment (Content-Disposition: attachment).
Credentials	Store SMTP user/password in environment variables or secrets.

ASCII Flow: Report Generation & Delivery

```csharp
[Client] ──▶ call "generateReport" ──▶ [MCP Server]
    │                                        ┣▶
load_csv(params["path"])
    │                                        ┣▶
pdf_bytes = build_pdf(data)
    │                                        ┣▶
send_email(to, subject, pdf_bytes)
    │                                        ┗▶ return
{"status":"sent"}
    │
[Email] ◀─ PDF report delivered
```

Step-by-Step Tutorial

A. Define & Register Your Tools

```jsonc
// manifest.json excerpt
{
  "methods": {
    "loadCSV": {
      "description": "Load CSV data into JSON
rows",
      "params": [{ "name":"path","type":"string"
}],
      "result": { "type":"array","items":{
"type":"object" } }
```

```json
        },
        "generatePDF": {
            "description": "Generate PDF bytes from JSON
data and template",
            "params": [
                { "name":"rows","type":"array" },
                { "name":"title","type":"string" }
            ],
            "result": { "type":"string","format":"base64"
}
        },
        "sendEmail": {
            "description": "Send an email with a PDF
attachment",
            "params": [
                { "name":"to","type":"string" },
                { "name":"subject","type":"string" },
                { "name":"body","type":"string" },
                {
"name":"attachment","type":"string","format":"base6
4" },
                { "name":"filename","type":"string" }
            ],
            "result": { "type":"object","properties":{
"status":{ "type":"string" } } }
        }
    }
}
```

Register in your server bootstrap:

python

```python
server.register_tool("loadCSV",   load_csv,
description="Load CSV", version="1.0.0")
server.register_tool("generatePDF", generate_pdf,
description="Build PDF", version="1.0.0")
server.register_tool("sendEmail",  send_email,
description="Send email", version="1.0.0")
```

B. Implement `load_csv`

```python
python

import pandas as pd
from mcp_framework import RPCError

def load_csv(params):
    (path,) = params
    try:
        df = pd.read_csv(path)
        return df.to_dict(orient="records")
    except FileNotFoundError:
        raise RPCError(code=-32060, message="CSV
file not found", data={"path": path})
    except Exception as e:
        raise RPCError(code=-32061, message="Failed
to load CSV", data={"detail": str(e)})
```

C. Implement `generate_pdf`

```python
python

import io, base64
from reportlab.platypus import SimpleDocTemplate,
Table, Paragraph, Spacer
from reportlab.lib.styles import
getSampleStyleSheet
from reportlab.lib.pagesizes import LETTER
from mcp_framework import RPCError

def generate_pdf(params):
    rows, title = params
    buffer = io.BytesIO()
    doc = SimpleDocTemplate(buffer,
pagesize=LETTER)
    styles = getSampleStyleSheet()
    elements = [Paragraph(title, styles["Title"]),
Spacer(1,12)]

    # Build table: header + data rows
    if not rows:
        raise RPCError(code=-32062, message="No
data to generate PDF")
```

```python
    header = list(rows[0].keys())
    data = [header] + [[str(r.get(c,"")) for c in
header] for r in rows]
    elements.append(Table(data, hAlign="LEFT"))

    try:
        doc.build(elements)
        pdf_bytes = buffer.getvalue()
        return base64.b64encode(pdf_bytes).decode()
    except Exception as e:
        raise RPCError(code=-32063, message="PDF
generation failed", data={"detail": str(e)})
```

D. Implement send_email

python

```python
import os, base64, smtplib
from email.message import EmailMessage
from mcp_framework import RPCError

SMTP_HOST = os.getenv("SMTP_HOST")
SMTP_PORT = int(os.getenv("SMTP_PORT", 587))
SMTP_USER = os.getenv("SMTP_USER")
SMTP_PASS = os.getenv("SMTP_PASS")

def send_email(params):
    to, subject, body, attachment_b64, filename =
params
    msg = EmailMessage()
    msg["Subject"] = subject
    msg["From"]    = SMTP_USER
    msg["To"]      = to
    msg.set_content(body)

    # Attach PDF
    pdf_bytes = base64.b64decode(attachment_b64)
    msg.add_attachment(pdf_bytes,
maintype="application", subtype="pdf",
filename=filename)

    try:
```

```
        with smtplib.SMTP(SMTP_HOST, SMTP_PORT) as
smtp:
            smtp.starttls()
            smtp.login(SMTP_USER, SMTP_PASS)
            smtp.send_message(msg)
        return {"status": "sent"}
    except Exception as e:
        raise RPCError(code=-32064, message="Email
send failed", data={"detail": str(e)})
```

Deep Dive & Best Practices

- **Template Engines:** For richer reports, integrate Jinja2 to render HTML and convert via WeasyPrint instead of ReportLab.
- **Large CSVs:** Stream rows (`chunksize=...`) to avoid memory spikes.
- **Retry Logic:** Wrap `send_email` with retry/backoff on transient SMTP errors.
- **Security:** Don't log raw attachment data; mask credentials in logs and use vaults for SMTP secrets.
- **PDF Styling:** Use stylesheets, add page numbers, and include charts (e.g., matplotlib → image embed).

Hands-On Exercise

1. **Extend** the PDF generator to include a **bar chart** of a numeric column:
   - Use matplotlib to draw the chart, save to PNG, embed in the PDF.
2. **Write a client script** that invokes the three tools in sequence to produce and send a weekly report.
3. **Add a caching layer** so repeated calls to `loadCSV` for the same file path within 5 minutes return cached data instead of reloading.

Section 13.1 Summary & Cheat Sheet

- **Tools & Signatures:**

Tool	Params	Returns
`loadCSV`	`[path]`	`[{...},...]`
`generatePDF`	`[rows,title]`	`base64-PDF`
`sendEmail`	`[to,subject,body,attachment,filename]`	`{"status":"sent"}`

- **Key Steps:**
    1. **Load CSV** → list of dicts.
    2. **Generate PDF** → base64 string.
    3. **Send Email** → SMTP with TLS + attachment.

Further Reading / Next Steps

- ReportLab User Guide: https://www.reportlab.com/docs/reportlab-userguide.pdf
- Jinja2 Templates: https://jinja.palletsprojects.com/
- WeasyPrint for HTML→PDF: https://weasyprint.org/
- Python `smtplib` docs: https://docs.python.org/3/library/smtplib.html
- In **Section 13.2**, we'll build an **Interactive ChatOps Agent** that integrates with Slack and MCP.

13.2 Context Aware Calendar Assistant

Section 13.2 Overview & Objectives

By the end of this section you will:

1. Define MCP tools for reading and writing calendar events via a standard API (e.g., iCalendar or Google Calendar).
2. Build a **context-aware calendar assistant** that can schedule, reschedule, and query events based on user context.
3. Implement natural-language handlers that translate between human requests and structured calendar operations.
4. Manage timezones, recurring events, and conflict detection with clear error handling.

Motivation & Context

Busy professionals rely on calendars to coordinate meetings, deadlines, and reminders. A **Context-Aware Calendar Assistant** goes beyond simple CRUD—it understands phrases like "find me an open slot next Wednesday afternoon" or "move my 3 PM meeting to tomorrow morning if possible," considering the user's existing schedule, work hours, and preferences. By exposing calendar operations as MCP tools, any client (chatbot, voice assistant, dashboard) can leverage the same capabilities in a consistent, discoverable way.

Fundamentals

Concept	Description
Event Schema	JSON Schema for calendar events (start, end, summary, attendees, recurrence).
Free/Busy Query	Tool to fetch busy blocks within a date range for conflict detection.
Timezones	Handling IANA zone names; converting between user local time and UTC.
Natural-Language Parsing	Converting user requests ("next Friday at 10") into concrete datetime ranges.
Conflict Resolution	Detecting overlapping events and proposing alternatives.

Step-by-Step Tutorial

1. **Define your manifest entries**

   jsonc

   ```
   {
     "methods": {
       "getFreeBusy": {
   ```

```
      "description": "Fetch busy intervals for
a user within a range",
      "params": [
        { "name":"user","type":"string" },
        {
"name":"start","type":"string","format":"date-
time" },
        {
"name":"end","type":"string","format":"date-
time" }
      ],
      "result": {
        "type":"array",
        "items": {
          "type":"object",
          "properties": {

"start":{"type":"string","format":"date-
time"},

"end":{"type":"string","format":"date-time"}
          }
        }
      }
    },
    "createEvent": {
      "description": "Create a calendar
event",
      "params": [
        { "name":"user","type":"string" },
        { "name":"event","type":"object" }
      ],
      "result": {
"type":"string","description":"Event ID" }
    },
    "updateEvent": { /* similar schema */ },
    "deleteEvent": { /* similar schema */ }
  }
}
```

2. Implement free/busy handler

python

```
from datetime import datetime
from mcp_framework import RPCError
from calendar_client import CalendarAPI  #
your wrapper

def get_free_busy(params):
    user, start_str, end_str = params
    try:
        start =
datetime.fromisoformat(start_str)
        end  =
datetime.fromisoformat(end_str)
    except ValueError:
        raise RPCError(code=-32070,
message="Invalid date-time format")

    busy = CalendarAPI(user).fetch_busy(start,
end)
    # busy: list of (start:datetime,
end:datetime)
    return [
        {"start": b[0].isoformat(), "end":
b[1].isoformat()}
        for b in busy
    ]
```

3. Natural-language intent handler

python

```
import re
from dateutil import parser as date_parser

def schedule_meeting_handler(params):
    """
    params: [user: str, text: str]
    """
    user, text = params
```

326

```python
    # Simple regex for "next X at Y":
    m = re.search(r"next (\w+) at
(\d{1,2}(?::\d{2})?\s*(?:AM|PM)?)", text,
re.IGNORECASE)
    if not m:
        raise RPCError(code=-32071,
message="Could not parse time from request")
    day_name, time_str = m.groups()
    # dateutil can resolve next weekday
    dt = date_parser.parse(f"{day_name}
{time_str}", default=datetime.now())
    # Check free/busy
    busy = get_free_busy([user,
dt.isoformat(), (dt +
timedelta(hours=1)).isoformat()])
    if busy:
        return {"status":"conflict",
"suggestion":"You are busy then"}
    event = {
      "start": dt.isoformat(),
      "end":    (dt +
timedelta(hours=1)).isoformat(),
      "summary": "Scheduled by Assistant"
    }
    eid = create_event([user, event])
    return {"status":"scheduled", "event_id":
eid}
```

4. **Register tools & handler**

python

```python
server.register_tool("getFreeBusy",
get_free_busy, …)
server.register_tool("createEvent",
create_event, …)
server.register_tool("scheduleMeeting",
schedule_meeting_handler,
                     description="Parse text
and schedule a meeting", version="1.0.0")
```

Deep Dive & Best Practices

Concern	Recommendation
Timezone Handling	Always store and communicate in UTC; convert to/from user's IANA zone once at ingress/egress.
Recurrence Rules	Use RFC 5545 iCalendar RRULE parsing libraries (e.g., `recurrence` package) for robust support.
Conflict Proposals	Offer multiple slots (e.g., next 3 open slots) instead of a single suggestion.
Validation	Validate event objects against JSON Schema before API calls to catch malformed inputs early.
Rate Limits	Cache free/busy results for short windows to avoid hitting calendar API quotas excessively.

Hands-On Exercise

1. **Enhance** `get_free_busy` to merge adjacent busy intervals to simplify conflict logic.
2. **Extend** the NLP parser to handle "tomorrow morning" or "Friday afternoon" phrases by mapping times of day.
3. **Write tests** mocking your `CalendarAPI` to verify conflict detection and event creation under various scenarios.

Section 13.2 Summary & Cheat Sheet

- **Core tools:**
  - `getFreeBusy(user, start, end)` → `[{start,end},…]`
  - `createEvent(user, event)` → `event_id`
  - `scheduleMeeting(user, text)` → `status/conflict or event_id`
- **Key patterns:**

  0. Parse text → concrete datetime
  1. Query free/busy → detect conflicts
  2. Create or suggest alternatives

- **Time handling:** keep UTC internally, convert at boundaries; leverage `dateutil` for parsing.

Further Reading / Next Steps

- Google Calendar API docs: https://developers.google.com/calendar
- iCalendar spec (RFC 5545): https://tools.ietf.org/html/rfc5545
- dateutil documentation: https://dateutil.readthedocs.io/
- In **Section 13.3**, we'll build a **Collaborative Document Agent** that uses MCP tools to manage shared notes and versioning.

13.3 Enterprise Search Agent (RAG with SQL/Vector DB)

Section 13.3 Overview & Objectives

By the end of this section you will:

1. Configure both a **relational database** (e.g., PostgreSQL) and a **vector store** (e.g., FAISS, Pinecone) as searchable backends.
2. Define MCP tools for **keyword SQL search**, **vector-based similarity search**, and **document retrieval**.
3. Implement a **Retrieval-Augmented Generation (RAG)** pipeline that:
   - Retrieves relevant records via SQL queries,
   - Fetches semantically similar embeddings from the vector store,
   - Aggregates and passes context to an LLM to answer enterprise queries.
4. Handle result ranking, deduplication, and fallback logic when one backend returns no hits.

Motivation & Context

Enterprises often have two kinds of knowledge: structured data in SQL tables (products, customers, transactions) and unstructured text (policies, manuals, emails). A **RAG Search Agent** combines both:

- **SQL search** surfaces precise, schema-driven data (e.g., "find orders over $10K last quarter").
- **Vector search** finds relevant documents even when queries are phrased differently (e.g., "refund policy").
  By merging these results and feeding them to an LLM, users get concise, contextual answers that draw on all corporate knowledge.

Fundamentals

Tool	Purpose
searchSQL	Execute parameterized SQL queries returning rows
searchVector	Query a vector store for top-k semantically similar docs
retrieveDoc	Fetch full text or metadata for a given document ID
generateAnswer	Call LLM with combined context to produce a final answer

Concept	Notes
Embeddings	Numeric representations of text (e.g., via OpenAI's `text-embedding-ada-002`).
Vector Store	FAISS, Pinecone, or similar; index embeddings with IDs for similarity search.
Result Aggregation	Merge SQL rows and vector hits, deduplicate on document IDs, rank by relevance score.
Prompt Construction	Concatenate top-n snippets (SQL fields as text + doc excerpts) within token limits.

Step-by-Step Tutorial

1. **Define Manifest Entries**

   jsonc

   ```
   {
     "methods": {
   ```

```json
    "searchSQL": {
      "description":"Run a safe parameterized
SQL search",
      "params":[
       {"name":"query","type":"string"},
       {"name":"params","type":"array"}
      ],
      "result":{
        "type":"array",
        "items":{"type":"object"}
      }
    },
    "searchVector": {
      "description":"Retrieve top-k similar
docs from vector store",
      "params":[

{"name":"query_embedding","type":"array","item
s":{"type":"number"}},
        {"name":"topK","type":"integer"}
      ],
      "result":{
        "type":"array",
        "items":{
          "type":"object",
          "properties":{
            "doc_id":{"type":"string"},
            "score":{"type":"number"}
          }
        }
      }
    },
    "retrieveDoc": {
      "description":"Fetch document content by
ID",

"params":[{"name":"doc_id","type":"string"}],
      "result":{"type":"object"}
    },
    "generateAnswer": {
      "description":"Generate an answer given
user question and context",
```

```
      "params":[
        {"name":"question","type":"string"},
        {"name":"context","type":"string"}
      ],
      "result":{"type":"string"}
    }
  }
}
```

2. **Implement `searchSQL` Handler**

python

```python
from mcp_framework import RPCError
from db import get_pg_conn

def search_sql(params):
    query, values = params
    # Whitelist allowed queries or use
prepared statements
    try:
        conn = get_pg_conn()
        with conn.cursor() as cur:
            cur.execute(query, tuple(values))
            cols = [desc[0] for desc in
cur.description]
            rows = [dict(zip(cols, row)) for
row in cur.fetchall()]
        return rows
    except Exception as e:
        raise RPCError(code=-32080,
message="SQL search failed", data={"detail":
str(e)})
```

3. **Implement `searchVector` Handler**

python

```python
import numpy as np
from vector_store import VectorIndex  # your
wrapper
```

```python
def search_vector(params):
    embedding, top_k = params
    try:
        results =
VectorIndex.query(np.array(embedding),
top_k=top_k)
        # each item: {"id":..., "score":...}
        return [{"doc_id": r["id"], "score":
float(r["score"])} for r in results]
    except Exception as e:
        raise RPCError(code=-32081,
message="Vector search failed",
data={"detail": str(e)})
```

4. **Implement `retrieveDoc` Handler**

python

```python
def retrieve_doc(params):
    (doc_id,) = params
    # could fetch from SQL or object store
    row = search_sql([ "SELECT title, content
FROM documents WHERE id=%s", [doc_id] ])[0]
    return row  # {"title":..., "content":...}
```

5. **Implement `generateAnswer` Handler**

python

```python
import openai, os
from mcp_framework import RPCError

openai.api_key = os.getenv("OPENAI_API_KEY")

def generate_answer(params):
    question, context = params
    prompt = f"""You are an enterprise search
assistant.
Use the following context excerpts to answer
the question.
Context:
{context}
```

```python
Question:
{question}

Answer concisely."""
    try:
        resp = openai.ChatCompletion.create(
            model="gpt-4o-mini",

messages=[{"role":"user","content":prompt}],
            temperature=0.0
        )
        return resp.choices[0].message.content
    except Exception as e:
        raise RPCError(code=-32082,
message="LLM generation failed",
data={"detail": str(e)})
```

6. Combine into a RAG Endpoint

python

```python
def enterprise_search_handler(params):
    user_query, = params
    # 1. SQL search for structured answers
    sql_results = search_sql([ "SELECT name,
description FROM products WHERE name ILIKE
%s", [f"%{user_query}%"] ])
    # 2. Embed query & vector search
    embedding =
openai.Embedding.create(model="text-embedding-
ada-002",
input=user_query)["data"][0]["embedding"]
    vec_results = search_vector([embedding,
5])
    # 3. Retrieve documents
    docs = [ retrieve_doc([r["doc_id"]]) for r
in vec_results ]
    # 4. Build context: include SQL rows and
doc snippets
    context_parts = []
    if sql_results:
```

334

```
        context_parts.append("Structured
Results:\n" + "\n".join(str(r) for r in
sql_results))
        for d in docs:

context_parts.append(f"{d['title']}\n{d['conte
nt'][:200]}...")
        context = "\n\n".join(context_parts)
        # 5. Generate answer
        answer = generate_answer([user_query,
context])
        return {"answer": answer, "sql_hits":
sql_results, "doc_hits": docs}
```

7. **Register All Tools**

python

```
server.register_tool("searchSQL", search_sql,
...)
server.register_tool("searchVector",
search_vector, ...)
server.register_tool("retrieveDoc",
retrieve_doc, ...)
server.register_tool("generateAnswer",
generate_answer, ...)
server.register_tool("enterpriseSearch",
enterprise_search_handler, ...)
```

Deep Dive & Best Practices

Concern	Recommendation
Query Safety	Never interpolate user input directly into SQL; use parameterized queries and a whitelist.
Embedding Costs	Cache query embeddings for repeated queries or use a local embedding service to reduce latency.
Result Fusion	Merge SQL and vector hits intelligently—e.g., promote SQL rows if schema high-priority.
Token Budget	Truncate context to fit within model limits; select top-k snippets by score or recency.

Concern	Recommendation
Fallback Logic	If neither backend returns hits, reply with a default "no results found" message.

Hands-On Exercise

1. **Benchmark** both backends: measure average latency for a typical SQL query and a vector search.
2. **Implement** a cache (e.g., Redis) for `retrieveDoc` to avoid repeated database calls.
3. **Write pytest** tests mocking both `searchVector` and `searchSQL` to simulate low- and high-relevance scenarios and verify answer generation uses the correct context.

Section 13.3 Summary & Cheat Sheet

- **Core tools:**

Tool	Purpose
`searchSQL`	Parameterized relational searches
`searchVector`	Semantic similarity search over embeddings
`retrieveDoc`	Fetch full document metadata/content by ID
`generateAnswer`	LLM-based synthesis given question + context
`enterpriseSearch`	Orchestrates RAG: SQL + vector + LLM

- **RAG Flow:**
    1. SQL search → structured data
    2. Embed & vector search → unstructured docs
    3. Retrieve docs → snippets
    4. Construct context → LLM answer

Further Reading / Next Steps

- Pinecone documentation: https://www.pinecone.io/docs/

- FAISS tutorial: https://github.com/facebookresearch/faiss/wiki
- Retrieval-Augmented Generation paper:
  https://arxiv.org/abs/2005.11401
- In **Section 13.4**, we'll build a **Collaborative Document Agent** with version control and conflict resolution.

13.4 Data Analysis Pipeline with MCP Tools

Section 13.4 Overview & Objectives

By the end of this section you will:

1. Expose MCP tools for data ingestion (`loadDataFrame`), transformation (`transformData`), visualization (`generateChart`), and export (`exportResults`).
2. Implement a **data analysis pipeline** that strings these tools together into an end-to-end workflow.
3. Handle large datasets via chunked processing and streaming results back to the client.
4. Return visualization artifacts (e.g., base64-encoded PNG) and data exports in a structured, reusable format.

Motivation & Context

Analysts often need to clean, aggregate, visualize, and share insights from data. By breaking each step into MCP-exposed tools, any client—chatbot, dashboard, or script—can orchestrate complex pipelines without embedding data logic. A standardized pipeline ensures reproducibility, composability, and clear separation of concerns.

ASCII Flow: Data Analysis Pipeline

```scss
[Client]
      ├──▶ loadDataFrame(path) ──▶ rows

      ├──▶ transformData(rows, pipeline) ──▶
transformed_rows
```

```
     ┗━▶ generateChart(transformed_rows, chart_spec)
 ━▶ chart_png

       ┗━▶ exportResults(transformed_rows, format) ━▶
 export_ref
```

Fundamentals

Tool	Params	Returns
loadDataFrame	path: string	rows: list[dict]
transformData	rows: list[dict], pipeline: list[op,args]	rows: list[dict]
generateChart	rows: list[dict], spec: dict	chart: base64-PNG string
exportResults	`rows: list[dict], format: string ("csv"	"json")`

Pipeline Operations	Description
filter	Keep rows matching a boolean expression
aggregate	Group by columns and apply aggregations (sum, mean, etc.)
sort	Order rows by specified columns
limit	Truncate result to top-N rows

Step-by-Step Tutorial

1. **Manifest Snippet**

   ```jsonc
   {
   ```

```
  "methods": {
    "loadDataFrame": {
      "description":"Load CSV into JSON rows",

"params":[{"name":"path","type":"string"}],

"result":{"type":"array","items":{"type":"obje
ct"}}
    },
    "transformData": {
      "description":"Apply transformations to
rows",
      "params":[

{"name":"rows","type":"array","items":{"type":
"object"}},

{"name":"pipeline","type":"array","items":{"ty
pe":"object"}}
      ],

"result":{"type":"array","items":{"type":"obje
ct"}}
    },
    "generateChart": {
      "description":"Render a chart as PNG",
      "params":[

{"name":"rows","type":"array","items":{"type":
"object"}},
        {"name":"spec","type":"object"}
      ],

"result":{"type":"string","format":"base64"}
    },
    "exportResults": {
      "description":"Export rows to CSV or
JSON and return reference",
      "params":[

{"name":"rows","type":"array","items":{"type":
"object"}},
```

```
{"name":"format","type":"string","enum":["csv"
,"json"]}
      ],
      "result":{"type":"string"}
   }
  }
}
```

2. Implement `loadDataFrame`

python

```python
import pandas as pd
from mcp_framework import RPCError

def load_data_frame(params):
    (path,) = params
    try:
        df = pd.read_csv(path)
        return df.to_dict(orient="records")
    except Exception as e:
        raise RPCError(code=-32090,
message="Failed to load CSV", data={"detail":
str(e)})
```

3. Implement `transformData`

python

```python
def transform_data(params):
    rows, pipeline = params
    df = pd.DataFrame(rows)
    for step in pipeline:
        op = step["op"]; args =
step.get("args", {})
        if op == "filter":
            df = df.query(args["condition"])
        elif op == "aggregate":
            df =
df.groupby(args["by"]).agg(args["agg"]).reset_
index()
```

```python
        elif op == "sort":
            df = df.sort_values(by=args["by"],
ascending=args.get("asc", True))
        elif op == "limit":
            df = df.head(args["n"])
        else:
            raise RPCError(code=-32091,
message=f"Unsupported op '{op}'")
    return df.to_dict(orient="records")
```

4. **Implement generateChart**

python

```python
import io, base64
import matplotlib.pyplot as plt
from mcp_framework import RPCError

def generate_chart(params):
    rows, spec = params
    df = pd.DataFrame(rows)
    plt.figure()
    chart_type = spec.get("type", "line")
    x, y = spec["x"], spec["y"]
    if chart_type == "line":
        plt.plot(df[x], df[y])
    elif chart_type == "bar":
        plt.bar(df[x], df[y])
    else:
        raise RPCError(code=-32092,
message=f"Unknown chart type '{chart_type}'")
    plt.xlabel(x); plt.ylabel(y);
plt.tight_layout()
    buf = io.BytesIO()
    plt.savefig(buf, format="png")
    plt.close()
    return
base64.b64encode(buf.getvalue()).decode()
```

5. **Implement exportResults**

python

```
import csv, json, tempfile
from mcp_framework import RPCError

def export_results(params):
    rows, fmt = params
    try:
        tmp =
tempfile.NamedTemporaryFile(delete=False,
suffix="."+fmt)
        if fmt == "csv":
            writer = csv.DictWriter(tmp,
fieldnames=rows[0].keys())
            writer.writeheader();
writer.writerows(rows)
        else:
            json.dump(rows, tmp)
        tmp.close()
        return tmp.name
    except Exception as e:
        raise RPCError(code=-32093,
message="Export failed", data={"detail":
str(e)})
```

6. **Orchestrate as a Pipeline**

python

```
def data_pipeline(params):
    path, pipeline, chart_spec, export_fmt =
params
    rows = load_data_frame([path])
    transformed = transform_data([rows,
pipeline])
    chart = generate_chart([transformed,
chart_spec])
    ref = export_results([transformed,
export_fmt])
    return {"chart": chart, "export_ref": ref}
server.register_tool("dataPipeline",
data_pipeline, description="End-to-end data
pipeline", version="1.0.0")
```

Deep Dive & Best Practices

Concern	Recommendation
Chunked Processing	For very large CSVs, process in chunks (`pd.read_csv(chunksize=…)`) and stream partial results.
Chart Styling	Accept spec parameters for colors, labels, and figure size to make charts more informative.
Temporary File Cleanup	Schedule background cleanup of exported files or return URLs to object storage instead of local FS.
Error Handling	Return partial outputs when non-critical steps fail (e.g., chart generation), with warnings.
Async Variants	Implement `async` versions using threads or `aiofiles` to avoid blocking the server loop.

Hands-On Exercise

1. **Extend** the pipeline to support a `"pivot"` operation in `transformData`.
2. **Add** support for a `"scatter"` chart in `generateChart`, mapping color by a third column.
3. **Write** an integration test that runs `dataPipeline` on a sample CSV and verifies that:
   - `export_ref` points to a valid file containing expected rows.
   - `chart` decodes to a non-empty PNG binary.

Section 13.4 Summary & Cheat Sheet

- **Tools & Signatures:**

Tool	Signature
`loadDataFrame`	`(path) → rows`
`transformData`	`(rows, pipeline) → transformed_rows`

Tool	Signature
`generateChart`	`(rows, spec) → base64-PNG`
`exportResults`	`(rows, format) → file_path`
`dataPipeline`	`(path, pipeline, spec, format) → {chart, export_ref}`

- **Pipeline Flow:**
    1. Load → 2. Transform → 3. Chart → 4. Export.

Further Reading / Next Steps

- Pandas performance:
  https://pandas.pydata.org/docs/user_guide/enhancingperf.html
- Matplotlib customization:
  https://matplotlib.org/stable/tutorials/index.html
- Server-side streaming patterns:
  https://asyncio.readthedocs.io/en/stable/stream.html

In **Section 13.5**, we'll explore **Collaborative Document Agents** with versioning and merging.

13.5 Lessons Learned & Optimization Tips

Section 13.5 Overview & Objectives

By the end of this section you will:

1. Reflect on key **lessons learned** from building real-world MCP pipelines and agents.
2. Apply **optimization tips** for performance, reliability, and developer productivity.
3. Recognize common **pitfalls** and how to avoid them in future projects.
4. Establish a continuous-improvement process using metrics, profiling, and feedback loops.

Motivation & Context

Every MCP project—from calendar assistants to RAG search agents—teaches valuable lessons about designing robust, maintainable, and performant systems. By codifying these insights, you can accelerate future development, reduce technical debt, and build agents that delight end users.

Fundamentals

Lesson Category	Key Insight
Performance	Cache expensive operations (e.g., manifest parsing, embeddings)
Reliability	Layer retry/backoff and circuit breakers around all external calls
Maintainability	Keep tools small and focused; apply single-responsibility principle
Observability	Instrument every tool with logs, metrics, and traces
Developer Experience	Provide runnable examples, clear error messages, and a fast feedback loop

Step-by-Step Optimization Path

1. **Measure Baseline**
   o Run end-to-end benchmarks (unit, integration, load tests).
   o Collect CPU, memory, latency, and error-rate metrics.
2. **Profile Critical Paths**
   o Use sampling profilers (py-spy) for production-like load.
   o Identify top 3 hotspots by cumulative time or memory usage.
3. **Optimize Incrementally**
   o **Cache** static data (e.g., parsed schemas, context lookups).
   o **Vectorize** data transformations with Pandas or NumPy.
   o **Batch** external calls where possible (e.g., bulk SQL, multi-request LLM streaming).
4. **Strengthen Resilience**
   o Add **circuit breakers** around each tool: open on X failures, reset after cooldown.

- o Implement **fallbacks** that degrade gracefully (e.g., stale cache).
- o Enforce **timeouts** on all I/O to prevent head-of-line blocking.

5. **Improve Developer Workflow**
   - o Write **self-contained examples** for each tool in a `examples/` folder.
   - o Use **reloadable manifests** and hot-reloading plugins for rapid iteration.
   - o Automate **linting**, **formatting**, and **type-checking** (e.g., `black`, `mypy`).

6. **Validate & Iterate**
   - o Re-run benchmarks and compare against baseline.
   - o Monitor **SLIs** and adjust thresholds or scaling rules.
   - o Collect user feedback and refine tool interfaces for clarity.

Deep Dive & Best Practices

Category	Optimization Tip
Manifest Loading	Cache the parsed JSON schema in memory; invalidate on file change
Batching Requests	Group multiple JSON-RPC calls into batch requests to reduce I/O overhead
Async Execution	Prefer `asyncio` for high-concurrency tools; avoid blocking calls inside handlers
Chunked Streaming	Stream large payloads incrementally via notifications to reduce memory spikes
Schema Validation	Compile and cache JSON Schema validators to speed up param checks
Tool Granularity	Extract common logic into shared libraries; keep MCP handlers as thin wrappers
Testing	Automate fault-injection tests in CI to catch regressions early
Documentation	Maintain up-to-date examples and a living manifest reference to help clients self-serve

---

Hands-On Exercise

1. **Benchmark** your slowest tool (identified via profiling) and apply one optimization pattern (e.g., caching or batching). Measure improvement.
2. **Inject a fault** (e.g., simulate a 50 ms delay in an external API) and verify your retry/circuit-breaker logic handles it gracefully.
3. **Clean up** your codebase: extract at least two utility functions into a shared module and update imports accordingly.
4. **Write a mini-case study** summarizing before/after metrics, lessons learned, and next steps for further tuning.

Section 13.5 Summary & Cheat Sheet

- **Measure → Profile → Optimize → Validate**: iterate in small, measured steps.
- **Cache & Batch**: reduce redundant work and I/O.
- **Async & Streaming**: handle high concurrency and large data efficiently.
- **Resilience Patterns**: timeouts, retries, circuit breakers, fallbacks.
- **Developer Workflow**: examples, hot-reload, linting, CI tests.

Step	Action
Baseline Metrics	Run end-to-end benchmarks
Profiling	Use `py-spy` or `cProfile`
Caching	Memoize manifest/schema/tool outputs
Batching	Combine JSON-RPC calls or DB queries
Async/Streaming	Adopt `asyncio` and chunked notifications
Resilience	Implement retries, backoff, circuit breakers
CI Fault Tests	Automate fault injection in your pipeline
Documentation	Keep examples, cheat sheets, and manifest docs up to date

Further Reading / Next Steps

- "Building Microservices" by Sam Newman (ch. on resilience)
- "High Performance Python" by Micha Gorelick & Ian Ozsvald
- Python's `functools.lru_cache` and `asyncio` patterns
- Profiling at scale with `py-spy` and `scalene`

- In **Chapter 14**, we'll look ahead at **Emerging Trends & Future Directions** for context-aware AI tools.

Chapter 14: Contributing to the MCP Ecosystem

14.1 Understanding the MCP Spec Repository

Section 14.1 Overview & Objectives

By the end of this section you will:

1. Navigate the official **MCP Specification** repository and its key components.
2. Understand the role of the **manifest schema**, **protocol definitions**, and **examples** folders.
3. Clone, build, and validate the spec locally to experiment with changes.
4. Identify how to propose updates or extensions via issues and pull requests.

Motivation & Context

The MCP Spec Repository is the single source of truth for everyone building MCP-compatible servers and clients. Whether you're adding a new feature, fixing a typo, or clarifying an edge-case, contributing upstream ensures consistency and accelerates adoption across the ecosystem.

Fundamentals

Component	Path / Location	Purpose
manifest.schema.json	`/schemas/manifest.schema.json`	Defines the JSON Schema for tool manifests.
protocol.md	`/docs/protocol.md`	Describes JSON-RPC extensions,

Component	Path / Location	Purpose
		header conventions, and flows.
examples/	/examples/	Sample manifests, client/server snippets, and use-cases.
CHANGELOG.md	/CHANGELOG.md	Records spec releases, breaking changes, and deprecations.
CONTRIBUTING.md	/CONTRIBUTING.md	Guidelines for reporting issues, coding style, and PRs.

Step-by-Step Tutorial

1. **Clone the Repository**

   bash

   ```bash
   git clone
   https://github.com/mcp-protocol/spec.git
   cd spec
   ```

2. **Install Dependencies & Validate Schema**

   bash

   ```bash
   npm install   # or pip install jsonschema-cli
   jsonschema-cli validate \
     --schema schemas/manifest.schema.json \
     --instance examples/basic-manifest.json
   ```

3. **Browse Key Files**

- o Open **schemas/manifest.schema.json**: note how `methods`, `params`, and `result` are defined.
- o Read **docs/protocol.md**: review header formats, notification vs. request rules.
- o Explore **examples/**: see minimal manifest, async examples, batch workflows.

4. **Make a Local Change**
   - o Edit `schemas/manifest.schema.json` to add a new optional field `deprecated`.
   - o Run `jsonschema-cli validate` again against all examples to catch regressions.

5. **Run the Test Suite**

   bash

   ```
   npm test    # verifies schema and documentation
   links
   ```

Deep Dive & Best Practices

Concern	Recommendation
Backward Compatibility	Follow semver: avoid removing or renaming fields in minor/patch releases.
Schema Documentation	Keep descriptions in JSON Schema up to date; they appear in generated docs.
Example Coverage	Add or update an example for every new schema feature to illustrate real-world usage.
CI Integration	Ensure your PR passes the spec's CI checks (schema validation, link validation, linting).

Hands-On Exercise

1. **Add a "deprecated" boolean** property to each `methods.*` entry in `schemas/manifest.schema.json`.
2. **Update one example** in `/examples` to mark a method as deprecated and rerun `npm test`.
3. **Submit a PR**: open an issue describing why deprecation flags help, implement the change, and push a branch for review.

Section 14.1 Summary & Cheat Sheet

- **Key Locations:**
  - `/schemas/manifest.schema.json` for manifest definitions
  - `/docs/protocol.md` for protocol rules
  - `/examples/` for real-world snippets
- **Local Workflow:**

  0. `git clone` → 2. `jsonschema-cli validate` → 3. edit → 4. `npm test`

- **Contribution Steps:**

  1. Fork & branch → 2. Make edits + add examples → 3. Run CI locally → 4. Open PR with description

---

Further Reading / Next Steps

- CONTRIBUTING guidelines: https://github.com/mcp-protocol/spec/blob/main/CONTRIBUTING.md
- JSON Schema best practices: https://json-schema.org/understanding-json-schema/
- SemVer specification: https://semver.org/
- In **Section 14.2**, we'll explore **Building and Publishing MCP Client Libraries** in multiple languages.

14.2 Writing & Publishing Extensions

Section 14.2 Overview & Objectives

By the end of this section you will:

1. Scaffold a new MCP extension package in your language of choice.
2. Implement custom tools and manifest snippets following MCP conventions.

3. Package, version, and publish your extension to a public registry (e.g., PyPI, npm).
4. Write clear README and API docs so other developers can discover and consume your extension.

Motivation & Context

Extensions let the community share reusable tools—database connectors, chat integrations, custom data-processing pipelines—without each project reinventing the wheel. A well-packaged extension:

- Follows MCP naming & versioning conventions.
- Bundles its own manifest fragments and schemas.
- Is easy to install (`pip install mcp-foo`, `npm install @mcp/foo`).
- Automatically registers its tools when imported.

Fundamentals

Concept	Description
Package Scaffold	Directory layout, metadata (`setup.py`/`package.json`), license, README.
Manifest Fragment	A `.json` snippet under `manifests/` describing new methods and types.
Entry Point	Language-specific mechanism (e.g., `entry_points` in Python, `main` in `package.json`) to auto-register tools.
Versioning	Semantic versioning (`MAJOR.MINOR.PATCH`) aligned with MCP protocol compatibility.
Publishing	Commands & credentials for package registries (PyPI, npm).
Documentation	Inline docstrings, generated API reference, examples in README.

Step-by-Step Tutorial

1. **Scaffold the Package**

bash

```
mkdir mcp-foo
cd mcp-foo
# Python example
python -m venv .venv && source
.venv/bin/activate
pip install setuptools wheel
cat > setup.py <<EOF
from setuptools import setup, find_packages
setup(
  name="mcp-foo",
  version="0.1.0",
  packages=find_packages(),
  install_requires=["mcp-framework>=1.0.0"],
  entry_points={
    "mcp_framework.tools": [
      "fooTool = mcp_foo.tools:register_tools"
    ]
  },
  author="You",
  description="MCP extension providing Foo
tools",
  long_description=open("README.md").read(),

long_description_content_type="text/markdown",
  classifiers=["Programming Language :: Python
:: 3"],
)
EOF
mkdir -p mcp_foo/tools mcp_foo/manifests
touch mcp_foo/__init__.py
```

2. **Define Your Manifest Fragment**

jsonc

```
// mcp_foo/manifests/foo_manifest.json
{
  "methods": {
```

```
    "fooEcho": {
        "description": "Echo back the input with
Foo branding",
        "version": "0.1.0",
        "params":[{
"name":"text","type":"string" }],
        "result":{ "type":"string" }
    }
  }
}
```

3. **Implement & Register Your Tools**

python

```python
# mcp_foo/tools.py
import json, pkg_resources
from mcp_framework import MCPServer

def foo_echo(params):
    (text,) = params
    return f"[Foo] {text}"

def register_tools(server: MCPServer):
    # Load manifest fragment
    manifest_data = json.loads(
      pkg_resources.resource_string(__name__,
"manifests/foo_manifest.json")
    )

server.register_manifest_fragment(manifest_dat
a)
    # Register handler
    server.register_tool("fooEcho", foo_echo,
description="Foo echo", version="0.1.0")
```

4. **Write Documentation & Examples**

markdown

```markdown
<!-- README.md -->
# mcp-foo
```

```
Provides a simple `fooEcho` MCP tool.

## Installation

```bash
pip install mcp-foo
```

Usage

python

from mcp_framework import MCPServer
import mcp_foo.tools # triggers registration
via entry point

server = MCPServer(...)
server.serve()
```

5. **Publish Your Package**

```
bash

# Python / PyPI
python setup.py sdist bdist_wheel
twine upload dist/*

# npm equivalent for JavaScript:
npm login
npm publish --access public
```

Deep Dive & Best Practices

Concern	Recommendation
Manifest Consistency	Keep your fragment's version in sync with your package version; bump minor for added tools.
Entry Points	Use your language's plugin mechanism so importing your package auto-registers tools.

Concern	Recommendation
Testing	Include a simple script in `examples/` that spins up an MCPServer with your extension loaded.
Documentation	Auto-generate API docs (Sphinx, TypeDoc) and publish them alongside the registry package.
Semantic Versioning	MAJOR for breaking changes, MINOR for new tools, PATCH for bug fixes in existing ones.

Hands-On Exercise

1. **Create** a second extension method (e.g., `fooReverse`) with its manifest entry and handler, bumping MINOR to `0.2.0`.
2. **Write** a quick integration test that installs your package (`pip install .`), launches an MCPServer with your extension, and calls `fooEcho` and `fooReverse`.
3. **Publish** the updated version to PyPI or npm, then install it in a fresh virtualenv and verify the tools appear in `server.fetch_manifest()`.

Section 14.2 Summary & Cheat Sheet

- **Scaffold:** use `setup.py`/`package.json`, `entry_points` or `main` hook.
- **Manifest Fragment:** place under `manifests/`, register via code.
- **Register Tools:** implement `register_tools(server)` to load fragment and call `register_tool`.
- **Versioning:** align fragment version with package version; follow SemVer.
- **Publishing:** build and upload to PyPI (`twine`) or npm (`npm publish`).

Step	Command / Code Snippet
Scaffold package	`setup.py` with `entry_points`/`package.json`
Manifest fragment	`manifests/foo_manifest.json`

Step	Command / Code Snippet
Tool registration	`server.register_tool(...)` in `register_tools`
Build & publish	`python setup.py sdist bdist_wheel && twine upload dist/*`
Integration test	`pip install mcp-foo;` `MCPClient(manifest_url=...); call fooEcho`

Further Reading / Next Steps

- setuptools entry points: https://packaging.python.org/specifications/entry-points/
- npm CLI docs: https://docs.npmjs.com/creating-and-publishing-unscoped-public-packages
- MCP Spec on Extensions: see `/docs/extensions.md` in the spec repo

In **Section 14.3**, we'll cover **Community Governance & Roadmap** to engage with the MCP community.

14.3 Community Governance & Best Practices

Section 14.3 Overview & Objectives

By the end of this section you will:

1. Understand the **governance model** guiding MCP's evolution—roles, decision processes, and release cadences.
2. Learn community **code of conduct**, issue triage, and contribution workflows.
3. Identify **best practices** for writing high-quality issues, PRs, and design proposals.
4. Discover communication channels and how to engage constructively with maintainers and fellow contributors.

Motivation & Context

A healthy open-source ecosystem thrives on clear governance and shared norms. Good community practices ensure that MCP remains stable, secure, and forward-looking, while welcoming new contributors and ideas. By aligning on processes and etiquette, you help MCP grow sustainably and inclusively.

Fundamentals

Aspect	Description
Governing Board	A small group of maintainers responsible for major decisions, release scheduling, and conflict resolution.
Working Groups	Topic-focused subteams (e.g., security, SDKs, docs) that shepherd proposals and design discussions.
RFC Process	"Request for Comments" workflow for proposing protocol changes: write an RFC, discuss publicly, and vote.
Code of Conduct	Behavioral expectations documented in `CODE_OF_CONDUCT.md`—ensuring respectful, harassment-free interactions.
Issue Triage	Labeling, prioritizing, and assigning new issues following defined templates and priority criteria.

Step-by-Step Engagement

1. **Filing a High-Quality Issue**
   o Use the **issue template**: include a clear **title**, **environment**, **steps to reproduce**, **expected vs. actual behavior**, and any **logs** or **config snippets**.
   o Assign relevant **labels** (bug, enhancement, proposal).
2. **Proposing an RFC**
   o Fork or checkout the `rfcs/` directory in the spec repo.
   o Draft an RFC Markdown file with: **motivation**, **design**, **alternatives**, **impact**, and **timeline** sections.
   o Submit a PR, tag or mention the appropriate working group, and solicit feedback.
3. **Participating in Reviews**
   o Read the project's **review checklist**: code style, tests, docs, backward compatibility.

- o Offer constructive feedback on PRs—reference specific lines and suggest alternatives.
- o Respect maintainers' time: ask clarifying questions in threads before doing heavy work.

4. **Joining a Working Group**
   - o Check the WORKING_GROUPS.md for open roles and meeting schedules.
   - o Introduce yourself on the shared mailing list or Slack channel, express interest, and commit to at least one issue or task.

5. **Voting & Releases**
   - o For breaking changes or major features, Voting Members cast votes per the **Governance Policy**.
   - o Releases follow a **time-based cadence** (e.g., quarterly minor, biannual major), with **alpha**, **beta**, and **stable** channels.

Deep Dive & Best Practices

Category	Best Practice
Respectful Communication	Assume good intent, be patient with newcomers, avoid sarcasm or heated language.
Transparent Decisions	Record design discussions and votes in publicly accessible meeting notes or RFC threads.
Inclusive Onboarding	Maintain up-to-date **"Good First Issue"** labels and documentation to lower entry barriers.
Documentation Quality	Every feature or change should be accompanied by examples, rationale, and migration guidance.
Security Disclosure	Use the private security mailing list or process outlined in SECURITY.md for vulnerabilities.

Hands-On Exercise

1. **Locate** the "Good First Issue" label in the MCP spec or framework repo and pick one to resolve.
2. **Draft** a small RFC proposal for adding a timeout field to the manifest schema, following the RFC template.
3. **Review** an open PR—add at least two constructive review comments, referencing the project's contribution checklist.

Section 14.3 Summary & Cheat Sheet

- **Governance:** Board makes strategic calls; working groups tackle specialized domains.
- **Contribution Workflow:**
  1. File issues with templates → triage →
  2. Draft RFCs for protocol changes → discuss/vote →
  3. Submit PRs with tests/docs → maintainers review → merge.
- **Community Norms:** Uphold the code of conduct, communicate respectfully, document thoroughly.

Activity	Resources / File Locations
Code of Conduct	`CODE_OF_CONDUCT.md`
Issue Templates	`.github/ISSUE_TEMPLATE/`
RFC Examples	`rfcs/` directory
Working Group Info	`WORKING_GROUPS.md`
Security Reporting	`SECURITY.md`

Further Reading / Next Steps

- Project Governance Doc: https://github.com/mcp-protocol/spec/blob/main/GOVERNANCE.md
- Contributor Covenant: https://www.contributor-covenant.org/
- OpenJS Foundation Community Guidelines: https://openjsf.org/code-of-conduct/
- In **Appendix A**, we'll provide **Cheat Sheets & Quick References** for manifest schema and JSON-RPC conventions.

14.4 Participating in RFCs & Spec Updates

Section 14.4 Overview & Objectives

By the end of this section you will:

1. Navigate the MCP RFC process—from drafting to voting to publication.

2. Draft and submit a spec change proposal using the official RFC template.
3. Engage in public discussion, iterate on feedback, and shepherd your RFC to acceptance.
4. Keep your implementation in sync with spec updates: tracking breaking changes, versioning, and client compatibility.

Motivation & Context

The MCP specification evolves through community-driven RFCs. Participating in this process ensures that new use-cases are supported, ambiguities are clarified, and the protocol grows in a coordinated, backward-compatible way. By learning how to contribute and react to spec changes, you'll help maintain interoperability across servers and clients.

Fundamentals

Term	Definition
RFC	"Request for Comments" document that proposes a concrete change or addition to the MCP spec.
Working Group	A focused team (e.g., protocol, SDK, security) that reviews and vets RFCs in its domain.
Draft → Candidate → Accepted	Lifecycle stages: initial proposal, community review, voting phase, final publication.
Spec Release	A versioned bump of the manifest schema and protocol docs incorporating accepted RFCs.
Compatibility Matrix	A published mapping of spec versions to library/client versions and known incompatibilities.

Step-by-Step Tutorial

1. **Locate the RFC Template**
   o In the spec repo's `rfcs/` directory find `0000-template.md`. Copy to a new file `0001-your-feature.md`.

2. **Draft Your RFC**
    - o Fill in sections:
        - ▪ **Title & Abstract** – concise summary.
        - ▪ **Motivation** – use-case and problem statement.
        - ▪ **Proposal** – precise schema or protocol changes, with examples.
        - ▪ **Backward Compatibility** – impact analysis and migration path.
        - ▪ **Drawbacks/Alternatives** – trade-offs considered.
3. **Submit & Label**

bash

```
git checkout -b rfc-your-feature
git add rfcs/0001-your-feature.md
git commit -m "RFC: Add foo bar feature"
git push origin rfc-your-feature
```

   - o Open a PR against `main`, apply labels `rfcs` and your relevant working group tag (`wg-protocol`).
4. **Engage in Review**
    - o Monitor comments on GitHub: respond in-thread, revise your draft.
    - o Tag participants with `@mcp-protocol/wg-protocol` for visibility.
5. **Voting & Acceptance**
    - o Once reviewers signal "LGTM," Working Group leads move the RFC to **Candidate**.
    - o A 7-day public comment period ensues, then a formal vote.
    - o On acceptance, merge the RFC, bump `manifest.schema.json` version, and update `CHANGELOG.md`.
6. **Update Your Implementation**
    - o In your server or client repo, bump supported spec version in `compatibility_matrix`.
    - o Add or adapt code to handle the new feature.
    - o Write tests exercising the RFC change and update documentation.

Deep Dive & Best Practices

Concern	Recommendation
Clarity & Precision	Use concrete examples (JSON snippets, message flows) to illustrate changes unambiguously.
Minimal Breaking Changes	Whenever possible, design additions as optional extensions to avoid forcing immediate client updates.
Version Tags	In your RFC header, specify `Manifest-Version:` `MAJOR.MINOR` that this change targets.
Cross-Ref Existing Issues	Link to any related GitHub issues or discussions in your motivation section.
Automate Testing	Provide a `test/rfc-0001.yaml` example manifest and client test that validate the new feature.

Hands-On Exercise

1. **Pick a Pending RFC** from the spec repo's issue tracker and leave at least two substantive review comments.
2. **Draft a Mini-RFC** to add a `timeout` field to every method in the manifest schema—follow the template and include examples.
3. **Simulate the Workflow** by opening a PR in a fork, labeling it, and soliciting feedback from a colleague or teammate.
4. **Implement & Test** the Schema Change in your local clone of the spec and ensure `jsonschema-cli validate` passes against all examples.

Section 14.4 Summary & Cheat Sheet

- **RFC Lifecycle:** Draft → Review → Candidate → Vote → Merge → Release.
- **Key Files:** `rfcs/0000-template.md`, updated schema in `schemas/manifest.schema.json`, `CHANGELOG.md`.
- **Labels & Tags:** use `rfcs`, `wg-*`, and version bump labels (e.g., `semver-major`).

- **Implementation Sync:** bump manifest version, update compatibility matrix, add tests/examples.

Step	File / Command
Scaffold RFC	`cp rfcs/0000-template.md rfcs/0001-your-feature.md`
Open PR	GitHub UI, label `rfcs`, request review from `wg-protocol`
Bump Schema Version	Edit `"version"` in `schemas/manifest.schema.json`
Update Changelog	Add entry under new spec version in `CHANGELOG.md`
Validate Examples	`jsonschema-cli validate --schema schemas/... --instance examples/*`

Further Reading / Next Steps

- MCP Spec CONTRIBUTING guidelines: `/CONTRIBUTING.md` → "RFC Process" section
- Example RFCs: browse `rfcs/0001-*.md` for patterns
- SemVer spec: https://semver.org/
- In **Chapter 14.5**, we'll conclude with **Staying Engaged**: community channels, events, and long-term roadmap involvement.

14.5 Roadmap: Future MCP Enhancements

Section 14.5 Overview & Objectives

By the end of this section you will:

1. Survey key **areas of growth** for the MCP protocol and ecosystem in the coming years.
2. Learn how to evaluate and prioritize **enhancement proposals** based on impact, feasibility, and compatibility.
3. Understand the process for **incubating new features**—from prototyping to community feedback to official rollout.
4. Begin sketching your own **long-term contributions** to shape MCP's roadmap.

Motivation & Context

The MCP ecosystem thrives on continuous innovation. As use-cases expand—from real-time streaming to domain-specific tools—having a clear roadmap ensures the protocol stays relevant, interoperable, and secure. By anticipating emerging trends (e.g., decentralized agents, formal verification, multi-modal contexts) and formalizing how they enter MCP, maintainers and contributors can steer development cohesively rather than reactively.

Fundamentals

Enhancement Area	Description
Streaming RPC	Native support for bidirectional, event-driven streams alongside JSON-RPC calls.
Typed Manifests	Schema-driven, code-generated bindings (e.g., TypeScript, Pydantic) for manifest safety.
Plugin Marketplace	A central registry where community-authored MCP extensions can be discovered and versioned.
Inter-Protocol Bridges	First-class adapters to gRPC, WebSockets, or AMQP for cross-platform interoperability.
Event Subscriptions	Declarative subscriptions (pub/sub) in the manifest for notifications and triggers.
Formal Verification	Tooling to statically check handler contracts and manifest conformance.
Multi-Modal Context	Standardized support for images, audio, and rich media in request/response payloads.
Governance Automation	Dashboards and bots to track RFC status, deprecations, and community engagement metrics.

Roadmap Incubation Path

1. **Identify & Prioritize**

- Gather stakeholder input: survey existing users about pain-points and feature requests.
- Score proposals on **impact**, **effort**, and **risk** to focus on quick wins and high-value initiatives.

2. **Prototype & RFC**
   - Spin up a minimal **proof-of-concept** implementation in a plugin or fork.
   - Draft an **RFC** outlining schema changes, example flows, and backwards-compatibility strategy.

3. **Community Feedback**
   - Open the prototype for early adopters via a **preview release** or **feature flag**.
   - Collect feedback in working-group meetings, hackathons, and issue threads; iterate rapidly.

4. **Specification & Release**
   - Finalize the **manifest schema** and **protocol docs** reflecting the new feature.
   - Release in a **minor** or **major** version bump per SemVer, with clear deprecation notices if needed.

5. **Ecosystem Support**
   - Provide **SDK updates**, **examples**, and **migrations guides** so server and client libraries adopt the change smoothly.
   - Host webinars or write blog posts to educate users about the new capabilities.

Deep Dive & Best Practices

Concern	Recommendation
Compatibility First	Whenever feasible, introduce new features as optional extensions or flags to avoid breaking clients.
Incremental Delivery	Break big enhancements (e.g., streaming RPC) into smaller phases: handshake, message framing, metadata, etc.
Automated Migration	Supply tooling (e.g., CLI scripts) to upgrade existing manifest files and client code.
Metrics-Driven	Instrument early prototype releases and measure adoption, error-rates, and performance impact.

Concern	Recommendation
Community-Led Governance	Rotate roadmap ownership among diverse working-group members to align priorities with real-world needs.

Hands-On Exercise

1. **Pick one enhancement area** from the table above and draft a two-paragraph **problem statement** and **high-level proposal**.
2. **Score** it against **impact** (user value), **effort** (complexity), and **risk** (breaking potential) on a scale of 1–5.
3. **Outline an incubation plan**: prototype steps, RFC outline, and community engagement channels.

Section 14.5 Summary & Cheat Sheet

- **Future Areas:** streaming RPC, typed manifests, plugin marketplace, inter-protocol bridges, event subscriptions, formal verification, multi-modal context, governance automation.
- **Roadmap Process:** identify → prototype → RFC → feedback → release → ecosystem support.
- **Key Practices:** incremental delivery, backward compatibility, metrics-driven decisions, community governance.

Step	Action
Identify	Survey users, prioritize by impact/effort/risk
Prototype	Build a minimal plugin or feature-flagged implementation
RFC	Draft and submit spec change with examples and compatibility plan
Collect Feedback	Preview release, working-group reviews, community discussion
Release & Educate	Version bump, SDK updates, docs, webinars

Further Reading / Next Steps

- "Roadmapping Products" by Bruce McCarthy for prioritization frameworks
- GitHub-Driven RFC processes: https://opensource.guide/starting-a-project/
- SemVer 2.0.0: https://semver.org/
- In **Appendix A**, you'll find **Cheat Sheets & Quick References** for manifest schema, JSON-RPC methods, and tool registration patterns.

Chapter 15: Next Steps & Advanced Topics

15.1 Microservices Architectures & Service Mesh

Section 15.1 Overview & Objectives

By the end of this section you will:

1. Understand the benefits and challenges of deploying MCP servers as microservices.
2. Learn core service-mesh concepts—sidecars, control plane, data plane.
3. Configure Istio (or Linkerd) to secure, route, and observe MCP service traffic.
4. Apply traffic-management policies: retries, circuit breaking, and mutual TLS.
5. Monitor mesh metrics and traces to ensure reliability and performance.

Motivation & Context

In a large organization, your MCP server won't live in isolation. You might run a dozen services—authentication, data tools, analytics—each in its own container. A **service mesh** adds a lightweight proxy to every pod. It handles networking, security, and observability so your MCP code can stay focused on business logic. Imagine routing calls to `mcp-server` through Istio, automatically retrying on failure, and collecting per-service metrics without touching your Python code.

Fundamentals

Concept	Description
Microservice	Small, single-purpose service (e.g., `mcp-server`) deployed independently in containers.

Concept	Description
Sidecar Proxy	Envoy-based proxy injected alongside your service to manage inbound/outbound traffic.
Control Plane	Central component (Istiod) that distributes mesh configuration (routing, certificates) to sidecars.
Data Plane	Network proxies (sidecars) that enforce policies and collect telemetry for each service instance.
VirtualService	Mesh resource defining HTTP/TCP routing rules to your microservices.
DestinationRule	Mesh resource for configuring policies like load-balancing, TLS settings, and circuit breakers per service.

ASCII Flow: Mesh-Enabled Call

```arduino
[Client] ──▶ Envoy(east-west) ──▶ MCP Server
sidecar ──▶ MCP Server app
          apply policies            apply app logic
          collect metrics           return response
```

Step-by-Step Tutorial

1. **Label Your Namespace for Sidecar Injection**

```bash
kubectl label namespace default istio-injection=enabled
```

2. **Annotate Your Deployment**

```yaml
apiVersion: apps/v1
kind: Deployment
metadata:
  name: mcp-server
  labels: { app: mcp }
```

```yaml
    annotations:
      sidecar.istio.io/inject: "true"
spec:
  replicas: 3
  template:
    metadata:
      labels: { app: mcp }
    spec:
      containers:
      - name: mcp-server
        image: myrepo/mcp-server:1.0
        ports: [{ containerPort: 4000 }]
```

3. **Apply a VirtualService** to Route Traffic

yaml

```yaml
apiVersion: networking.istio.io/v1beta1
kind: VirtualService
metadata:
  name: mcp-vs
spec:
  hosts: ["mcp.local"]
  http:
  - route:
    - destination:
        host: mcp-
server.default.svc.cluster.local
        port: { number: 4000 }
    retries:
      attempts: 3
      perTryTimeout: 2s
      retryOn: gateway-error,connect-failure
```

4. **Define a DestinationRule** with Circuit Breaking

yaml

```yaml
apiVersion: networking.istio.io/v1beta1
kind: DestinationRule
metadata:
  name: mcp-dr
```

```
spec:
  host: mcp-server.default.svc.cluster.local
  trafficPolicy:
    connectionPool:
      http:
        http1MaxPendingRequests: 100
        maxRequestsPerConnection: 50
    outlierDetection:
      consecutiveErrors: 5
      interval: 10s
      baseEjectionTime: 30s
```

5. **Enable Mutual TLS** (optional)

yaml

```
apiVersion: security.istio.io/v1beta1
kind: PeerAuthentication
metadata:
  name: default
spec:
  mtls:
    mode: STRICT
```

6. **Verify Traffic and Telemetry**
   o Access on-mesh dashboard:

   bash

   ```
   istioctl dashboard kiali
   ```

   o Observe retries, latencies, and failures per pod.

Watch out: if you enforce STRICT mTLS, all clients (including test scripts) must present valid certificates.

Deep Dive & Best Practices

Concern	Recommendation
Granular Policies	Apply retries and timeouts per-route in VirtualService to avoid global settings that mask issues.
Circuit Breakers	Tune outlier-detection to prevent cascading failures under brief spikes.
mTLS & AuthZ	Use strict mTLS in production; define `AuthorizationPolicy` resources for per-service ACLs.
Observability	Collect Envoy metrics (via Prometheus) and distributed traces (via Jaeger) to pinpoint bottlenecks.
Resource Overhead	Sidecars consume CPU/memory—size your replicas accordingly and monitor proxy resource usage.

Hands-On Exercise

1. **Deploy** the annotated MCP server and VirtualService/DestinationRule.
2. **Simulate a Failure** by scaling one pod to zero:

   ```bash

   kubectl scale deployment mcp-server --
   replicas=0
   ```

   Then restore and observe retries in Kiali or Prometheus metrics.

3. **Enable mTLS** and configure a test client with certificates to call the service successfully.
4. **Explore Traffic Shifting**: update `VirtualService` to split 10% of traffic to a `canary` subset, and roll back if errors spike.

Section 15.1 Summary & Cheat Sheet

- **Namespace Label:** `istio-injection=enabled`
- **Deployment Annotation:** `sidecar.istio.io/inject: "true"`
- **VirtualService:** define `hosts`, `route`, `retries`

- **DestinationRule:** configure `connectionPool`, `outlierDetection`
- **mTLS:** use `PeerAuthentication` (STRICT mode) and `AuthorizationPolicy`

Resource	Key Snippet
VirtualService retries	`retries: { attempts:3, perTryTimeout:2s, retryOn:... }`
Circuit Breaker	`outlierDetection: { consecutiveErrors:5, baseEjectionTime:30s }`
mTLS STRICT	`PeerAuthentication.spec.mtls.mode: STRICT`
Traffic Shift	`weight: 10` in additional `route` entries

Further Reading / Next Steps

- Istio documentation: https://istio.io/latest/docs/
- Linkerd quick start: https://linkerd.io/2/getting-started/
- "The Service Mesh Book" by Christian Posta
- Envoy proxy concepts: https://www.envoyproxy.io/docs/
- In **Section 15.2**, we'll explore **Serverless MCP Servers** for event-driven, autoscaling deployments.

15.2 Message Queues (RabbitMQ, Kafka) Integration

Section 15.2 Overview & Objectives

By the end of this section you will:

1. Define MCP tools for **publishing** and **subscribing** to message queues (RabbitMQ, Kafka).
2. Configure Python clients (`pika` for RabbitMQ, `kafka-python` for Kafka) to connect, send, and receive messages.
3. Integrate queue-based handlers into your MCP server for asynchronous event processing.
4. Implement acknowledgment, error handling, and retry logic to ensure reliable delivery.

Motivation & Context

Synchronous RPC calls suit many workflows, but for long-running tasks, fan-out notifications, or decoupled services, **message queues** provide resilience and scalability. By integrating RabbitMQ or Kafka as backends for MCP events, you can:

- Offload heavy work (e.g., report generation) to background workers.
- Broadcast notifications (e.g., "new user registered") to multiple subscribers.
- Guarantee at-least-once or exactly-once delivery semantics depending on your needs.

ASCII Flow: Publish & Subscribe

css

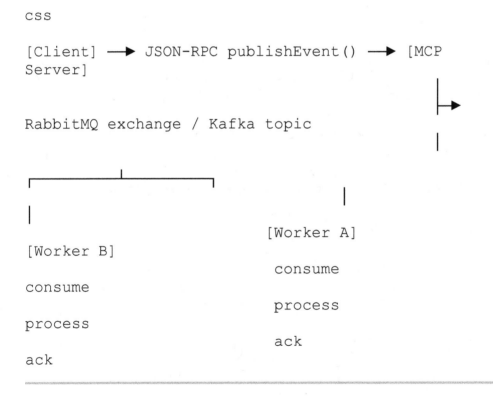

```
[Client] ──▶ JSON-RPC publishEvent() ──▶ [MCP
Server]
                                              │
                                              └▶

                                              │
RabbitMQ exchange / Kafka topic


  ┌──────────────┴──────────────┐
                                              │
  │
                                    [Worker A]
[Worker B]
                                      consume
consume
                                      process
process
                                      ack
ack
```

Fundamentals

Concept	RabbitMQ (`pika`)	Kafka (`kafka-python`)
Producer	`channel.basic_publish( exchange, routing_key, body)`	`producer.send(topic, value)`
Consumer	`channel.basic_consume( queue, callback, auto_ack=False)`	`consumer = KafkaConsumer(topic, group_id=…)`
Exchange / Topic	Exchange types: `direct`, `fanout`, `topic`, `headers`	Topics with partitions and consumer groups
Acknowledg ment	`channel.basic_ack(deli very_tag)`	Automatic vs. manual `consumer.commit()`
Durability	Durable queues/exchanges, persistent messages	`enable_auto_commit =False`, `acks='all'` on producer
Error Handling	NACK / requeue on exception	Seek to retry, dead-letter topic patterns

Step-by-Step Tutorial

A. Define Manifest Methods

jsonc

```
{
  "methods": {
    "publishEvent": {
      "description": "Publish a message to a named
queue or topic",
      "params": [
        {
"name":"backend","type":"string","enum":["rabbitmq"
,"kafka"] },
        { "name":"destination","type":"string" },
        { "name":"message","type":"object" }
      ],
      "result": {
"type":"string","description":"Message ID or
offset" }
    },
```

```
    "subscribeEvents": {
      "description": "Register a subscription
handler for incoming messages",
      "params": [
        {
"name":"backend","type":"string","enum":["rabbitmq"
,"kafka"] },
        { "name":"destination","type":"string" }
      ],
      "result": {
"type":"string","description":"Subscription
started" }
    }
  }
}
```

B. Implement RabbitMQ Integration

python

```python
# mcp_server/handlers/mq.py
import json, threading
import pika
from mcp_framework import RPCError

RABBIT_URL = "amqp://guest:guest@localhost:5672/"

def publish_event(params):
    backend, dest, message = params
    if backend != "rabbitmq":
        raise RPCError(code=-32090,
message="Unsupported backend")
    conn =
pika.BlockingConnection(pika.URLParameters(RABBIT_U
RL))
    channel = conn.channel()
    channel.exchange_declare(exchange=dest,
exchange_type='fanout', durable=True)
    body = json.dumps(message)
    channel.basic_publish(
        exchange=dest,
        routing_key='',
```

```python
        body=body,

properties=pika.BasicProperties(delivery_mode=2)    #
persistent
    )
    conn.close()
    return "published"

def subscribe_events(params):
    backend, dest = params
    if backend != "rabbitmq":
        raise RPCError(code=-32091,
message="Unsupported backend")
    def _worker():
        conn =
pika.BlockingConnection(pika.URLParameters(RABBIT_U
RL))
        channel = conn.channel()
        channel.exchange_declare(exchange=dest,
exchange_type='fanout', durable=True)
        result = channel.queue_declare('',
exclusive=True)
        queue_name = result.method.queue
        channel.queue_bind(exchange=dest,
queue=queue_name)
        def callback(ch, method, props, body):
            try:
                msg = json.loads(body)
                # Here call your handler, e.g.,
server.dispatch("handleEvent", [msg])
                # ...

ch.basic_ack(delivery_tag=method.delivery_tag)
            except Exception:

ch.basic_nack(delivery_tag=method.delivery_tag,
requeue=True)
        channel.basic_consume(queue=queue_name,
on_message_callback=callback, auto_ack=False)
        channel.start_consuming()
    thread = threading.Thread(target=_worker,
daemon=True)
```

```
    thread.start()
    return f"subscribed to {dest}"
```

C. Implement Kafka Integration

```python

from kafka import KafkaProducer, KafkaConsumer
from mcp_framework import RPCError

KAFKA_SERVERS = ["localhost:9092"]

producer = KafkaProducer(
    bootstrap_servers=KAFKA_SERVERS,
    value_serializer=lambda v:
json.dumps(v).encode('utf-8'),
    acks='all'
)

def publish_event_kafka(params):
    backend, topic, message = params
    if backend != "kafka":
        raise RPCError(code=-32092,
message="Unsupported backend")
    fut = producer.send(topic, message)
    record_metadata = fut.get(timeout=10)
    return
f"{record_metadata.topic}:{record_metadata.partitio
n}:{record_metadata.offset}"

def subscribe_events_kafka(params):
    backend, topic = params
    if backend != "kafka":
        raise RPCError(code=-32093,
message="Unsupported backend")
    def _worker():
        consumer = KafkaConsumer(
            topic,
            bootstrap_servers=KAFKA_SERVERS,
            group_id="mcp-group",
            auto_offset_reset='earliest',
            enable_auto_commit=False,
```

```python
            value_deserializer=lambda m:
json.loads(m.decode('utf-8'))
        )
        for msg in consumer:
            try:
                # server.dispatch("handleEvent",
[msg.value])
                consumer.commit()
            except Exception:
                # on failure, optionally seek back
or log
                pass
    thread = threading.Thread(target=_worker,
daemon=True)
    thread.start()
    return f"subscribed to {topic}"
```

D. Register in Server Bootstrap

python

```python
from mcp_server.handlers.mq import publish_event,
subscribe_events
from mcp_server.handlers.mq import
publish_event_kafka, subscribe_events_kafka

server.register_tool("publishEvent", publish_event,
description="Publish to RabbitMQ", version="1.0.0")
server.register_tool("subscribeEvents",
subscribe_events, description="Subscribe RabbitMQ",
version="1.0.0")
server.register_tool("publishEvent",
publish_event_kafka, description="Publish to
Kafka", version="1.0.0")
server.register_tool("subscribeEvents",
subscribe_events_kafka, description="Subscribe
Kafka", version="1.0.0")
```

Deep Dive & Best Practices

Concern	Recommendation
Connection Management	Reuse long-lived connections; avoid opening/closing per message to reduce latency.
Message Durability	Use persistent messages and durable queues/exchanges or `acks='all'` to prevent data loss.
Error Handling & Retries	On processing failure, NACK with requeue or send to a dead-letter queue for later inspection.
Scaling Consumers	For RabbitMQ, use multiple consumers per queue; for Kafka, use consumer groups across partitions.
Ordering Guarantees	RabbitMQ per-queue ordering; Kafka per-partition ordering—design partitions for ordering needs.

Hands-On Exercise

1. **Publish** a test message via `publishEvent("rabbitmq", "events", {"hello":"world"})` and verify a background subscriber prints it.
2. **Simulate a Failure** in the callback (raise an exception) and confirm the message is requeued/directed to the dead-letter queue.
3. **Scale Out** by running two subscriber threads for a Kafka topic with 2 partitions; observe balanced consumption across partitions.

Section 15.2 Summary & Cheat Sheet

- **RabbitMQ**
  - **Publish:** `basic_publish(exchange, '', body, persistent)`
  - **Subscribe:** `basic_consume(queue, callback, auto_ack=False)` + `basic_ack/nack`
- **Kafka**
  - **Producer:** `producer.send(topic, message, acks='all')`
  - **Consumer:** `KafkaConsumer(..., enable_auto_commit=False)` + `commit()`

Tool	Key Snippet
RabbitMQ Pub	`channel.basic_publish(exchange, '', json.dumps(msg))`
RabbitMQ Sub	`channel.basic_consume(...); channel.start_consuming()`
Kafka Prod	`producer.send(topic, msg).get()`
Kafka Cons	`for m in consumer: process; consumer.commit()`

Further Reading / Next Steps

- RabbitMQ tutorials: https://www.rabbitmq.com/getstarted.html
- Kafka Python docs: https://kafka-python.readthedocs.io/
- Best practices: "Designing Data-Intensive Applications" by Martin Kleppmann
- In **Section 15.3**, we'll explore **Serverless Architectures** for MCP using AWS Lambda and Azure Functions.

15.3 WebSockets & Real Time Context Streaming

Section 15.3 Overview & Objectives

By the end of this section you will:

1. Establish a **WebSocket** endpoint alongside your MCP server to handle bidirectional, low-latency streams.
2. Implement a **context-streaming tool** that pushes real-time updates (notifications) to connected clients.
3. Handle WebSocket specifics—handshake, subprotocol negotiation, ping/pong, and clean shutdown.
4. Integrate the streaming layer with your MCP framework so that RPC calls and streams share the same context and authentication.

Motivation & Context

Traditional JSON-RPC over HTTP is request/response only. For use-cases like live chat, real-time data feeds, or collaborative editing, you need

persistent connections that can deliver server-side events immediately. WebSockets provide a full-duplex channel in a single TCP connection, allowing your MCP server to both receive client RPCs and **push** notifications as context changes.

Fundamentals

Concept	Description
Handshake	Initial HTTP→WebSocket upgrade request/response, including optional `Sec-WebSocket-Protocol`.
Subprotocol	Client/server agree on "mcp-stream" protocol so messages carry JSON-RPC frames or events.
Ping/Pong	Heartbeat frames to detect dead peers and keep NAT mappings alive.
Backpressure	Applying flow control so slow clients don't overwhelm server buffers—use `await` on sends.
Clean Close	Graceful connection teardown with close codes and proper resource cleanup.

ASCII Flow: Bidirectional WebSocket Stream

pgsql

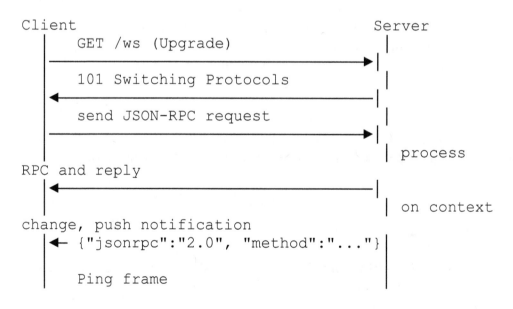

```
Client                                          Server
      |     GET /ws (Upgrade)                    |
      |----------------------------------------->|
      |     101 Switching Protocols              |
      |<-----------------------------------------|
      |     send JSON-RPC request                |
      |----------------------------------------->|
      |                                          | process
RPC and reply
      |<-----------------------------------------|
      |                                          | on context
change, push notification
      |<- {"jsonrpc":"2.0", "method":"..."}      |
      |     Ping frame                           |
```

Pong frame

Step-by-Step Tutorial

python

```python
# mcp_server/streaming.py
import asyncio
import json
import websockets
from mcp_framework import RPCError

CONNECTED = set()  # track active WebSocket
connections

async def ws_handler(websocket, path):
    # 1. Subprotocol check
    if websocket.subprotocol != "mcp-stream":
        await websocket.close(code=1002,
reason="Unsupported subprotocol")
        return

    # 2. Register connection
    CONNECTED.add(websocket)
    try:
        async for message in websocket:
            # 3. Handle inbound JSON-RPC frames
            try:
                frame = json.loads(message)
                response = await dispatch(frame)  #
your MCP dispatch
                await
websocket.send(json.dumps(response))
            except RPCError as e:
                await
websocket.send(json.dumps(e.to_message()))
            except Exception:
                err = RPCError(code=-32603,
message="Internal error")
```

```python
            await
websocket.send(json.dumps(err.to_message()))
    finally:
        # 4. Cleanup
        CONNECTED.remove(websocket)
```
python

```python
# server.py (excerpt)
import asyncio, websockets
from mcp_server.streaming import ws_handler

async def start_servers():
    # Start JSON-RPC HTTP server...
    # Start WebSocket server for streams
    ws_srv = await websockets.serve(
        ws_handler, "0.0.0.0", 8765,
        subprotocols=["mcp-stream"],
ping_interval=30, ping_timeout=10
    )
    await
asyncio.gather(http_server.serve_forever(),
ws_srv.wait_closed())

if __name__ == "__main__":
    asyncio.run(start_servers())
```
python

```python
# Pushing notifications from your MCP tools
from mcp_server.streaming import CONNECTED
import json

def notify_context_update(update: dict):
    payload = {
        "jsonrpc": "2.0",
        "method": "contextUpdate",
        "params": [update]
    }
    message = json.dumps(payload)
    # Broadcast asynchronously
    for ws in list(CONNECTED):
        asyncio.create_task(ws.send(message))
```

Watch out: Use `await ws.send(...)` or `asyncio.create_task` to avoid blocking; catch and remove closed connections.

Deep Dive & Best Practices

Concern	Recommendation
Authentication	Perform token validation during the HTTP upgrade (e.g., check `Authorization` header).
Flow Control	Respect `websocket.pong_waiter()` and handle slow clients by bounding `CONNECTED` size or buffering.
Error Handling	On `ConnectionClosed`, ensure tasks aren't left dangling; wrap sends in `try/except`.
Scalability	For multi-instance servers, use a pub/sub backend (Redis, Kafka) to fan-out notifications.
Protocol Versioning	Include a version field in your streaming protocol (`"mcp-stream-v1"`) to allow future upgrades.

Hands-On Exercise

1. **Secure** your WebSocket endpoint by checking a JWT passed in `Sec-WebSocket-Protocol` or a query param during upgrade.
2. **Implement** a tool `streamMetrics` that, when called, starts sending periodic metric snapshots via `contextUpdate`.
3. **Test** with a simple HTML/JavaScript client:

```js
const ws = new
WebSocket("ws://localhost:8765/ws", "mcp-
stream");
ws.onmessage = e => console.log("Update:",
JSON.parse(e.data));
ws.send(JSON.stringify({ jsonrpc:"2.0",
method:"streamMetrics", id:1 }));
```

Section 15.3 Summary & Cheat Sheet

- **WebSocket Server:** use `websockets.serve(ws_handler, …, subprotocols=["mcp-stream"])`.
- **Handshake:** verify `websocket.subprotocol` and implement auth.
- **Inbound Frames:** parse JSON, dispatch RPC, and reply.
- **Outbound Notifications:** broadcast JSON-RPC notifications over active connections.
- **Heartbeat:** configure `ping_interval`/`ping_timeout` to detect dead peers.

Task	Code Snippet
Serve WebSockets	`await websockets.serve(ws_handler, host, port, subprotocols…)`
Handle messages	`async for message in websocket: …`
Broadcast notification	`asyncio.create_task(ws.send(json.dumps(payload)))`
Configure ping/pong	`ping_interval=30, ping_timeout=10`

Further Reading / Next Steps

- WebSockets RFC 6455: https://tools.ietf.org/html/rfc6455
- `websockets` Python library docs: https://websockets.readthedocs.io/
- Building real-time apps with WebSocket and asyncio: https://realpython.com/python-web-sockets/
- In **Section 15.4**, we'll cover **Serverless MCP** deployments on AWS Lambda and Azure Functions.

15.4 Hybrid Cloud & Edge Deployments

Section 15.4 Overview & Objectives

By the end of this section you will:

1. Architect an MCP deployment that spans both public cloud and edge locations.
2. Package and provision your MCP server for small-footprint edge devices (e.g., k3s, IoT gateways).
3. Implement **cloud-edge synchronization** of manifests, code updates, and context data.
4. Design fallback and offline modes so edge nodes continue to serve requests when disconnected.

Motivation & Context

Edge computing brings your context-aware AI tooling closer to where data is generated—industrial sensors, retail kiosks, or remote offices—reducing latency and bandwidth costs. A hybrid cloud + edge architecture lets you:

- Run latency-sensitive handlers locally on edge devices.
- Offload heavy computation or shared state to the cloud.
- Gracefully handle intermittent connectivity with local caching and queueing.

Fundamentals

Concept	Description
Edge Node	A lightweight host (e.g., Raspberry Pi, industrial gateway) running a minimal Kubernetes or container runtime.
Cloud Control Plane	Central service that manages edge deployments, configuration, and versioning of MCP components.
Data Synchronization	Mechanism for propagating manifests, code updates, and state between cloud and edge (e.g., GitOps, MQTT).
Offline Mode	Edge-only operation using local cache and queue; buffers requests until cloud is reachable.
Cloud Bursting	Fallback to cloud servers for heavy workloads or shared tools when edge capacity is exceeded.

Concept	Description
Device Provisioning	Secure onboarding of edge nodes via certificates, tokens, or a bootstrap service.

Step-by-Step Tutorial

1. **Prepare an Edge-Optimized Container**

   ```dockerfile
   FROM python:3.10-slim AS builder
   WORKDIR /app
   COPY requirements.txt .
   RUN pip install --no-cache-dir -r
   requirements.txt
   COPY . /app

   FROM python:3.10-slim
   WORKDIR /app
   COPY --from=builder
   /usr/local/lib/python3.10/site-packages
   /usr/local/lib/python3.10/site-packages
   COPY . /app
   # Drop to non-root for edge security
   RUN useradd -m edgeuser && chown -R edgeuser
   /app
   USER edgeuser
   CMD ["python", "-m", "mcp_server.server", "--
   config", "/etc/mcp/config.yaml"]
   ```

2. **Deploy k3s on the Edge Device**

   ```bash
   # On your edge device (e.g., Raspberry Pi)
   curl -sfL https://get.k3s.io | sh -
   sudo kubectl create namespace mcp-edge
   # Push image to a local registry or use a
   pull-through cache
   ```

3. **GitOps-Style Manifest Delivery**

- o Store your `mcp-deployment.yaml` in a Git repo.
- o Install <u>Flux</u> or Argo CD on k3s to sync that repo to the `mcp-edge` namespace.
- o Updates to your manifest (new image tag, config changes) get applied automatically on edge.

4. **Implement Offline Caching & Queueing**

```python
# In your request handler wrapper
try:
    result = dispatch_to_cloud(method, params)
except NetworkError:
    # Fallback: handle locally or enqueue for later
    local_result = dispatch_locally(method, params)
    enqueue_for_sync({"method":method, "params":params})
    return local_result
```

5. **Cloud Bursting Configuration**
   - o In `config.yaml`, list heavy tools to offload:

```yaml
offload:
  - tool: generatePDF
  - tool: executeLongTask
cloud_endpoint: https://mcp-cloud.example.com
```

   - o Edge server checks this list and proxies those calls to the cloud.

Deep Dive & Best Practices

Concern	Recommendation
Security	Use mutual TLS or IoT certificates to authenticate edge nodes; rotate credentials periodically.
Resource Constraints	Limit memory/CPU usage on edge; prefer async handlers and minimal dependencies.
Data Consistency	Employ idempotent operations and include timestamps to reconcile state after reconnection.
Monitoring & Alerts	Relay edge node health and metrics back to your cloud monitoring (Prometheus federation).
Version Skew	Tag your edge image versions clearly; use semantic versioning and allow side-by-side upgrades.

Hands-On Exercise

1. **Provision** a k3s cluster on two Raspberry Pi devices and deploy your MCP server via Flux.
2. **Simulate Disconnection:** unplug the network on one Pi, send several RPC requests, then reconnect and verify queued calls sync to the cloud.
3. **Configure Cloud Bursting:** mark `generatePDF` for offload, invoke it on the edge device, and confirm the job runs on your cloud instance instead.

Section 15.4 Summary & Cheat Sheet

- **Edge Packaging:** multi-stage Docker for minimal final image.
- **Deployment:** k3s + GitOps (Flux/Argo CD) for zero-touch updates.
- **Offline Fallback:** local dispatch + enqueue on network failure.
- **Cloud Bursting:** proxy selected tools to cloud endpoints.
- **Security:** mTLS/IoT cert-based node authentication.

Feature	Key Config / Code Snippet
Edge container	multi-stage Docker + non-root user
k3s install	`` `curl https://get.k3s.io ``
GitOps sync	Flux or Argo CD pointing to Git repo
Offline queue	`enqueue_for_sync(...)` in request wrapper

Feature	Key Config / Code Snippet
Offload list	`offload:` section in `config.yaml`

Further Reading / Next Steps

- k3s lightweight Kubernetes: https://k3s.io/
- Flux GitOps guide: https://fluxcd.io/docs/
- AWS IoT Greengrass for edge: https://aws.amazon.com/greengrass/
- Azure IoT Edge: https://azure.microsoft.com/services/iot-edge/
- In **Section 15.5**, we'll explore **Serverless MCP** deployments on AWS Lambda and Azure Functions.

15.5 Preparing for Production Compliance & Audits

Section 15.5 Overview & Objectives

By the end of this section you will:

1. Identify the key **compliance frameworks** (e.g., SOC 2, GDPR, HIPAA) that apply to your MCP deployment.
2. Implement **audit logging** with immutability and tamper-evidence for all tool invocations.
3. Enforce **data retention** and **access controls** to meet regulatory requirements.
4. Automate **evidence collection** and reporting for security reviews and audits.

Motivation & Context

Organizations in finance, healthcare, and government must prove they handle data securely and consistently. Imagine a SOC 2 audit where an external assessor demands to see every API call, who made it, and what they accessed—complete with unalterable logs and documented retention policies. By baking compliance and audit readiness into your MCP server, you'll reduce risk, speed up reviews, and maintain customer trust.

Fundamentals

Concept	Description
Compliance Framework	A set of standards and controls (SOC 2, GDPR, HIPAA) you must adhere to for your industry.
Audit Log	Append-only record of every action, timestamped and tagged with context (`request_id`, `user_id`).
WORM Storage	"Write Once, Read Many" storage (e.g., S3 Object Lock) that prevents log deletion or tampering.
Data Retention	Policy defining how long logs and data must be kept before secure deletion.
Role-Based Access	Grant permissions based on user roles; deny all others to minimize unauthorized access.

ASCII Flow: Audit-Ready Request

pgsql

```
Client Request ──▶ MCP Server ──▶ append audit log
record ──▶ dispatch handler ──▶ append result log
         |
|        
         |_____ stored in immutable WORM
storage ◀──────────┘
```

Step-by-Step Tutorial

1. **Enable Structured Audit Logging**

   python

   ```python
   # audit_logging.py
   import logging, json
   from datetime import datetime

   class AuditFormatter(logging.Formatter):
       def format(self, record):
           return json.dumps({
   ```

394

```python
            "timestamp":
datetime.utcnow().isoformat() + "Z",
            "level": record.levelname,
            **record.extra
        })

def
setup_audit_logger(path="/var/log/mcp_audit.lo
g"):
    handler = logging.FileHandler(path)
    handler.setFormatter(AuditFormatter())
    logger = logging.getLogger("mcp_audit")
    logger.setLevel(logging.INFO)
    logger.handlers.clear()
    logger.addHandler(handler)
    return logger

# In server startup
audit_logger = setup_audit_logger()
```

Watch out: ensure `/var/log` is on WORM storage or mounted with immutable flags.

2. **Log Every RPC Call**

python

```python
# in your request dispatch wrapper
def audited_dispatch(method, params, context):
    record = {
        "request_id": context.request_id,
        "user_id": context.user_id,
        "method": method,
        "params": params
    }
    audit_logger.info("rpc_call",
extra={"extra": record})
    result = dispatch_to_handler(method,
params)
    record["result"] = "success"
    audit_logger.info("rpc_result",
extra={"extra": record})
```

```
    return result
```

Pitfall: don't log sensitive fields in `params`; mask or omit them per policy.

3. **Configure WORM in AWS S3**

   ```yaml
   # terraform snippet for S3 Object Lock
   resource "aws_s3_bucket" "audit_logs" {
     bucket = "mcp-audit-logs"
     object_lock_configuration {
       object_lock_enabled = "Enabled"
       rule {
         default_retention {
           mode = "GOVERNANCE"
           days = 365
         }
       }
     }
     versioning { enabled = true }
   }
   ```

   o Upload rotated log files daily via CI/CD or cron.
4. **Implement Role-Based Access Control**

   ```python
   # auth.py
   from mcp_framework import RPCError

   ROLE_PERMISSIONS = {
     "admin": {"*"},
     "auditor": {"getAuditLogs"},
     "user": {"chat", "createEvent",
   "readContext"}
   }

   def enforce_permissions(method, context):
       allowed =
   ROLE_PERMISSIONS.get(context.role, set())
   ```

```
    if method not in allowed and "*" not in
allowed:
        raise RPCError(code=-32001,
message="Permission denied", data={"method":
method})
```

- o Call `enforce_permissions` before dispatching each RPC.
5. **Automate Evidence Export**

```bash
bash
```

```bash
# daily_cron.sh (run via cron or CI)
aws s3 cp /var/log/mcp_audit.log s3://mcp-
audit-logs/$(date +%Y-%m-%d)-audit.log
```

- o Generate a digest checksum and store it for integrity verification:

```bash
bash
```

```bash
sha256sum /var/log/mcp_audit.log >
/var/log/mcp_audit.log.sha256
```

Deep Dive & Best Practices

Concern	Recommendation
Log Tampering	Use WORM storage with object-lock and versioning; store checksums in a separate system.
Retention Enforcement	Automate deletion jobs based on policy; track deletions in a separate audit trail.
Access Reviews	Periodically review IAM roles and permissions; log all role changes.
Encryption at Rest	Ensure audit logs and backups are encrypted (e.g., S3 SSE-KMS).
Audit Trail Completeness	Include both request and response logs; capture failed calls and exceptions explicitly.

Hands-On Exercise

1. **Set up** an S3 bucket with **Object Lock** enabled for 180 days, and configure your server to rotate logs there nightly.
2. **Implement** a `getAuditLogs` tool that reads logs from S3 (read-only) and returns a filtered time window.
3. **Simulate** a permission violation by calling a method as a `user` role and verify the error and audit entry both occur.

Section 15.5 Summary & Cheat Sheet

- **Compliance Frameworks:** SOC 2, GDPR, HIPAA.
- **Audit Logging:** structured JSON, `mcp_audit` logger, request/response entries.
- **WORM Storage:** S3 Object Lock, versioning, daily rotation, checksum.
- **Access Control:** role-based checks via `enforce_permissions`.
- **Automation:** cron/CI scripts for upload, retention, and evidence generation.

Task	Code/Config Snippet
Audit Logger Setup	`setup_audit_logger("/var/log/mcp_audit.log")`
RPC Auditing Wrapper	`audit_logger.info(..., extra={"extra": record})`
S3 Object Lock	`object_lock_configuration { default_retention { mode="GOVERNANCE" days=365 }}`
Role Enforcement	`enforce_permissions(method, context)`
Evidence Upload	`aws s3 cp /var/log/... s3://bucket/$(date)-audit.log`

Further Reading / Next Steps

- AWS S3 Object Lock:
  https://docs.aws.amazon.com/AmazonS3/latest/dev/object-lock-overview.html
- NIST 800-53 Audit Logging:
  https://csrc.nist.gov/publications/detail/sp/800-53/rev-5/final
- SOC 2 Trust Services Criteria:
  https://www.aicpa.org/interestareas/frc/assuranceadvisoryservices/soc2.html
- GDPR Logging Guidance: https://gdpr.eu/audit-logs/

In **Appendix A**, you'll find **Cheat Sheets & Quick References** for JSON-RPC, manifest schema, security patterns, and more.

Appendix

Appendix A: JSON RPC 2.0 Quick Reference

A.1 Message Types

- **Request**: client→server, expects a response
- **Notification**: client→server, no response
- **Response**: server→client, includes `result` or `error`
- **Batch**: array of any mix of the above

A.2 Common Fields

Field	Type	Required?	Description
`jsonrpc`	string	Yes	Must be exactly `"2.0"`
`method`	string	Yes (req)	Name of the method to invoke (omit in responses)
`params`	array or object	No	Positional or named parameters for the `method`
`id`	string, number, or null	Yes for requests & responses	Unique identifier pairing requests with responses; omit in notifications
`result`	any	Yes in success response	The successful result value
`error`	object	Yes in error response	Error object with `code`, `message`, and optional `data`

A.3 Request Object

```jsonc
// Request
{
  "jsonrpc": "2.0",
  "method": "subtract",
  "params": [42, 23],
```

```
  "id": 1
}
```

- **jsonrpc**: "2.0"
- **method**: procedure name
- **params**: positional ([...]) or named ({"a":42,"b":23})
- **id**: must not be null for requests expecting a reply

A.4 Notification

jsonc

```
// Notification (no "id")
{
  "jsonrpc": "2.0",
  "method": "updateStatus",
  "params": {"status":"ready"}
}
```

- No id → server must not send a response

A.5 Response Object

- **Success**

  jsonc

  ```
  {
    "jsonrpc": "2.0",
    "result": 19,
    "id": 1
  }
  ```

- **Error**

  jsonc

  ```
  {
  ```

```
  "jsonrpc": "2.0",
  "error": {
    "code": -32601,
    "message": "Method not found",
    "data": null
  },
  "id": 1
}
```

A.6 Error Object Fields

Field	Type	Description
code	integer	Predefined or custom error code
message	string	Short, human-readable description
data	any	Additional information (optional)

Common Error Codes

Code	Name	Meaning
-32700	Parse error	Invalid JSON was received
-32600	Invalid Request	The JSON sent is not a valid Request object
-32601	Method not found	Method does not exist or is not available
-32602	Invalid params	Invalid method parameter(s)
-32603	Internal error	Internal JSON-RPC error
-32000 to -32099	Server error range	Implementation-defined server-side errors

A.7 Batch Requests & Responses

- A batch is an array of Request/Notification objects
- Server returns an array of corresponding Responses (omit responses for Notifications)

jsonc

```
[
  { "jsonrpc":"2.0", "method":"sum",
"params":[1,2,4], "id":"1" },
  { "jsonrpc":"2.0", "method":"notify",
"params":[7]              },
  { "jsonrpc":"2.0", "method":"subtract",
"params":[10,5],    "id":"2" }
]
```

Might yield:

jsonc

```
[
  { "jsonrpc":"2.0","result":7,     "id":"1" },
  { "jsonrpc":"2.0","result":5,     "id":"2" }
]
```

A.8 Quick Examples

Simple call
Request:

json

```
{"jsonrpc":"2.0","method":"echo","params":["hi"],"id":42}
```

Response:

json

```
{"jsonrpc":"2.0","result":"hi","id":42}
```

Notification

json

```
{"jsonrpc":"2.0","method":"logEvent","params":{"event":"start"}}
```

Error

json

```
{"jsonrpc":"2.0","error":{"code":-
32601,"message":"Method not found"},"id":99}
```

Batch

json

```
[
  {"jsonrpc":"2.0","method":"ping","id":1},
  {"jsonrpc":"2.0","method":"ping"},

{"jsonrpc":"2.0","method":"add","params":[5,7],"id"
:2}
]
```

A.9 Best Practices

- Always validate incoming frames against schema.
- Use named `params` for clarity in complex methods.
- Maintain strictly increasing or unique `id` values.
- Return exactly one Response per Request in batch.
- Never leak internal errors—map them to defined error codes and messages.

B. MCP Manifest Schema Cheat Sheet

Appendix B: MCP Manifest Schema Cheat Sheet

B.1 Top-Level Manifest Structure

jsonc

```
{
  "protocol_version": "1.0.0",   // MCP protocol
version
  "version": "MAJOR.MINOR.PATCH",// manifest
semantic version
```

```jsonc
  "name": "my-mcp-server",      // optional, human-readable identifier
  "description": "…",           // optional, brief summary
  "methods": { … },             // RPC-capable tools
  "notifications": { … },       // server-initiated events
  "subscriptions": { … }        // pub/sub definitions
}
```

Field	Type	Required?	Description
protocol_version	string	Yes	MCP protocol compatibility tag
version	string	Yes	Manifest's own SemVer version
name	string	No	Identifier for server or package
description	string	No	Short human description
methods	object	Yes	Map of method-name → method definition
notifications	object	No	Server-sent notification definitions
subscriptions	object	No	Declarative pub/sub topics

B.2 Method Definition

jsonc

```
"methods": {
  "toolName": {
    "version": "1.2.0",
    "description": "What the tool does",
    "deprecated": false,            // optional
    "params": [                     // positional
or named parameters
      { "name": "foo", "type": "string",
"required": true },
      { "name": "bar", "type": "integer",
"required": false }
    ],
```

```
    "result": {                              // JSON-Schema
for the return value
      "type": "object",
      "properties": {
        "baz": { "type": "number" }
      },
      "required": ["baz"]
    }
  }
}
```

Field	Type	Required?	Description
version	string	Yes	Method SemVer
description	string	Yes	Human-readable summary
deprecated	boolean	No	Mark method as phased out
params	array	Yes (can be empty)	List of parameter schemas
result	object (JSON Schema)	Yes	Schema for successful response payload

B.3 Parameter Schema

Field	Type	Required?	Description
name	string	Yes	Parameter identifier
type	string	Yes	JSON type (string,number,boolean,array,object)
required	boolean	No	Defaults to true if omitted
enum	array	No	Restrict allowed values
format	string	No	Additional semantic hint (date-time,base64,...)

B.4 Result Schema

- Any valid JSON Schema object
- Common shortcuts:
  - Primitive: { "type":"string" }
  - Array:

    ```jsonc
    { "type":"array", "items": {
    "type":"object" } }
    ```

  - Enum:

    ```jsonc
    { "type":"string",
    "enum":["on","off","auto"] }
    ```

B.5 Notifications & Subscriptions

- **Notifications** (server→client events):

```jsonc
"notifications": {
  "eventName": {
    "description": "When something happens",
    "params": [ {
"name":"data","type":"object" } ]
  }
}
```

- **Subscriptions** (pub/sub semantics):

```jsonc
"subscriptions": {
  "topicName": {
    "description": "Stream of updates",
```

```
        "params": [ {
    "name":"filter","type":"string" } ],
        "result": { "type":"object" }
      }
    }
```

B.6 Best Practices & Tips

- **SemVer discipline**: bump MAJOR for breaking schema changes, MINOR for new optional fields, PATCH for fixes.
- **Explicit `required`**: list required params in both `params` array and JSON Schema `required` lists.
- **Use named params** for clarity when more than 2–3 parameters.
- **Leverage $ref**: extract common schemas into separate files and reference them to avoid duplication.
- **Document examples**: include a minimal example manifest in your `/examples` folder.
- **Validate on startup**: load and validate the manifest against your JSON Schema before serving.

B.7 Minimal Example Manifest

jsonc

```
{
  "protocol_version": "1.0.0",
  "version": "0.1.0",
  "name": "example-server",
  "methods": {
    "echo": {
      "version": "1.0.0",
      "description": "Return the input text",
      "params": [ { "name":"text","type":"string" }
],
      "result": { "type":"string" }
    }
  }
}
```

Keep this cheat sheet handy for quick authoring and review of MCP tool manifests!

Appendix D: Sample Dockerfiles & GitHub Actions Workflows

D.1 Multi-Stage Dockerfile for Production

```dockerfile
dockerfile

# Stage 1: build dependencies
FROM python:3.10-slim AS builder
WORKDIR /app

# Install build-time dependencies
RUN apt-get update && apt-get install -y --no-
install-recommends \
    build-essential \
  && rm -rf /var/lib/apt/lists/*

# Install Python dependencies into a portable layer
COPY requirements.txt .
RUN pip install --no-cache-dir -r requirements.txt

# Stage 2: final image
FROM python:3.10-slim
WORKDIR /app

# Copy installed packages from builder
COPY --from=builder /usr/local/lib/python3.10/site-
packages /usr/local/lib/python3.10/site-packages

# Copy application code
COPY . .

# Create non-root user
RUN useradd -m appuser && chown -R appuser /app
USER appuser

EXPOSE 4000
CMD ["python", "-m", "mcp_server.server"]
```

Notes:

- Keeps final image minimal.
- Installs build-only tools in builder stage.
- Uses non-root user for security.

D.2 Development Dockerfile with Live-Reload

dockerfile

```
FROM python:3.10-slim
WORKDIR /app

# Install dependencies
COPY requirements.txt .
RUN pip install --no-cache-dir -r requirements.txt
watchdog

#
COPY . .

# Install optional dev tool for live reload
RUN pip install --no-cache-dir ptvsd

# Default command mounts current directory and
restarts on changes
CMD ["watchmedo", "auto-restart", "--directory=.",
"--pattern=*.py", "--", "python", "-m",
"mcp_server.server"]
```

Notes:

- Uses `watchdog`'s `watchmedo` to restart on file changes.
- Ideal for local iterative development.

D.3 Sample `docker-compose.yml`

yaml

```
version: "3.8"
services:
  mcp-server:
    build:
      context: .
      dockerfile: Dockerfile
    image: mcp-server:latest
    ports:
      - "4000:4000"
    env_file:
      - .env
    volumes:
      - ./logs:/var/log/mcp
    depends_on:
      - redis
  redis:
    image: redis:6-alpine
    ports:
      - "6379:6379"
```

Notes:

- Mounts logs for local inspection.
- Includes a Redis dependency for caching or pub/sub.

D.4 GitHub Actions Workflow: CI/CD (`.github/workflows/ci-cd.yml`)

yaml

```
name: CI/CD Pipeline

on:
  pull_request:
    branches: [ main ]
  push:
    branches: [ main ]

jobs:
```

```yaml
test:
  runs-on: ubuntu-latest
  strategy:
    matrix:
      python-version: [3.9, 3.10, 3.11]
  steps:
    - uses: actions/checkout@v3

    - name: Set up Python ${{ matrix.python-version }}
      uses: actions/setup-python@v4
      with:
        python-version: ${{ matrix.python-version }}

    - name: Install dependencies
      run: |
        python -m pip install --upgrade pip
        pip install -r requirements.txt
        pip install pytest pytest-cov

    - name: Lint with flake8
      run: |
        pip install flake8
        flake8 mcp_server tests

    - name: Run pytest
      run: pytest --cov=mcp_server --cov-report=xml

    - name: Upload coverage report
      uses: actions/upload-artifact@v3
      with:
        name: coverage-report
        path: coverage.xml

  build-and-push:
    needs: test
    if: github.event_name == 'push' && github.ref == 'refs/heads/main'
    runs-on: ubuntu-latest
    steps:
```

```yaml
    - uses: actions/checkout@v3

    - name: Log in to Docker Hub
      uses: docker/login-action@v2
      with:
        username: ${{ secrets.DOCKERHUB_USER }}
        password: ${{ secrets.DOCKERHUB_TOKEN }}

    - name: Build and push Docker image
      uses: docker/build-push-action@v3
      with:
        context: .
        push: true
        tags: |
          ${{ secrets.DOCKERHUB_USER }}/mcp-server:latest
          ${{ secrets.DOCKERHUB_USER }}/mcp-server:${{ github.sha }}

  deploy:
    needs: build-and-push
    if: github.event_name == 'push' && github.ref == 'refs/heads/main'
    runs-on: ubuntu-latest
    steps:
      - name: Set up kubectl
        uses: azure/setup-kubectl@v3
        with:
          version: 'latest'

      - name: Configure kubeconfig
        run: echo "${{ secrets.KUBE_CONFIG }}" > $HOME/.kube/config

      - name: Update deployment image
        run: |
          kubectl set image deployment/mcp-server mcp-server=${{ secrets.DOCKERHUB_USER }}/mcp-server:${{ github.sha }} --record

      - name: Wait for rollout
```

```
        run: kubectl rollout status deployment/mcp-
server
```

Notes:

- `test` job on PRs ensures linting and tests pass.
- `build-and-push` builds Docker image and pushes to registry on merges to `main`.
- `deploy` updates Kubernetes Deployment with new image and waits for rollout.

Keep these templates as a starting point—customize paths, credentials, and tools to fit your project's needs.

Appendix E: Further Reading & Community Links

Official MCP Resources

- **MCP Specification Repository** (GitHub): https://github.com/mcp-protocol/spec
- **MCP Framework (Python)**: https://github.com/mcp-protocol/mcp-framework-py
- **MCP RFCs Directory**: https://github.com/mcp-protocol/spec/tree/main/rfcs

---

Community & Communication

- **MCP Slack Workspace**: https://mcp-protocol.slack.com/
- **Mailing List**: mcp-protocol@lists.example.org
- **Discord Server**: https://discord.gg/mcp-protocol
- **GitHub Discussions**: https://github.com/mcp-protocol/spec/discussions
- **Issue Tracker**: https://github.com/mcp-protocol/spec/issues

---

Learning & Tutorials

- **JSON-RPC 2.0 Spec**: https://www.jsonrpc.org/specification
- **Semantic Versioning (SemVer)**: https://semver.org/
- **"Building Microservices" by Sam Newman** (Resilience patterns)
- **Real-time Python with WebSockets** (Real Python): https://realpython.com/python-web-sockets/
- **Prometheus & Grafana Hands-On** (Prometheus docs): https://prometheus.io/docs/introduction/overview/

Ecosystem & Extensions

- **Shadcn/UI Tailwind Components**: https://ui.shadcn.com/
- **FastAPI for HTTP-based MCP Servers**: https://fastapi.tiangolo.com/
- **Testcontainers-Python** (Integration testing): https://github.com/testcontainers/testcontainers-python
- **Py-Spy Profiler**: https://github.com/benfred/py-spy

Contributing & Governance

- **CONTRIBUTING.md** (Spec Repo): https://github.com/mcp-protocol/spec/blob/main/CONTRIBUTING.md
- **Governance Policy**: https://github.com/mcp-protocol/spec/blob/main/GOVERNANCE.md
- **Code of Conduct**: https://github.com/mcp-protocol/spec/blob/main/CODE_OF_CONDUCT.md

---

Keep exploring these resources to deepen your understanding, stay up to date, and actively engage with the MCP community!